Soapmaking

For Fun & Profit™

Maria Given Nerius

PRIMA HOME

An Imprint of Prima Publishing

PRIMA PUBLISHING and colophon are registered trademarks of Prima Communications, Inc.

The FOR FUN & PROFIT™ logo is a trademark of Prima Communications, Inc.

Some of the projects discussed herein involve the use of chemicals. The improper handling or unsafe use of such chemicals can result in serious bodily injury or death. These chemicals should be kept away from and out of reach of children and animals. Also, it is important to follow the manufacturer's safety recommendations and use standard safety precautions, such as the use of proper safety glasses and gloves, in using such chemicals and creating the projects described in this book.

Prima Publishing and the author hope that you enjoy the projects discussed in this book. While we believe the projects to be safe and fun if proper safety precautions are followed, all such projects are done at the reader's sole risk. Prima Publishing and the author cannot accept any responsibility or liability for any damages, loss, or injury arising from use, misuse, or misconception of the information provided in this book.

Library of Congress Cataloging-in-Publication Data

Nerius, Maria.
  Soapmaking for fun & profit / Maria Nerius; series editor Barbara Brabec.
      p.   cm.
  Includes index.
  ISBN 0-7615-2042-2
  1. Soap.
  I. Title. II. Title: Soapmaking for fun and profit.
  TP991.N35 1999
  668'.12—dc21   99-39228
                                                                                      CIP

99 00 01 02 ii 10 9 8 7 6 5 4 3 2 1
Printed in the United States of America

How to Order

Single copies may be ordered from Prima Publishing,
P.O. Box 1260BK, Rocklin, CA 95677; telephone (916) 632-4400.
Quantity discounts are also available. On your letterhead, include
information concerning the intended use of the books and
the number of books you wish to purchase.

Visit us online at www.primalifestyles.com

Contents

THE FOR FUN & PROFIT SERIES™

Decorative Painting For Fun & Profit

Holiday Decorations For Fun & Profit

Knitting For Fun & Profit

Quilting For Fun & Profit

Soapmaking For Fun & Profit

Woodworking For Fun & Profit

Introduction

AS A CHILD, I WAS KNOWN in my neighborhood as the best mud pie maker in Indiana, maybe in the entire world. I was quite proud of this distinction. My mother, on the other hand, wasn't quite so pleased. I was often sent to the showers to clean up once or twice a day. I often thought myself clever when I cleaned myself simply by wetting my hands and then proclaiming my hands clean. But somehow, Mom always knew. She sent me back for a real cleaning. I soon learned to appreciate the process of becoming clean. A big part of that process was soap. Little did I know then that making soap would become a pleasure, a hobby, and a source of gift giving for me as an adult. I still believe that you can't know the true joy of being clean if you haven't also enjoyed the exquisite pleasure of getting positively dirty. In addition to making soap, I highly recommend making mud pies.

Americans in general love being clean and show a passion for anything used in the cleansing ritual. One reason that the household-cleaning aisles of grocery stores are stocked from floor to ceiling with every soap imaginable is that, as a nation, we are obsessed with everything that aids us in being clean. Would freshly washed sheets smell as wonderful without soap? Would a baby's skin smell so sweet without soap? Would cars sparkle so brightly after washing without soap?

When I first heard about handmade soaps, I wasn't convinced it was anything more than a selling gimmick for small cottage industries. People who sold their handmade soaps proclaimed the benefits of using all natural ingredients, but I felt that life was complicated enough without having to worry about soap containing potentially harmful or unnecessary additives or ingredients. I considered it the responsibility of our government and manufacturers to regulate soap. Despite some of my cynical thoughts, I still found myself in awe of handmade soaps and the people who made them. As I learned more about soap and soapmaking, I began to see the wonderful benefits of knowing exactly what goes in a product that would eventually touch my skin. For example, many people have allergies or skin reactions to detergents and soaps. Making handmade soap allows the soap crafter to control the ingredients and additives in the household's main cleaner, the family-size bar of soap.

The History of Soapmaking

The archaeological record shows that the Babylonians were making soap around 2800 B.C. The first known written mention of soap has been found on Sumerian clay tablets dating from about 2500 B.C., which mention using soap to wash wool. Another Sumerian tablet describes soap made from water, alkali, and cassia oil. There is further evidence that the Phoenicians were using soap around 600 B.C. These early references to soap and soapmaking show that soap was used to clean textile fibers, such as wool and cotton, in preparation for weaving them into cloth. In addition, the ancient Egyptians bathed regularly with a soaplike substance made from a combination of animal and vegetable oils with alkaline salts.

According to ancient Roman legend, the word *soap* comes from the name Mount Sapo, where animals were sacrificed. The rain washed a mixture of melted animal fats and wood ashes into the Tiber River, where the soapy mixture was discovered to be useful for washing clothes and skin. Soap also was used in the extremely popular Roman baths, built around 312 B.C. The Romans are thought to have acquired the knowledge of soap from the Gauls. With the fall of the Roman Empire, the popularity of soap and bathing in Europe went into decline. The joy and pleasure of bathing and soap didn't return to everyday life in Europe until several centuries later.

Soapmakers' guilds began to spring up in Europe during the seventh century. Secrets of the trade were closely guarded and rarely shared, and the training and promotion of craftsmen within the trade were highly regulated. Southern European countries, such as Italy, Spain, and France, were early production centers for soap because they had an excellent supply of oil from olive trees and barilla ashes, which they used to make lye. These olive-oil-based soaps became known as Castile soaps.

The English began soap crafting during the twelfth century. Unfortunately, soap was heavily taxed as a luxury item, so it was readily available only to the rich. In 1853, when the English soap tax was repealed, a boom in the soap trade coincided with a change in social attitudes toward personal cleanliness.

In colonial America, soapmaking was considered women's work. Each year, women would set aside a time, usually just before spring-cleaning time, to make soap from ashes, animal and cooking grease that had been saved during the winter, and rainwater. The process involved trickling rainwater through the ashes to make lye. The fats and grease were boiled and rendered and mixed together with the lye, forming the thick substance that was perfect for making soap.

The commercial production of soap didn't start until the early 1600s, when enterprising soapmakers from England began arriving in the New World. These early soap entrepreneurs made the rounds of local households to purchase stored fat. They then sold the soap back to the homes. Called tallow chandlers and soap boilers, they at first peddled soap door to door. Eventually general stores distributed soap, selling it from enormous blocks. Customers would indicate how much they wanted, and that amount was cut off the block.

More than 150 years passed before some enterprising souls decided to produce soap for mass distribution and consumption. In

1806 William Colgate opened a soapmaking concern in New York called Colgate & Company, which became the first great soapmaking company in America. In the 1830s the company began selling individual bars in uniform weights. Soon other soapmaking companies were born and added perfumes, deodorants, and antibacterial ingredients to the soaps. Since that time, scientific achievements in the chemistry of soapmaking made soap a popular and easy-to-obtain commodity that could be used for everything from bathing to washing clothes to cleaning the home.

In the 1970s there was a resurgence of people wanting to make their own soaps, especially with natural and herbal ingredients. Simplified techniques and easy-to-find supplies have made soapmaking easier. Consumers bored with mass-produced and mass-marketed products have welcomed the arrival of small-scale soap crafters, who enjoy at least 3 percent of the specialty soap market. The creativity of crafting soap has given rise to a love for the product and an increased demand for specialty soaps.

The fact that you have purchased this book indicates that you're interested in the delightful craft of soapmaking. This book covers a wide spectrum of advice and wisdom from my own personal experiences and experiences of other soap crafters. Whether you decide to do soapmaking as a hobby or choose to earn an income from it, this book will cover all the bases, giving you enough information to develop your skills. The only thing left out is the little yellow rubber ducky.

Using This Book

The following chapters provide the information and instructions you'll need to get started on some good clean fun. Because the goal of this book is to help you have fun and learn more about a craft, it provides a great deal of information about the different ingredients and additives you can use to personalize your soap. This book will cover what is called the cold process of soapmaking, which is the most common way to create soap from scratch. The step-by-step instructions were carefully written and are easy to follow. You'll also learn the convenience of using the hand-milled and melt-and-pour soapmaking methods. Part 2 covers how to make a profit from your soap, from prices to marketplaces to advertising. The Glossary provides a list of soapmaking jargon and Resources provides references for further reading. I've also included informational sidebars, Handy Hints to help you along your way, and whimsical facts about soapmaking and crafting in the Did You Know? boxes you'll see throughout.

Resources are available to the beginning and advanced soapmaker. Magazines and books with recipes and hints about soapmaking are widely available.

The appendix lists plenty of information about Web sites, news groups, and mailing lists. In addition, I've also included basic instructions on how to find valuable resources on the Web. The topic of the Internet and soapmaking is covered in chapter 9. It's a bit ironic that something as old-fashioned as making soap by hand is being taught and rediscovered through the use of the highest technological means, the information superhighway.

My one goal in writing this book is to communicate the wonders of the traditional craft of soapmaking. To make your adventure easier, I've included extensive information about ingredients and additives used to create a new recipe or contribute to a soap base. When I started making soap, I had to reference several books to learn more about essential oils, herbs, saponification oils, and colorants. With *Soapmaking for Fun & Profit,* everything is at your fingertips. Enjoy!

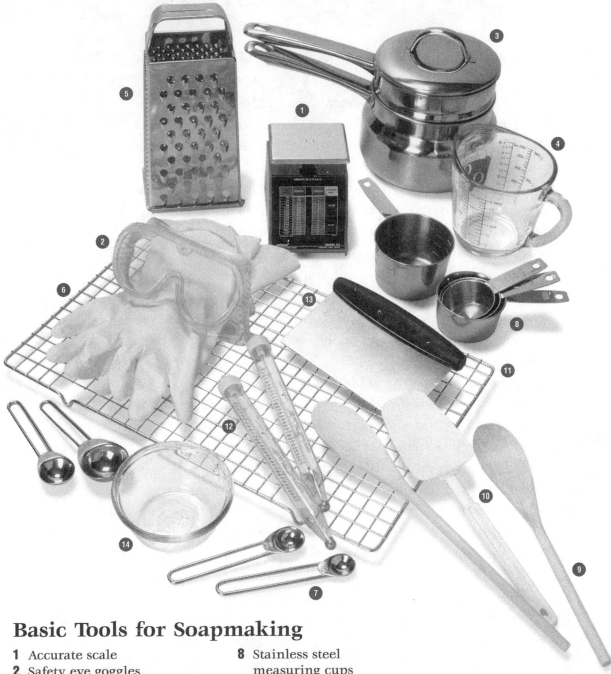

Basic Tools for Soapmaking

1 Accurate scale
2 Safety eye goggles
3 Double boiler
4 Glass measuring cup
5 Hand grater, large
6 Rubber gloves
7 Stainless steel
   measuring spoons

8 Stainless steel
   measuring cups
9 Wooden spoons
10 Rubber spatula
11 Drying rack
12 Two candy or
   cake thermometers
13 Soap cutter
14 Small glass bowl(s)

Part One

For Fun

The Joy of Soapmaking

▼▼

IN THIS DAY AND AGE, with soap so readily available at relatively inexpensive prices in local grocery stores and drugstores, you might wonder why anyone would bother to make soap by hand. I understand this point of view completely because I used to have the same opinion. Many people are happy with the really good stuff sold at finer department stores and boutiques; it's pricey but worth the cost for the high-quality ingredients and scents. Before I started exploring the craft of soapmaking, I was more concerned with the variety of scents and textures that homemade soaps possess than the cosmetic value or chemical makeup of the soap. At heart, I'm a wanna-be artist, not a rocket scientist.

I began to change my tune when a good friend and respected colleague sent me a bar of her hand-milled soap. The soap had a wonderful, fluffy lather and smelled so fresh and invigorating, unlike any of the commercial bars I used. My curiosity was piqued, and I did the only thing I knew to do: I started looking for everything and anything about soapmaking. The practical, logical side of me had some serious questions. *Who has the time to make handmade soap? Why make something that's so easy to buy and most likely*

CARI'S STORY

Cari Bourassa of Sunshine Soapworks in Florida started the art of soapmaking in November of 1998 and still thinks it is so much fun! She was looking for some new ideas for homemade Christmas presents for family and friends, and she read a recipe in a magazine for soap made with melted-down grated soap from the grocery store, herbs, and oatmeal. After that she was hooked! "It was fascinating to me that I could take a bowlful of oils, herbs, and fragrances and turn them into a bar of soap, so I read all the books I could find on soapmaking."

Soon Cari became pregnant with her second child and wanted to make a soap to use for her newborn. She searched around and found the most mild ingredients. She finally formulated a basic recipe of olive oil, castor oil, chamomile tea, and chamomile flowers, but accidentally added more chamomile flowers than the recipe called for. The soap was too abrasive

cheaper to buy than to make? What's the big deal about making sure anything added to soap is pure and natural? Aren't most chemicals just elements found in nature?

A few days into my research of soapmaking, I had some major concerns about my personal safety and health because soap made from scratch uses lye, a caustic and potentially harmful substance. Again my mind went into overdrive. *I'm an accident waiting to happen. Working with harsh ingredients like lye would be foolish and asking for trouble. What if something goes wrong and the house burns down?* Although I don't recall any newspaper headlines announcing the tragic mass loss of skin and limbs through soapmaking, I didn't want to go down in history as the first soapmaker to take out a

and actually left tiny scratches on her hands, so she gave that batch to her neighbors for their new "baby" puppy.

"My advice to newcomers is don't let a small setback frustrate you and don't be afraid to try something new. There are almost an unlimited amount of ingredients—exotic oils and fragrances—that you can put into a bar of soap. Each batch has so many variables that make it unique—how it lathers, the texture, the consistency, the color and fragrance. Also, learn from your failures. Read as much as you can and check your library or the Internet for articles on different aspects of the craft. Save a bar of your very first batch to look back on."

whole neighborhood. I had every excuse ready for anyone who tried to convince me that soap was easy to make. Even my husband expressed concern that I might get careless with lye and end up hurting myself. Yet, I was strongly attracted to the beauty and art of soapmaking. I was drawn to the challenge of making soap from basic ingredients. I also wanted to feel the satisfaction my foremothers must have felt—they must have taken great pride in providing their community with a healthy, cleansing batch of soap.

You've probably figured out by now that I haven't blown up my neighborhood. The real warning about soapmaking is that it is addictive. Once you understand the basics of making soap, the fun really begins. Once you read all the instructions twice, you relax and can't wait to start your first batch. Once you make your first batch or two, you get overwhelming urges to create your own recipes. Experimenting with different ingredients, colorants, and scents will become a pleasure and satisfy the creative passions of artistic and personal expression. You'll take special pride in seeing your efforts turn a mixture of wholesome ingredients into a bar of soap.

Learning the Lingo

You'll have to learn a few new words before you gather your ingredients and set up your home soap factory. I've provided a complete glossary in the back of the book, but the following should be enough to familiarize you with the basics. Some words appear to be interchangeable, but if read in context, words like *oil* and *fragrance* do have specific meanings. When in doubt, read the sentence or paragraph again.

Additives: Ingredients added to a soap batch that add a specific quality or property. Additives include superfatting oils, essential oils, colorants, fragrance oils, botanicals, and fruits.

Aroma: The scent of an essential oil, fragrance oil, botanical/plant, or fat/oil. Interchangeable with the word *scent*.

Basic soap (also called soap base): Soap made from the basics of fats/oils and lye with no additives. Also refers to hand-milled soap or melt-and-pour soap before it is remelted and additives are introduced.

Cold process (CP): A method of creating handmade soap where the saponification process takes place in the absence of a direct heat source.

Detergents: Cleansers in which petroleum derivatives have been substituted for animal fats or vegetable oils. Soaps are not called detergents, and detergents may not be called soap.

Essential oils: Oils distilled directly from plants.

FDA: Federal Department of Agriculture.

Fixatives: Any substance that stabilizes fragrances and allows for slower dissipation of the aroma.

Fragrance oils: Synthetic oils produced to have the same aroma as essential oils.

Hand milled: A method of creating handmade soap by grating a basic soap and remelting it with water.

Hot process (HP): A method of creating handmade soap where the fats/oils and lye are actively boiled. The entire process is done over a heat source.

Melt and pour (MP): A method of creating handmade soap by melting a purchased soap base in a double boiler or in the microwave.

Rebatching: The process of reconstituting a cured or partially cured soap. It is a means of salvaging a batch of soap if you don't like the way it turns out and is also used to enhance fragrance and color and increase the shelf-life of other additives.

Recycling: Grating, cubing, or cutting scraps and leftover pieces of soap into shapes to be added to a new soap batch.

Remelted: Recycled, hand-milled, or melt-and-pour soap batches.

Saponification: The chemical process that occurs when fats/oils are combined with lye to create soap.

Seizing: The process of soap quickly becoming solid before the soap batch is poured into a mold or hand shaped into soap balls.

Superfatting: Adding extra oils and fats after a soap batch has traced to create a richer, milder soap. Extra oils or fats can also be added to hand-milled soaps once the grated soap is melted.

Trace: The stage in hot-process and cold-process soapmaking when the soap mixture leaves a line, or trace, across the top of the mixture before blending back into the mixture. The time it takes for the soap to trace varies with the fats and oils used in the recipe. Hot-process and cold-process soap batches must trace before they can be poured into a mold.

What Is Involved in Soapmaking?

Soap forms during a chemical reaction called *saponification,* which happens when you combine an acid (fats or oils) with an alkali (sodium hydroxide, or lye). For saponification to occur, the acid and the alkali must be in liquid form. The sodium hydroxide is mixed with water, fats are melted, and the two liquids are combined to make soap. It's fascinating to watch the fats/oils and lye as they chemically react with one another, drastically changing form to create thick, creamy soap.

Making soap from scratch is most often done using the cold-process rather than the hot-process method. While hot-process was commonly used by our soapmaking forebears, cold-process is more widely used today and is the method taught in this book. The "cold" in cold-process is a comparative term; the process does involve heat. In both methods, the fats/oils and the lye are hot when combined. Hot-process soapmaking actively boils the combined ingredients over a heat source for the entire saponification, whereas in cold-process no external heat is used other than to melt the fat/oils. Both processes have their pros and cons, and you may decide after

Are You Using Soap?

Next time you buy a bar of soap, note whether the word *soap* is even used on the labeling or packaging. Much to my surprise, many "soaps" on the market aren't really soaps at all. Rather they are detergent bars. Only the substance that has been created through saponification may be called soap. All other substances will be called bars, as in *cleaning bar, family bar,* or *moisturizing bar.*

you master cold-process soapmaking that you want to give hot-process a try.

If the idea of working with chemicals is a little intimidating, you can start your soapmaking endeavor with a simpler method, such as hand-milling or melt-and-pour. In hand-milling, you purchase an unscented, commercially made soap and then grate it, mix it with water, and melt it down. Melt-and-pour is similar except that you use a commercial soap base that does not need to be mixed with water in the melting process.

There is some debate about whether using the hand-milled and melt-and-pour methods is really soapmaking when it seems more like just remaking the soap, but allow me to offer the following analogy. Making a cake from scratch and preparing a cake from a mix produces two cakes that may taste slightly different, but hardly anyone will say the difference is dramatic. Although it's wonderful to make a cake from scratch, making a cake from a mix can be just as gratifying if done with imagination and creativity. Much of the fulfillment of anything handmade is in the tasteful and imaginative presentation of what we make. You may decide after reading this book that you don't want to make soap from scratch, maybe due to time constraints or maybe to avoid working with a caustic material like lye. Using hand-milled or melt-and-pour methods can be just as rewarding and can result in soap that is just as wonderful.

Soapmaking isn't just creating soap—it is inventing your own little scented, colored, original masterpiece. You are in charge of how your soap smells, feels, and looks. Once your cold-process soap batch has traced or your hand-milled or melt-and-pour soap is lique-fied, it's time for experimentation and fun with ingredients. This is the stage where you have the chance to make your handmade soap special and unique by introducing various additives and fillers. These aren't used simply to bulk up a soap recipe, nor are they nec-essarily chemical ingredients as is often implied on commercial soaps; each has qualities to give your soap more benefits or charac-ter. You can add an almost endless list of things to your soap, includ-ing oils for superfatting, essential and fragrance oils, colorants, fresh or dried herbs, pressed flowers, fruits, vegetables, and spices. Chapter 2 discusses all of these options in detail.

After you have the perfect blend of ingredients, it's time for the finishing touches. Your soap batch can be poured into a plain box mold or a decorative mold, or it can be hand-shaped into balls once the soap has cooled. Molds come in all shapes and sizes, and you can even use many household items as molds. You can also create wonderful and interesting effects by layering or marbling different colors of soaps. You can slice, shred, or chop up colored soaps and mix the bits and pieces into a white soap base for an unusual kalei-doscope effect. You can imprint soap with images from rubber or metal stamps. Once it is cured, you can paint, decoupage, or stencil your soap. There's no limit to what you can create with your imagi-nation and a little experimentation.

One of the best things about soapmaking is that almost nothing is wasted. If you don't like the way your soap turns out, you can re-batch it by grating it down, melting it with water, and adding new ingredients. Soap slivers left over after you cut your soap into bars and unused portions of other batches can also be recycled by adding them to the rebatch.

Pleasures and Benefits of Soapmaking

Our great grandmothers made soap outdoors in large pots over open fires, but most of us will be making our soap indoors in our kitchens. Unlike our ancestors, we have the option to use modern conveniences like food processors and different types of blenders. We can also use soap base or commercially made soap bars to eliminate the need to work with lye. We don't have to take advantage of these things; it's simply a matter of choice, a choice our ancestors didn't have. I think that if they had the option, many of our forebears would have gladly figured out how to trade other farm products for soap base rather than labor over hot cooking pots!

You'll reap countless rewards for spending a few hours creating handmade soaps. Family and friends will fuss over your handcrafted gifts and goodies. The sense of accomplishment builds esteem. In an age of mass production there's a charm in creating with one's hands and heart. Trends of nostalgia and the desire for the "good old days" follow all of us into the twenty-first century. Soapmaking is rich with traditions and folklore. It's a learned trade that commands respect and interest, and it's a craft that allows one to develop advanced skills and take pride in one's self-sufficiency.

There is so much fun that lies ahead of you! Like a great chef on a mission, you will enjoy spending time gathering all types of ingredients for your soaps. Enjoy the pleasure of finding the right

Did you know???

Commercial soap manufacturers must depend on many additives, fillers, and chemicals to make their soap. Some commercial fillers and additives can make soap harsh to sensitive skin or may contain ingredients that cause allergic reactions. Scents in commercial soaps and detergents are often used to mask the odors of harsh ingredients.

scent that pleases your nose. Relax and relish the challenge of mixing herbs or flowers, spices or oils. Making soap isn't a race to cross the finish line first; it is a journey that provides as much creative release in the process as it provides gratification as the end result.

What This Book Has to Offer

This book not only gives you the basic step-by-step instructions for soapmaking, it also serves as a timeless reference. One of the main requests I've had from hobbyists and professional soapmakers is for one book full of well-rounded, complete information on ingredients. Most soapmakers neither want nor need a library of books to cover fats/oils, essential oils, fragrance oils, additives, fillers, and preservatives. Therefore, I've compiled the efforts of my research in the ingredients listed in chapter 2. The second half of the book offers plenty of practical advice and information on how to make money from your soap if you decide to sell it.

Now that you know a little about soapmaking, it's time to gather the ingredients and get started!

chapter

2

Getting Started

▼▼

RECIPES ARE CHALLENGES TO THE soapmaker, who is a lighthearted chef always on the lookout for a new oil, scent, or ingredient. The soapmaker's quest is to get all the proportions and measurements just right for that perfect bar of soap. The goal for each soap batch is to have flawlessness and high quality in terms of the soap's hardness, color, tint, and texture. But remember that not all recipes and experiments work out. Some batches of soap may need to be rebatched or in some cases must be carefully wrapped and properly disposed of. Don't ever let a failure get you down or turn you away from trying again. The final destination might seem to be the goal, but don't forget to enjoy the scenery. In other words, stretching your creative wings by trying a new recipe is part of the journey, not a bump in the road.

This chapter provides a great deal of information about the variety of ingredients used in soapmaking. Read this information not to memorize it but to understand the ingredients you'll be selecting, storing, and using for your recipes. Understanding why different ingredients are needed or wanted in a soap recipe gives you a better foundation on which to build your skills. The ingredients used in soapmaking have not changed significantly since the first soap

13

batch was made. However, this chapter explains how modern advances in manufacturing, packaging, preserving, shipping, and marketing have broadened the ingredients readily available to you.

Basics of Any Soap Batch

All soapmaking processes basically cover the same areas. Following is a brief description of the things you'll need to familiarize yourself with when making soap.

Lye

For cold-process soapmaking, you will need sodium hydroxide, the chemical used to make lye. Sodium hydroxide generally comes in the form of beads or crystals. The terms *sodium hydroxide* and *lye* are sometimes used interchangeably to refer to the solid form of the chemical. Try not to let this confuse you. Whether the product you purchase is labeled as sodium hydroxide or as lye, you will have to combine it with water before adding it to the fats/oil. In this book, I always refer to the solid crystals as sodium hydroxide and to the liquid solution as lye.

When I first decided to give soapmaking a try, finding sodium hydroxide was an adventure. I hunted high and low. Sodium hydroxide is a chemical, so I figured a pharmacist would know where to find it. But all the pharmacists I asked gave me strange looks and said they did not sell the product. When I finally located a specialty pharmacy, the response was similar, but with a twist. This pharmacist said that although the pharmacy carried the product, she wouldn't sell it to me to make soap. For a controlled science experiment she might have relinquished the chemical, but not for a home project like soapmaking. I finally snapped. I told her that every book and recipe I found on soapmaking clearly listed sodium hydroxide. Why

Irritants and Allergens: A List of Well-Known Culprits

Be aware that many people have allergies or sensitive skin. Some oils may irritate the skin or cause the allergies to flare up.

- Common irritants include, but are not limited to, almond oil and almonds, botanicals, cocoa butter, coconut oil, glycerin, honey, lanolin, and powdered orrisroot.

- Essentials oils that tend to irritate delicate skin include basil, cajeput, camphor, cedarwood, citronella, clove, eucalyptus, juniper, lemongrass, orange, oregano, peppermint, pine, rosemary, spearmint, tea tree, thyme, verbena, and wintergreen.

- Never add the following to a soap batch: fabric dyes, basket reed dyes, bleach, ammonia, seeds with hard or sharp shells, sand, gravel, or shoe polishes.

would all the authors, soapmakers, and recipes call for an ingredient that I couldn't find?

The pharmacist seemed to realize I'd reached the end of my soap rope. She explained that when she used sodium hydroxide, she wore a professional safety suit, which included a glass pane in the hooded helmet. How could she sell me such a volatile chemical, knowing I didn't have such safety precautions?

Defeated, I followed the only other option I could think of: I posted a request for information on several Internet mailing lists. Less than an hour later, I had my answer. Red Devil drain cleaner, which was sold in every store I had visited, lists its one ingredient as 100% lye. If you can't find this drain cleaner, you can always do what Majestic Mountain Sage, a soapmaking supply company, advises on their Web site. Look up Chemicals in your local yellow pages and call any companies that specialize in small quantities. Ask for the technical grade, not the lab grade. Eventually you'll find a company that will sell it to you, although you may end up buying a 50-pound bag. Some mail-order companies also sell sodium hydroxide, but the shipping is subject to a hazardous materials fee and the amount you can purchase is usually limited to 20 pounds.

My days tracking down the sodium hydroxide gave me some insight into the safety measures needed when making soap from scratch. Carefully read Safety Tips in chapter 3 before starting your first efforts at making soap. Working with sodium hydroxide is not dangerous if you understand and appreciate the risks involved and follow all instructions to the letter.

> ## Handy Hint
>
> Post the safety measures in Safety Tips in chapter 3 near your work area and review them before every soapmaking session.

Fats and Oils

Fats and oils play a variety of roles in soapmaking. In the cold-process method you will need to select a fat, oil, or combination of both to mix with the lye. Fats and oils are also added after a cold-process batch has traced or a hand-milled or melt-and-pour batch is melted to superfat the soap. These fats and oils will not be saponified and will retain much of their therapeutic value. Essential and fragrance oils, which will be discussed later, can also be used to provide scent. I've listed all the fats and oils together to show you all the options available. I've also included specific qualities of each fat and oil. If you find that you don't like a certain fat or oil for soapmaking, you can often use whatever is left over for food preparation, cooking, or baking.

Fats and oils used in soapmaking can be found in most grocery stores, health food stores, or specialty and gourmet food shops

Cautions for Essential Oils

When using essential oils, fragrance oils, and other fats/oils in a soap recipe, use caution. Although common sense is very helpful, it's a good idea to use the many resources available to find out as much as you can.

- Research each essential oil before mixing your own blends. Not all essentials work well together, and some essentials are too harsh to use in products that will be used on your skin.

- Do not touch or use pure essential oils on your skin. Essential oils must be diluted before using directly on the skin.

- Use plastic gloves when mixing oils. Remove and clean gloves after every use, and wash hands immediately after using oils.

- Avoid rubbing your eyes or skin when using the oils. If essential or fragrance oil comes in contact with your skin or eyes, flush immediately with cool water.

- Never take essential or fragrance oils internally and never add them to items that will be ingested. Although some essential oils may be used for internal use when diluted, never assume it is safe to ingest any essential oil.

- Children have more delicate skin than adults do. Consult a book on essential oils or aromatherapy before using essential oils in products for children. Keep all essential oils out of the reach of children.

- Pregnant women should consult a doctor or health care specialist before using or handling any products that contain essential oils.

- Anyone with epilepsy or asthma must consult a doctor or health care specialist before handling essential oils. Certain essential oils can cause medical or health conditions to flare up. The essential oils that most often cause problems (but not only these) are aniseed, camphor, cinnamon, eucalyptus, fennel, hyssop, rosemary, sage, star anise, and essential oils made from flowers.

(either in the cooking area or with dietary or medicinal supplies). If you can't find a certain fat or oil, try using one with similar properties or qualities, or refer to Resources for a list of the many mail-order sources that sell hard-to-find oils. The price varies from fat to fat and from oil to oil, although most are fairly reasonable. As a general rule, the less expensive fats and oils are used for saponification while the more costly ones are used in superfatting soaps.

The amount of sodium hydroxide required to saponify a particular fat or oil varies considerably, so it is extremely important to know exactly what you are working with. To calculate the amount of sodium hydroxide you will need, you must make exact measurements, in weight, of the fats and oils you are using. Too much sodium hydroxide and an excess amount of lye will remain in the soap, burning and irritating your skin. Too little sodium hydroxide and the saponification will not occur, leaving you with a soupy mess. The proper amounts are explained further in chapter 4.

Many fats and oils must be refrigerated after opening. When using a refrigerated fat or oil for superfatting, measure the amount needed and allow it to warm to room temperature. When using the fat or oil for saponification, it will be heated over a heat source, so you don't need to warm it to room temperature. Some oils settle when left to stand, so shake the bottle before use.

Many of the oils listed are considered base oils or carrier oils, which means that the oil itself has little or no scent or flavor. Base oils are used in massage oils, bath oils, lotions, and soap. A carrier oil dilutes essential oils without damaging the aroma or scent. Carrier oils inhibit evaporation and are quickly absorbed into the skin.

Almond oil: An easy-to-find, all-purpose oil that contains vitamins and minerals. It is an unscented, skin-softening lotion that is rich in protein and that is easily absorbed by skin. It is used as a carrier oil, in saponification, and for superfatting.
Uses: balms, bath oils, cooking, cosmetics, lotions, massage oils, and soap.

Apricot kernel oil: Has many of the same properties found in almond oil, including benefits to sensitive skin. It's a light,

soft oil with a slight fragrance and is rich in vitamins and minerals. It is used as a carrier oil, in saponification, and for superfatting.
Uses: cooking, cosmetics, creams, bath oils, lotions, and soap.

Avocado oil: An oil with a light scent and a hue the shade of honey. It adds vitamins, protein, lecithin, and fatty acids to the soap batch. It's especially rich in vitamins A, D, and E and must be refrigerated after opening. It is used as a carrier oil, in saponification, and for superfatting.
Uses: bath oils, cooking, cosmetics, lotions, and soap.

Baby oil: A delicate, soothing oil with a soft fragrance. It is often mixed with floral fragrances. It is used as a carrier oil and in superfatting. It's rarely used in saponification.
Uses: bath oils, creams, lotions, massage oils, and soap.

Beef fat/Tallow: Animal fat that must be rendered before use or purchased already rendered from a distributor. It is used mainly in saponification. It creates a hard, mild soap. It traces quickly to produce a white soap, which works well.
Uses: candles, cooking, and soap.

California walnut oil: Golden-colored oil with a distinct aroma. It is highly favored for its light quality. Refrigerate after opening. It is used as a carrier oil and for superfatting.
Uses: bath oils, cooking, and soap.

Canola oil/Canolive oil: Canolive oil is a blend of canola oil and extra virgin olive oil. It has a light golden hue and the distinct smell of olive oil. Refrigerate after opening to keep the light flavor of the oil intact. It is used in saponification and for superfatting.
Uses: cooking and soap.

Castor oil: An oil rich in fatty acids that lubricates the skin and acts as a humectant and combines with other oils. Used more frequently in glycerin soaps; only small amounts of castor oil are used in other soap batches. It is used both in saponification and for superfatting.

Uses: lotions, medicines, lubricants, and soap.

Cocoa butter: A soothing oil that is solid at room temperature. It has emollient qualities and the soft aroma of white chocolate. It adds hardness to a soap batch. It is used for superfatting.

Uses: bath oils, chocolate, cosmetics, creams, lotions, massage oils, and soap.

Coconut oil: A light, odorless oil that is solid at room temperature. Good for moisturizing, but only in small quantities. It adds a quick lather and cleansing quality to soap. It is used as a carrier oil, in saponification, and for superfatting.

Uses: balms, candles, cooking, creams, lotions, and soap.

Corn oil: A light oil with a soft golden color and little or no scent. It is used in saponification and for superfatting. Although it isn't frequently used in soapmaking, it is easy to find.

Uses: cooking and soap.

Cottonseed oil: Has emollient qualities but can spoil quickly, turning rancid. When used in soapmaking, a preservative should be added to the soap. It is used as a carrier oil and for superfatting.

Uses: balms, cooking, cosmetics, and soap.

Emu oil: A difficult-to-find but wonderful oil that is an emollient and a moisturizer. It has many excellent qualities, including being an anti-inflammatory and hypoallergenic. It is good for superfatting and is also used as a carrier oil and in

Handy Hint

Always read the labeling on the packaging for fats and oils. You may find that a fat or an oil is actually a combination of fats and oils.

saponification. Although it's a specialty oil and may be hard to find, it's growing in popularity with soapmakers.
Uses: anti-inflammatory, moisturizing, and emollient.

Grape seed oil: A light, almost odorless oil that is rich in vitamins (mainly vitamin E), minerals, and linoleic acid. It is used as a carrier oil, in saponification, and for superfatting.
Uses: balms, bath oils, cooking, creams, lotions, and soap.

Hazelnut oil: A moisturizing oil that is easily absorbed by the skin. It is light, almost odorless, and one of the most highly unsaturated vegetable oils. It is used as a carrier oil and for superfatting.
Uses: balms, cooking, creams, and soaps.

Hemp seed oil: An oil prized for its soothing qualities and for healing dried skin. Its high linoleic content means that it is vulnerable to spoilage. It may be easier to find in some parts of the United States than in others. It is used as a carrier oil, in saponification, and for superfatting.
Uses: paint, soap, and varnish.

Lard: A cheap, easy-to-find fat that produces white soap that creates large bubbles when used. It is solid at room temperature and has a fatty scent that can be covered with fragrance. It is used in saponification.
Uses: cooking and soap.

Lime oil: A light green oil that is a combination of canola, olive, and lime oils. It has a sweet, pleasant lime aroma. It is used in saponification and for superfatting.
Uses: cooking and soap.

Linseed oil: An oil used mainly in liquid or soft soaps.
Uses: linoleum, paint, soap, and varnish.

Macadamia nut oil: A light, almost odorless oil used for its emollient qualities. It is used as a carrier oil, in saponification, and for superfatting.
Uses: bath oils, cooking, cosmetics, and soap.

Olive oil: One of the best and most accessible moisturizers. A heavy-scented oil that varies in color, grade, and quality. Grade A is recommended for soapmaking. It is used in saponification and for superfatting. Castile soaps are made using olive oils.
Uses: cooking and soap.

Palm kernel oil: Similar to coconut oil in that it gives a lot of lather. It adds hardness to the soap. It is used as a carrier oil, in saponification, and for superfatting. It is often used in rebatching or recycling a soap batch that is too soft.
Uses: balms, cooking, cosmetics, and soap.

Palm oil: Also referred to as vegetable tallow. A universal oil, with a pale yellow hue, that adds firmness to soap. It is used as a carrier oil, in saponification, and for superfatting.
Uses: cooking and soap.

Peanut oil: A highly unsaturated oil with a very distinct aroma that helps condition dry skin. If not stored in the refrigerator after opening, it can easily become rancid. It's used in saponification and for superfatting.
Uses: cooking and soap.

Pumpkin seed oil: A light-bodied oil with a moss-green color. It is high in vitamins and minerals and has little or no scent. When added to soap during superfatting, it adds a natural, earthy color. It is used as a carrier oil, in saponification, and for superfatting.
Uses: cooking and soap.

Safflower oil: An oil light in color and in scent used for its moisturizing qualities. It has a limited shelf life and must be refrigerated after opening. It is used as a carrier oil, in saponification, and for superfatting.
Uses: cooking, cosmetics, and soap.

Sesame oil: An oil with a strong nutty smell that is praised for its moisturizing properties. It is used in saponification and for superfatting.
Uses: cooking, cosmetics, creams, and soap.

Shortening/Vegetable oil: A blend of various oils and fats commonly available at grocery stores. It leads to a soft soap batch, so it's often used in combination with other types of oils that help harden the soap. It is favored by soapmakers who choose not to use animal fats or by-products. The time to trace is longer than for animal fats. It is used in saponification.
Uses: cooking, cosmetics, and soap.

Soybean oil: A light, almost odorless, and easy-to-find oil that is not often used in soapmaking. It is used as a carrier oil, in saponification, and for superfatting.
Uses: cooking, paint, soap, and varnish.

Sunflower oil: A good, less-expensive substitute for olive oil. It contains vitamin E and is a good moisturizer. It tends to soften the soap batch, so it should be used with other oils that harden for balance. It is used as a carrier oil, in saponification, and for superfatting.
Uses: cooking and soap.

Wheat germ oil: An oil rich in vitamins A, D, and E, all of which are nourishing to the skin. It is used as a carrier oil, in saponification, and for superfatting.
Uses: cooking, massage oils, and soap.

Additional Ingredients for Your Soap

The funnest thing about soapmaking is adding your ingredients and making it just the way you want it. Following is everything you need.

Scent and Fragrance

Selecting your own fragrance or scent to add to a soap batch is a treat. As an enthusiastic gardener and herb crafter, this side of soapmaking really appeals to me. My friend Marie Browning from Victoria, British Columbia, coined the term *fragrance crafting,* and I think it's a perfect description. You can choose from dozens of different botanicals and naturals and a wide array of essential and fragrance oils. I tend to use fresh herbs and flowers from my own garden. Dried herbs and pressed flowers work well too, adding texture to soaps in addition to fragrance. Other wholesome ingredients include dried fruits and vegetables or spices.

The most common method for adding fragrance to a soap batch is the use of essential oils and fragrance oils. Keep in mind that *fragrance* and *fragrance oils* are two separate ideas. I use *fragrance* and *scent* interchangeably to refer to the aroma a soap will have. *Fragrance oil,* however, refers to the synthetic oil used to create an aroma.

Essential oils and fragrance oils are not the same, and the recipes in this book clearly note which type of oil to use. When creating your own recipes, it is important to know the pros and cons of each.

Essential oils are distilled directly from botanicals such as petals, leaves, berries, flowers, twigs, bark, stems, wood, spices, roots, fruits, and rinds. Many soapmakers think it would be fun to make their own essential oils, but the incredible amount of raw materials and time needed to make just a small amount makes this impractical. However, you may choose to make infusions and decoctions from botanicals—processes that are much simpler and less expensive than creating essential oils from scratch. (See chapter 4 for descriptions of how to make infusions and decoctions.)

Because of the tedious processes involved in making essential oils, these oils tend to be more expensive than fragrance oils. However, all essential oils must be diluted before touching the skin, so what may seem like a small amount of oil for the cost will be more than enough to use in many soap recipes.

The less expensive alternative to essential oils is fragrance oils. Fragrance oils are synthetic and thus don't have to be made from a specific plant. For this reason, they are available in a wider variety of scents and blends than are essential oils. The choice of whether to use essential oils or fragrance oils is a personal one. Try to find a local outlet or a mail-order source for both and request samples so you can see if you find any differences between the two types of scents. As with all product lines, you'll find that you favor one over another. Or you may prefer essential oils for some fragrances and fragrance oils for others.

It is extremely important that you do not confuse perfumes and potpourri oils with essential oils or fragrance oils, as the difference is significant. Perfumes are diluted with alcohol and formulated to be placed directly on the skin. The alcohol base in perfumes is not suitable for use in any method of soapmaking. Potpourri oil is too harsh to be used in soapmaking and should never be used on skin. It was not designed to come in contact with skin and will likely be aggravating to all skin types. Some scent or fragrance supplies may include *perfume oil* or *perfume fragrance oil* on the label. Before ordering, always ask whether the product can be used in soapmaking.

> **Handy Hint**
>
> A few drops of pure essential oil will go a long way. If you're like me, you'll be tempted to add just a few more drops than are recommended in a soap recipe. Don't give in to this temptation! Essential oils are very potent and the additional oil won't make a difference in the soap fragrance but might be irritating to your skin.

Buying Oils for Scents and Fragrances

Your nose will play a substantial role in the selection of a fragrance or blend of fragrances for your soap. When buying essential and fragrance oils, carefully read all labels. Products that proclaim to be essential oils must be made only from natural sources. Synthetics must be labeled as such and are called fragrance oils or fragrance perfume oils. Some wording on labels can be tricky to decipher, but reliable sources for essential and fragrance oils will not muddy the labeling. When in doubt, ask the supplier how the oil was made and if anything was added to the oil while it was processed. Even if the supplier isn't the manufacturer of the oils, he or she should be able to answer your questions.

Buying higher quality essential and fragrance oils should be considered a wise investment. Both can be used for multiple purposes, not just soapmaking. For example, you may choose to use a scent in a soap batch and coordinate your soap with a bath oil, lotion, hair shampoo, or rinse.

Specific Scents

When creating your own scents, take the main scent and add blenders—scents that enhance the main scent. (See chapter 4 for more information about blending or creating scents from essential and fragrance oils.) To allow the slow release of the aroma over time, use a fixative with the scent blend. The fixatives used in this book include soap base, base and carrier oils, salts, botanicals, and lotion base. When you first start to mix your own scents, it might be best to use fixatives with no scent. As you become more familiar with blending oils, try fixative oils with distinct aromas that will add interest to the new blend. Refer to the list above of common carrier and base oils, which can be used as fixatives. See Resources for a detailed description of how to use different materials as fixatives.

The following list of fragrances and scents commonly used in soap serves as a one-stop reference for your soapmaking needs. The properties of each scent are included as well. The scents listed can be found as both essential oils and fragrance oils.

Allspice: Anesthetic, analgesic, muscle relaxant; stimulating, warming.

Anise: Aids in digestion and respiration; muscle relaxant, insect repellant; clarifying, head clearing, warming.

Basil: Aids in digestion and respiration, increases concentration; muscle relaxant; clarifying, head clearing, refreshing, soothing, stimulating, uplifting.

Bay: Antibacterial, anti-inflammatory; relaxing, soothing.

Bergamot: Aids in digestion and respiration; antiseptic; clarifying, uplifting.

Carrot seed: Aids in circulation and digestion; antiseptic, muscle relaxant; revitalizing, toning.

Cedarwood: Antiseptic, astringent; calming, harmonizing, sedating, soothing, strengthening, toning.

Chamomile: Aids in digestion; muscle relaxant; balancing, calming, refreshing, relaxing, soothing.

Cinnamon: Aids in digestion and respiration; antiseptic, astringent; toning.

Clary sage: Astringent; calming, euphoric, relaxing, soothing, toning, uplifting, warming.

Clove: Aids in respiration; antiseptic; warming.

Cypress: Aids in circulation and respiration; astringent; cooling, refreshing, relaxing, stimulating.

Eucalyptus: Analgesic, anti-inflammatory, antiseptic, decongestant; cleansing, cooling, head clearing, invigorating, refreshing, uplifting.

Fennel: Aids in digestion; carminative.

Frankincense: Aids in respiration; comforting, rejuvenating, relaxing, warming.

Geranium: Anti-inflammatory, antiseptic, diuretic; harmonizing, refreshing, relaxing, toning, warming, balancing.

Ginger: Aids in circulation, digestion, and immunities; antiseptic; refreshing, stimulating.

Grapefruit: Antiseptic, astringent, diuretic; invigorating, refreshing, stimulating, toning.

Hyssop: Decongestant.

Jasmine: Builds confidence, enhances sensuality; relaxing, soothing, warming.

Juniper: Aids in circulation and appetite; diuretic, muscle relaxant; balancing, cleansing, cooling, refreshing, relaxing, stimulating, warming.

Lavender: Aids in respiration and digestion; antiseptic, antibacterial, decongestant, muscle relaxant; calming, head clearing, refreshing, relaxing, stimulating, soothing, warming.

Lemon: Aids in circulation; antiseptic, antibacterial, astringent, diuretic; cooling, motivating, refreshing, stimulating, uplifting.

Lemongrass: Cooling, fortifying, refreshing, toning.

Lime: Aids in circulation, digestion, and immunities; antiseptic, deodorizer; cooling, rejuvenating, stimulating.

Mandarin: Aids digestion and circulation; antiseptic, diuretic; sedating, stimulating.

Marjoram: Aids in respiration and digestion; muscle relaxant; calming, fortifying, sedating.

Melissa: Insect repellant; calming, refreshing, sedating, uplifting.

Myrrh: Aids in respiration and digestion; astringent, antiseptic, anti-inflammatory, antifungal, expectorant; rejuvenating, strengthening, toning.

Neroli: Aids in circulation and digestion, enhances sensuality; antibacterial; calming, healing to skin, relaxing, sedating.

Orange: Calming, cooling, healing to skin, refreshing, relaxing.

Patchouli: Anti-inflammatory; enhances sensuality; relaxing, sedating.

Peppermint: Aids in digestion and respiration; anti-inflammatory, muscle relaxant; cooling, head clearing, refreshing, warming.

Petitgrain: Cooling, refreshing, relaxing.

Pine: Aids in respiration; antiseptic, deodorizer; cooling, invigorating, refreshing, stimulating.

Rose: Aids in digestion, enhances sensuality, builds confidence; antiseptic, antibacterial, anti-inflammatory, astringent; balancing, relaxing, soothing.

Rosemary: Aids in respiration, circulation, and digestion; muscle relaxant; clarifying, invigorating, refreshing, stimulating, uplifting.

Sage: Antiseptic, diuretic; relaxing.

Sandalwood: Aids in digestion, builds confidence; calming, grounding, healing to skin, relaxing, sedating, softening, warming.

Spearmint: (less potent than peppermint) Antiseptic, astringent, expectorant, muscle and nerve relaxant; stimulating.

Tangerine: Calming, cooling, refreshing, relaxing.

Tea tree: Aids in digestion, immunities, and respiration; antifungal, antiseptic, decongestive; healing to skin.

Thyme: Aids in circulation, immunities, and respiration; antiseptic, disinfectant, muscle relaxant; cleansing, refreshing.

Vanilla: Enhances sensuality; calming, relaxing, soothing, warming.

Wintergreen: (less potent than peppermint) Astringent, anti-inflammatory, diuretic; cooling, refreshing, stimulating.

Ylang-ylang: Enhances sensuality; antiseptic; relaxing, sedating, soothing.

Color and Hue

Different fats and oils give soap a natural range of colors, from pale golds to pure whites. Although there is a simple beauty in a hand-made soap that uses no additional colorants, adding color can be fun and creative. There are many options when it comes to adding color to your soap. As with essential and fragrance oils, colorants may be natural or synthetic. You may choose to use fresh fruits and vegetables, dried herbs and spices, or commercial colorants. Choosing ingredients for colors is a personal preference.

When adding color, it is important to know that the color of the soap when it is first poured into the mold may not be the color of the soap after it dries and cures. All colors lighten during the drying

Additional Essential and Fragrance Oils

Apple blossom	Heather	Mango	Plum
Bluebonnet	Honey	Mulberry	Raspberry
Cantaloupe	Honeydew	Narcissus	Sweet pea
Earl Grey tea	Kiwi	Papaya	Watermelon
Forget-me-not	Lilac	Peach	Wisteria
Freesia	Lily of the valley	Pear	
Gardenia	Magnolia	Pink grapefruit	

and curing stage. Also, once dried and cured, all colors in soap fade over time.

Pureed or liquefied fruits and vegetables can be used to provide light color to a soap batch. Strawberries and cherries add a delicate red or rose color to soap. Liquefied skin of cucumbers, aloe vera, or sweet green pepper creates a pale mint to sage green hue. But keep in mind that the color of fresh fruits and vegetables does not hold up in the saponification process, so add a natural preservative, such as vitamin E, grapefruit seed extract, carrot root oil, or wheat germ oil, to the soap batch. Using fresh fruits and vegetables does shorten the shelf life of the soap, but using these natural colorants adds to the wholesome nature of a soap recipe. In a cold-process recipe, the puree of fresh fruits or vegetables must be calculated as a liquid (you must subtract this measurement from the amount of water used to make the lye).

Finely chopped or powdered fresh herbs and other botanicals give a speckled dash of color and add bulk to a natural soap. Although infusions or decoctions of herbs don't give a great deal of color to a soap batch, they can give a gentle hue to white soaps.

Cold-process soapmaking is rather harsh, and few colors survive pure, but the results can be interesting. Use no more than 1 to 2 tablespoons of infusion of fresh herbs per pound of soap. (See more about fresh herbs, infusions, and decoctions in chapter 4.) As with fruit and vegetable purees, you will have to subtract the amount of the infusion or decoction from the total amount of water needed to make the lye.

Finely ground dried herbs and spices add slight speckling, bulk, interest, and texture to soap. Each herb has its own qualities and properties (use the list of essential oils to guide you). Whether you use cold-process, hand-milled, or melt-and-pour recipes, use no more than 1 to 3 tablespoons per pound of soap.

If you opt to use commercial or synthetic colorants, there are many options available to you. Commercial soap colorants are usually sold in blocks or disks. If you cannot obtain commercial soap colorant, you may opt to use slivers of candle colorant or even shaved crayons. Whichever option you choose, the method for preparing the color is the same. Place the color in a block of soap base with a few tablespoons of oil. Place the colorant and soap in a microwavable glass container and melt at a low heat setting for 10- to 20-second intervals until the colorant is completely melted. If using soap colorant, read the packaging to determine the amount of colorant needed per pound of soap.

Fillers and Additives

Soapmakers can use just about anything and everything to add other qualities to soap. Some additives are used purely for aesthetic purposes, while others give the soap qualities such as moisturizing or cleansing. For example, using oatmeal in a soap batch not only adds an interesting texture, but also works as a natural exfoliant. Herbs or flower petals added to soap give interest and color and can act as natural astringents or moisturizers.

Additional ingredients are added at trace for cold-process soaps and just before melt-and-pour soaps are poured into a mold. If added too soon in cold-process soap batches, many of the qualities and properties of added ingredients are lost to saponification. For better results, many soapmakers recommend rebatching cold-process soap before using additives.

Because you can use just about anything in soap, it's almost impossible to list every additive. Of course, there are some limitations. You don't want to use anything that dries out the skin or that acts as an irritant or allergen to people with sensitive skin. See the sidebar on page 15 for some ingredients that are known to be irritants and allergens. The following list gives some examples of products to use as additives.

Almond: Adds interest and texture; acts as natural exfoliant. Can be used in all methods of soapmaking. Use no more than 1 teaspoon of finely ground nut per pound of soap.

Aloe Vera: Available fresh (as a plant) or sold as a gel; soothes dry, chapped, or burned skin.

Apricot: Adds interest and light color; contains many vitamins and minerals; acts as a skin softener. Soak dried apricots in water for several hours, then liquefy it. Can be used for cold-process and melt-and-pour soapmaking. Use no more than 1 to 2 tablespoons of liquefied fruit per pound.

Apricot kernel oil: Rich in vitamins and minerals; softens delicate skin. Used for superfatting.

Avocado oil: Rich in vitamins, protein, and fatty acids; soothes dry skin. Used for superfatting.

Banana: Adds aroma; rich in vitamins and minerals; soothes and softens skin.

Beeswax: Adds interest and scent to soap; acts as an emulsifier; speeds up trace in hot-process soaps; makes for a harder-bodied soap. Use no more than 1 ounce per pound of soap.

Benzoin: (available powdered) Acts as a fixative.

Borax: Adds cleansing power; acts as disinfectant and water softener. Can be used for any soapmaking method. Use no more than 1 teaspoon per pound of soap.

Bran: Adds bulk, interest, slight color speckling, and texture; acts as natural exfoliant (slightly abrasive to delicate skin). Can be used for any method of soapmaking. Use no more than 1 to 2 tablespoons of finely ground bran per pound of soap.

Carrot: Adds interest and a light color to cold-process and melt-and-pour soaps; full of vitamins; soothes chapped and dry skin. Must be liquefied before being added to soap batch.

Carrot root oil: Antioxidant; rich in vitamins A and C; good for dry or delicate skin. Used for superfatting.

Cinnamon: Adds speckled color and scent to soap; calming; use sparingly.

Cocoa butter: Adds interest and scent (similar to white chocolate); acts as an emollient; soothing.

Coffee: Adds bulk, interest, scent, slight color speckling, and texture to soap; helps remove odors from skin. Can be used for any soapmaking method. Use no more than 1/4 to 1/2 cup of finely ground coffee per pound of soap.

Cornmeal: Adds bulk, texture, and light color to cold-process and melt-and-pour soaps; acts as an exfoliant. Can be used for any soapmaking method. Use no more than 1 tablespoon per pound of soap.

Cucumber: Acts as an astringent; adds cleansing power and light scent to cold process and melt-and-pour soaps. Can use cucumber skin finely grated or liquefied.

Distilled water: Preferred water in all soapmaking processes; used to avoid impurities of tap water.

Evening primrose oil: Used for superfatting.

Flower petals: Add bulk, interest, slight color speckling, and texture; depending on the flower, some petals add qualities; discolor in cold-process soapmaking. Can be used for any soapmaking method. Use no more than 1 to 2 tablespoons of finely ground dried petals per pound of soap.

French clay: (also referred to as bentonite) Adds interest, light color, and smoothness; available in pink, gray, and green; avoid using on dry or delicate skin; draws dirt from skin. Can be used for any soapmaking method. Use no more than 1 tablespoon per pound of soap.

Fuller's earth: Adds light brown color, cleansing power, and denseness to soap; avoid using on dry or delicate skin. Can be used for any method. Use no more than 1 tablespoon per pound of soap.

Ginger: Acts as an astringent and a deodorizer; refreshing; use very sparingly.

Glycerin: Used for superfatting.

Goat's milk: Substitute for water; soothing to all skin types; rich in vitamins.

Grapefruit seed extract: Acts as an antioxidant and deodorizer; antibacterial, natural preservative; speeds up trace.

Hazelnut: Adds interest and texture to soap; acts as a gentle exfoliant. Can be used for any soapmaking method. Use no more than 1 teaspoon of finely ground nut per pound of soap.

Honey: Acts as an emollient; softens soap.

Jojoba oil: Acts as a humectant and moisturizer. Used for superfatting.

Kukui nut oil: Acts as a moisturizer; soothes chapped, dry, or delicate skin. Used for superfatting.

Lanolin: Softens and soothes; avoid for anyone allergic to wool. Used for superfatting.

Lemon: Adds interest and speckling to soap; antibacterial; substitute juice for water. Can be used for any soapmaking method. Use no more than 1 tablespoon of finely grated dried or fresh peel per pound of soap.

Lime: Adds interest and light speckling to soap; substitute juice for water; Can be used for any soapmaking method. Use no more than 1 tablespoon of finely grated dried or fresh peel per pound of soap.

Loofah sponge: Acts as a natural exfoliant.

Milk: Substitute for water; soothes all skin types; rich in vitamins.

Mustard powder: Adds color; avoid for children or anyone with delicate skin; opens skin pores. Can be used for any soapmaking method. Use no more than 1 teaspoon per pound of soap.

Oatmeal: (baby oatmeal or ground rolled oats) Adds bulk and texture; acts as a gentle exfoliant. Can be used for any soapmaking method. Use no more than 1/2 cup per pound of soap.

Orange: Adds interest and speckling; substitute juice for water. Can be used for any soapmaking method. Use no more than 1 tablespoon of finely grated fresh or dried peel per pound of soap.

Orrisroot: Acts as a fixative and preservative.

Powdered goat milk: Filler; moisturizes and softens.

Powdered milk: Filler; moisturizes and softens.

Pumice: Adds texture; abrasive for stubborn stains; not recommended for delicate skin. Can be used for any soapmaking method. Use no more than 1 to 2 tablespoons per pound of soap.

Rose hip oil: Moisturizer, natural preservative; soothing. Used for superfatting.

Seaweed: (dried, powdered, or in sheets) Adds interest and light speckling; high in minerals and vitamins. Can be used for any soapmaking method. Use no more than 1 to 5 tablespoons per pound of soap.

Shea butter: Moisturizer; soothing; will not saponify. Used for superfatting.

Spices: Add interest, color, and speckling; some are too harsh for skin. Unless otherwise stated in recipe, can be used for any soapmaking method. Use no more than 1/4 to 1/2 teaspoon per pound of soap.

Vitamin E oil: Acts as an antioxidant and natural preservative. Used for superfatting.

Wheat germ: Adds bulk, interest, texture, and light speckling; gentle exfoliant. Can be used for any soapmaking method. Use no more than 1 to 3 tablespoons per pound of soap.

Wheat germ oil: Acts as an antioxidant and emollient; use for delicate skin or as facial soap. Used for superfatting.

White clay (kaolin): Acts as an astringent; adds cleansing power; avoid for dry or delicate skin. Can be used for any soapmaking method. Use no more than 1 tablespoon per pound of soap.

When it's time for you to try your first recipe, you may want to refer back to this chapter for pointers. It's also a good idea to review this information whenever you work on batches of hand-made soaps.

Setting Up Your Personal Workspace

▼▼

IF YOU PLAN WELL and utilize the space available to you, you won't need a huge work area for making soap. It's important that your work area remain uncluttered. In some of the steps of soapmaking, you will need to work quickly and efficiently. The less clutter, the better off you are. As you think about how to set up your work area, keep a few things in mind. It's best to set up your equipment in the kitchen. (However, because the kitchen tends to be the family meeting place, be sure to explain what you will be doing and how making soap is done.) Because soapmaking requires a heat source for melting, your stove or heat source should be no more than three easy steps from the work area. This way you can melt substances as needed while keeping flammable ingredients away from the heat. Your sink or running water should be within two or three easy steps from the work area. When creating soap from scratch, you must be able to open windows or use a fan to increase air circulation and ventilation. Cold-process recipes require making lye, which must be mixed in a well-ventilated area. You may even consider making the lye outside of your home.

Good lighting is necessary for soapmaking. Insufficient lighting leads to mistakes. Good lighting comes into play when watching for trace in a cold-process batch of soap. Trace often requires a good eye to detect, and poor lighting can cause you to miss it entirely. Good lighting also helps you avoid spills when pouring the soap into molds. When working with colorants, it is best to work with full-spectrum light; otherwise, you may think you have a soft shade of blue when what you really have is teal. It's not a disaster and the soap is quite usable, yet for the artist in all of us it can be frustrating. The perfect work area should be near a large window with soft or diffused light or under fluorescent lighting that uses a full spectrum of color in the tubes. Unfortunately most of us aren't that lucky. Feel free to take your colorants outside to see the true color you're mixing. If you're careful, you can stir the batch to trace outside or near a window. But if you decide to work outside, avoid direct sunlight and prolonged exposure to the heat of the sun. Temperature and humidity can affect a batch of soap, so it's better to work in an area where you have more control over such factors. Room temperature should be from 69 to 90 degrees Fahrenheit. Humidity causes some soap to sweat and prolongs the time needed to dry and cure.

The best ergonomic way to craft is to work in a half-circle, which means that all your materials, supplies, and equipment are laid out in a half-circle in front of you. Do not place any of your supplies on the floor. Everything should be in your field of vision and within easy reach, so less energy is used in making the soap. The work area should be at about waist level. It's best if you stand while making soap, but if you have physical limitations and must sit, remember to place your supplies so you won't accidentally spill any ingredients.

You may want to cover the surface of your work area with old newspapers or a plastic tablecloth, particularly when you pour the soap into molds. Also keep moist kitchen towels or sponges within easy reach. (Dry sponges don't pick up spills as quickly as damp ones do.)

Spilled soap wipes up easily with a wet sponge, and most ingredients won't damage countertops. The exceptions are sodium hydroxide and lye, which are both very caustic. Covering your work area makes cleanup easier—all you have to do is throw out the newspaper or wipe down the plastic tablecloth. Many grocery stores and party supply shops also sell disposable plastic tablecloths that can be used many times before being thrown out.

Basic Equipment

You probably already have most of the equipment and tools needed for soapmaking in your home or kitchen. If you don't have a particular item, everything on the basic equipment list can be found at a grocery store, a kitchen or food specialty shop, or any store with a homeware department. Glass is perfect for this craft because it won't hold any fragrance transference, and lye won't leach into the glass. If you clean glass tools thoroughly, they can be used for soapmaking and then returned to the kitchen for food preparation. The only stage in which glass isn't used is when the soap batch is poured into the mold. Glass molds are too rigid and don't allow the soap to dry evenly. If any metal, plastic, or wooden utensil comes in contact with sodium hydroxide, lye, or essential oils, that utensil cannot be returned to the kitchen for food preparation. Also, be sure to clean and rinse glass droppers immediately after use to keep the essential oils from eroding the rubber in the dropper.

Handy Hint

Keep a few loose paper towels in a front pocket of your work apron or just to the side of your work area for little "spill" emergencies.

Equipment Needed for Soapmaking

- Dish towels, paper towels, or sponges
- Double boiler
- Glass mixing bowls, large
- Glass bowls, small
- Glass droppers
- Glass measuring cups
- Heat-resistant glass measuring bowls (4- to 8-cup)
- Hand grater, large
- Nonstick cooking spray or other release agent
- Rubber gloves
- Paring knife or potato peeler, sharp
- Thin-bodied knife or soap blade, sharp
- Metal measuring spoons
- Molds
- Wooden spoons or dedicated utensils
- Drying rack (wooden or metal)

Additional Equipment Needed for Cold-Process Soapmaking

- Accurate scale (food or postage)
- Two candy or cake thermometers
- Old towels or blanket
- Eye goggles or other protection

Other Options

- Large saucepan of any metal combined with large heat-resistant glass measuring bowl (4 to 8 cups) to replace a double boiler
- Food processor to replace the hand grater
- Microwave (many melt-and-pour soaps can be melted in the microwave)
- Spice grinder/coffee grinder

- Apron to protect clothing
- Work clothes (long-sleeve shirt and pants)

Ingredients used in soapmaking should never be heated directly over an open flame or heat element. Use a double boiler, or a mock double boiler (place a heat-resistant glass measuring bowl or cup into a pan of water). When using a double boiler, fill the bottom pan with 2 inches of water (double boilers can vary in size, so adjust the water measurement to the size of your double boiler). Bring the water to a gentle boil on medium heat. Once the boiling begins, reduce the heat. When the boiling has stopped, place the top pan of the double boiler in place. If water from the bottom pan spills over, remove some of the water from the bottom pan before placing the top boiler into the bottom pan. Add the ingredients to be melted to the top pan of the double boiler. This way the ingredients will warm at the same rate as the top pan.

When using the heat-resistant glass measuring bowl as a substitute for a double boiler, place the glass bowl in the large cooking pan. Add enough water to surround one-third of the glass bowl. Remove the glass measuring bowl from the pan, allow the water to come to a gentle boil, and then reduce the setting to low heat. Place the glass bowl in the water and immediately put the ingredients to be melted into the glass bowl.

When mixing sodium hydroxide with water, it is best to use a large heat-resistant glass measuring cup. This will give you more control when it comes time to add the lye to the melted fats/oils. I'll repeat the following rule several times in this book, but it's an important step to remember in soapmaking: **Always add sodium hydroxide *to* water. *Never* add water to sodium hydroxide.** By following this rule you have better control over the reaction. It's also important that you do not dump the entire measurement of sodium

Handy Hint

Before beginning the soapmaking process, gather and measure all ingredients required.

General Maintenance and Care Rules for Tools

- Each tool should have its own place. Jamming all tools in a drawer is a disaster waiting to happen. That special little mold or brush is going to get crushed by that soap cutter at some point. As a rule of thumb, put like tools in like containers—molds with molds, scissors with scissors, and so on.

- Oil or lubricate your metal tools often. The worst problem with tools is rust. A light coat of oil or wax will protect the metal from moisture.

- Protect the edges on sharp tools. There is nothing worse than a nicked blade. These problems cause the piece being cut to have tattered edges instead of nice, clean cuts. If a blade is broken, dull, or nicked, replace it or have it sharpened.

- Always clean your tools after use. A dirty tool is much harder to clean the next day. Always leave a little time at the end of the day for cleaning both your work area and your tools.

- Last and most important is to read the tool manufacturer's instructions, which were written to ensure long tool life and to prevent unnecessary wear and tear. Believe it or not, the manufacturer wants the tool to last. With the high labor costs associated with tool returns and customer complaints, it is in everyone's best interest to read the directions, no matter how simple the tool may be.

hydroxide into the water all at once. Instead add small amounts at a time while stirring and mixing the solution.

Large glass bowls also work well to hold grated soap while hand milling. Smaller glass bowls (also called custard cups) are good for holding measured items like colorants, essence oils, botanicals, and other ingredients that you will be adding to your soap batch. It's important not to mix the additional ingredients together. Keep each in its own bowl until it's time to mix them into the soap batch.

Most recipes use drops as the unit of measurement for oils. Glass droppers, which can be found at stores that sell science project supplies, health foods and vitamins, and fragrances, accurately measure essential oils, fragrance oils, and other small amounts of liquid additives. It's best to use glass droppers that have measurements displayed on them. Many essential oils and fragrance oils come in bottles with plastic dropper disks in the top of the bottle for oil to drip out of. In most cases, these stoppers aren't accurate gauges for measuring because it is often difficult to control the drops of oil coming out. When blending essential oils, it's better to use a glass dropper so that all your measurements are the same.

Use glass or plastic measuring (liquid measure) cups for ingredients like water, and metal measuring (dry measure) cups for ingredients like grated soap or soap base. Because metal cannot be used for food preparation once it comes in contact with caustic substances like sodium hydroxide, I recommend dedicating a set of measuring cups (dry measure) to soapmaking.

In cold-process soapmaking *all* ingredients are measured by weight, not with measuring cups or spoons. The success rate of your cold-process soap batches is tied directly to exact measurements of ingredients, especially for sodium hydroxide. A majority of the problems with cold-process soap is directly related to an incorrect amount of lye in the soap batch. Use a calibrated scale to measure the weights. You can find these scales at an office supply store or specialty food shop. The scales sold at most grocery stores or chain discount stores are not exact enough for measuring sodium hydroxide, water, or fats/oils. Calibrate the scale to zero by setting an empty container (for example, a glass bowl) on the scale and hand setting the scale's needle to zero. Once you've calibrated the scale, add the ingredient to be measured to the container. This gives you the most accurate measurement of an ingredient.

Handy Hint

Any time you place a new container on a scale (always set the scale with an empty container), remember to calibrate the scale for that container. If you think you may forget, put a small label on the top of the scale as a reminder to calibrate the scale each time you change containers.

Use a hand grater or food processor to grate or shave the soap or soap base when making hand-milled or melt-and-pour soap or when rebatching cold-process soap. Grating the soap makes it easier to melt. Blocks or even small chunks of soap or soap base take at least 30 minutes to melt, but grated soap melts in about 15 to 20 minutes and grated soap base melts in less than 10 minutes. Stainless steel graters work much better than plastic graters.

Warning: If you grate a cold-process soap in the rebatching process, remember that the grater cannot be used for food preparation afterward because trace of lye may still be present. Also, the grater must not be made of aluminum because lye will destroy the aluminum.

A paring knife is useful for cutting small slivers of color from a block of wax colorant. A paring knife is also used to shape a soap bar or to remove the top layer of soap bars for aesthetic purposes. Use a sharp, thin-bodied knife to cut, slice, or remove soap from molds. Another tool for cutting soap is a vegetable cutter, which has either a straight or wavy blade. You can buy this tool in grocery stores or kitchen specialty stores, where it is sold as a scraper or vegetable cutter. This same item is sold by some soap suppliers as a soap cutter—they are all the same tool but with different names.

Use wooden spoons to stir and mix ingredients during soapmaking. Even though the wood will eventually chip, splinter, or crack, I use wooden spoons mainly because they are easy to obtain and inexpensive. Clearly mark the spoons used for soapmaking so they are not accidentally used in food preparation.

Molds used in soapmaking are as varied as the recipes used to make soap. Most soapmakers prefer square or rectangular boxes to give the soap bars straight lines and sharp corners. The most basic mold is a large, rectangular wooden box with a removable lid and wooden dividers. The large wooden molds come in a variety of sizes, from a 12-bar to a 40-bar mold. For cold-process soaps, new soapmakers prefer clear plastic molds because you can see the soap through the plastic and detect any problems. Some molds have removable separators that section off a larger box into smaller rectangular (soap-bar size) units. Any rectangular box, including cardboard boxes, lined with plastic can be used as a soap mold.

If you prefer something other than a rectangular bar of soap, consider the dozens and dozens of commercial soap molds that are sold at art supply stores and craft retail shops. You can also use molds that are used for candy making, paper casting, candlemaking, or plaster casting. Be sure the mold is flexible enough to make releasing the soap easy. Avoid extremely rigid molds, such as those made of glass, and never use aluminum when working with cold-process soaps. In the past, soapmakers used cast-iron molds, but cast iron must be properly seasoned or conditioned, and even then, small bits of the cast iron may find a way into your soap. Avoid molds made from any material that can't keep its shape under extreme heat, such as foam cups or thin-bodied paper cups. Shallow molds may be tempting, but most shallow molds make a soap that easily slips out of one's hands and doesn't last very long.

Test any plastic for warping or melting before pouring an entire batch of soap into it. Soap made with any method can be shaped into a soap ball, which gives soap a rustic, country charm. Cold-process soap should not be hand shaped until it is rebatched, unless you use rubber gloves for the process.

Cold-process soap recipes call for two thermometers because you must track two temperatures simultaneously: One thermometer measures the temperature of the fats/oils being melted and the other measures the temperature of the lye. The mixtures cannot be combined until each cools to between 90 and 130 degrees Fahrenheit. Buy thermometers that can detect temperatures from 75 to 220 degrees Fahrenheit. Make sure your thermometer is accurate. Water at sea level boils at 212 degrees Fahrenheit, so check to see if your thermometer reads the correct heat of boiling water. If you live at a higher altitude, water boils at a lower temperature. Buy glass-encased thermometers such as candy thermometers, which are sold at grocery stores, craft retail outlets, cake shops, and specialty kitchen shops. Avoid any thermometer that has exposed aluminum.

Clean your equipment and tools with warm water and dish soap. It's better to wash your equipment and tools by hand rather than putting them in the dishwasher. The soaps you make are for cleaning and washing skin, and most leave a moisturizing or protective coating on your skin and on the tools used to create them. Putting equipment and tools directly into the dishwasher after a session of soapmaking will leave a dull residue on every item in the dishwasher, and you'll end up having to handwash the entire load!

Safety First and Foremost

Any nonporous kitchen utensils that you use for soapmaking can be returned to the kitchen for safe use in cooking after you have thoroughly cleaned them. Items such as wooden spoons or plastic measuring cups should not be used in food preparation once you have used them with sodium hydroxide or lye. Clearly label any porous utensils with permanent marker or tie a colored yarn or ribbon to the utensil. If you find you enjoy soapmaking, it is best to buy utensils that are dedicated solely to your soapmaking craft.

When I first started researching cold-process soapmaking, I spent days and days reading and making phone calls to experts about sodium hydroxide, chemicals, and chemical reactions. I memorized each step of the recipes. I wrote out the steps several times to double-check my memory. I gathered all my supplies and arranged all my equipment, tools, and ingredients in the garage, with the doors open for maximum ventilation. I used a hot plate for my heat source and had the garden hose ready to go. With a quick squeeze of my shaking finger, I could hose down the work area in seconds.

I covered my body from head to toe with old clothing. I pulled my hair back in a tight bun, slid the safety goggles over my own glasses, snapped on rubber gloves, and adjusted the filter mask over a bandanna I'd tied around my face. I learned to move like a ballerina while feeling like a tank! I posted biohazard signs on each side of my garage and scared home the children playing in the streets. I measured everything twice and told my husband to stand back—I was going to make soap.

There was only one problem. I was so afraid of sodium hydroxide that I was not enjoying myself one little bit. At one point I thought the fumes were overwhelming me until my husband told me I might feel better if I stopped hyperventilating. I thought my brain would never hold all the information I needed to make soap. After reading what felt like a full set of encyclopedias from A to Z, I forgot the most basic of instructions: I forgot to breathe!

I did learn a valuable lesson that I wish to share with you, crafter to crafter, soapmaker to soapmaker, human being to human being. Don't freak out! Read the precautions listed on the next page and prepare yourself thoroughly. Most of these safety precautions are for cold-process soapmaking, and to a lesser degree the hand-milled and melt-and-pour methods. When you're learning a new craft, it may at first seem as difficult as learning a second language. But after a few batches, you'll begin to feel like a native.

Soapmaking is not dangerous if you read all the instructions, carefully prepare your equipment and materials, and take all safety

> ## Handy Hint
> Make a copy of the soap recipe you're attempting rather than leaving this book near your work area. Write the recipe on an index card or use a copy machine, then slip the recipe into a plastic sleeve, or tape the recipe card at eye level on a cabinet door or on the top of your range. This way the recipe will lie flat in your work area (books always seem to move, flip, or get splattered with oil).

precautions seriously. Before you even attempt to make your first batch of soap, read all the safety precautions and advisories. Chemicals aren't to be taken lightly, and chemical reactions are serious situations that demand your complete attention. But once you know what you're doing, you can relax and enjoy all the methods of soapmaking. Chapter 4 puts all this soap knowledge to work by explaining the how-to's and what-fors of cold-process, hand-milled, and melt-and-pour soapmaking.

Safety Tips

- Always wear rubber gloves when handling sodium hydroxide or any other chemical ingredient of soapmaking, including essential or fragrance oils. Wear the gloves through the entire process of making soap, including taking soap out of molds or turning soap on a drying rack. Hand-milled and melt-and-pour soaps can be removed from molds without gloves.

- Always add a chemical to water; *never* add water to a chemical! Adding water to a chemical can create a massive heat expansion that is not easy to control and that can blow up like a volcano. In soapmaking, this means you will add your measured amount of sodium hydroxide to the water.

- Never put sodium hydroxide or lye into aluminum. The aluminum doesn't stand a chance and will become black and pitted! It's best to avoid all metals when working with lye.

- Never touch hands or rubber gloves to your face or skin while making soap. Sodium hydroxide and lye are caustic materials that will burn your skin if they come in contact with it. Rinse and remove gloves and then wash your hands if you must do something other than soapmaking during the process.

■ Remove jewelry from hands and pull hair out of your face.

■ Wear eye protection while working with a heat source or when mixing any ingredients. Make sure all skin is protected from possible splashes.

■ Work in a well-ventilated area and never stand directly over the container when you introduce sodium hydroxide to water. Toxic fumes and extreme heat are created during the chemical reaction. *Do not* add all the sodium hydroxide at once; instead stir it gradually into the water.

■ Children must be closely supervised if involved with the soapmaking process. Children should be given protective wear, including rubber gloves and eye goggles. Children under the age of 12 should not be allowed to participate in cold-process soapmaking.

■ Never leave soap over heat unattended. Let the answering machine get the phone and let the doorbell ring until you can remove the soap from the heat element. Never leave a batch of soap unattended while waiting for the soap to trace.

■ Never take cautionary or safety precautions too lightly. Getting careless or too familiar with a caustic material can and will lead to serious accidents. Be aware of your surroundings when working with a chemical. Post poison control phone numbers near your work area.

■ Allow cold-process soap to cure for the recommended time listed in the recipe. If the recipe doesn't give any guidelines, wait at least two to four weeks before using the soap. Most soaps using lye remain caustic for at least a week after being removed from a mold. Hand-milled and melt-and-pour soaps don't need to be cured but do need 72 hours to two weeks to dry before use. Once soap is cured, check for any defects (see troubleshooting tips on page 293 for help with this). Always test the batch of soap with a pH strip before using the soap, giving the soap as a gift, or selling the soap to a customer.

- Never pour soap down the drain. Allow the pot or measuring cup to cool and scrape any excess soap left in the container into a garbage bag or other disposable container. Dispose of any failed cold-process batches with care, as they may still contain lye.

- Be aware of allergies. Perform a skin test before using a cured soap. Place a small amount of lather on a sensitive area of your skin, such as the inside wrist or inside elbow. If the skin becomes red and irritated, you are allergic to an ingredient. Possible causes for allergic reactions: almonds, almond oil, cocoa butter, coconut oil, glycerin, honey, lanolin, and orrisroot.

chapter 4

Creative How-To's

▼▼

MOST SOAPMAKERS FEEL THAT creating soap is a simple task, and for the most part it is. However, some parts of the process require a little more thought and procedure. This chapter will discuss the fun parts of soapmaking, as well as provide the simplest ways to work with the more "detailed" parts of the process.

Saponification Calculations and SAP Values

The saponification process that occurs when fats, oils, or a combination of both are mixed with lye to create the compound known as soap is a fairly complex chemical reaction. You don't need to understand the fine details of the reaction to make cold-process soap, but you do need to follow the instructions carefully. The most important rule is never get creative with the measurements for cold-process soaps. The amount of fats and oils *must* be calculated precisely as this measurement is used to calculate the proper amount of sodium hydroxide needed to complete the saponification process. The amount of sodium hydroxide will then determine the amount of water needed to make the lye. If too much lye is added to the recipe, the resulting soap will be too caustic to use. If not enough lye is added, the soap will never harden properly and might go rancid.

Each fat or oil has a saponification (SAP) value, which is used to calculate the amount of sodium hydroxide needed in a particular recipe. Saponification values are given in the list of oils on page 56. Please note that if you are using a soap recipe found in this book or other reliable source, the SAP calculation has already been done for you, but it is always smart to do your own calculations as a double-check before you make the recipe.

I'm not a mathematician, scientist, chemist, or particularly bright when it comes to numbers, fractions, or decimal points. Formulas and calculations make me dizzy. I admire and respect traditional art-and-craft methods and those purists who follow the old ways to the letter, but I'm not a purist. I believe in using modern methods in my work, home, and leisure activities. My goal is to make this calculation easy to understand.

The saponification table below provides the amount of sodium hydroxide required to saponify the number of ounces of the particular fat or oil. Keep in mind that this book uses measurements in weighted ounces, not grams. You can use a conversion chart to change measurements to the metric system if that is easier for you. (I should have paid attention to the new math while I was in school, but I didn't.)

When working in ounces, the formula for determining the amount of sodium hydroxide needed is:

$A \times B = C$

A = ounces of fat/oil

B = saponification value

C = amount of sodium hydroxide needed for saponification, rounded up/down to the nearest quarter ounce

The SAP value for olive oil is used in this example:

10 ounces olive oil × 0.0134 = 1.34 ounces sodium hydroxide;
round up to 1.5 ounces

If you use a recipe that calls for a combination of fats and oils, you must follow these steps to find the amount of sodium hydroxide needed for saponification:

Saponification Chart

1. Find the saponification value of each fat or oil.
2. Multiply the weight of each fat or oil by its own SAP value.
3. Total the results and round up or down to the nearest quarter ounce.

This example uses olive oil, coconut oil, and vegetable shortening. The total amount of fats/oils is 32 ounces, using the following formula:

$A + B + C = D$

A = 8 ounces olive oil × 0.134 (SAP value) = 1.072 ounces

B = 12 ounces coconut oil × 0.190 (SAP value) = 2.28 ounces

C = 12 ounces vegetable shortening × 0.136 (SAP value)
= 1.632 ounces

D = total amount of sodium hydroxide needed for saponification
= 4.984 ounces, rounded up to 5 ounces

Water

The original soapmakers didn't have a specific calculation to determine how much water to use with sodium hydroxide to make lye. Either that or they chose not to put a calculation in writing. The soapmakers started from scratch, adding more water or more sodium hydroxide as needed during the process. The first documentation of a calculation for the amount of water needed was called the Baume (Be) scale after Antoine Baume who measured the

Fat/Oil	SAP Value
Almond oil, sweet almond oil, *Prunus amygdalus* oil	0.136
Apricot kernel oil, *Prunus armeniaca* oil	0.135
Arachis oil, peanut oil, earth nut oil, katchung oil	0.136
Avocado oil, *Persea americana* oil	0.133
Babassu, Brazil nut oil	0.175
Bayberry or myrtle wax	0.069
Beef tallow, beef fat, beef suet, dripping	0.140
Beeswax	0.069
Borage oil	0.136
Brazil nut oil, babassu oil	0.175
Canola oil, rapeseed oil, coiza oil, rape oil, ramic oil	0.124
Carnauba wax	0.069
Castor oil, ricinus oil	0.128
Chicken fat	0.138
Cocoa butter	0.137
Coconut oil, *Cocos nucifera* oil	0.190
Cod liver oil	0.132
Corn oil, maize oil	0.136
Cottonseed oil	0.138
Deer tallow, venison fat	0.139
Evening primrose oil, *Oenothera biennis* oil	0.136
Flaxseed oil	0.135
Goat tallow, goat fat	0.139
Goose fat	0.136
Grape seed oil, grapefruit seed oil, *Vitis vinifera* oil	0.123–0.135 (varies widely)
Hazelnut oil, *Corylus avellana* oil	0.136
Hemp oil, hemp seed oil	0.137
Herring oil, fish oil	0.136
Java cotton, kapok oil	0.137
Jojoba oil	0.069
Karite butter, shea butter	0.128
Kukui oil	0.135
Lanolin, sheep wool fat	0.074

Fat/Oil	SAP Value
Lard, pork tallow, pork fat	0.138
Linseed oil, flaxseed oil	0.136
Macadamia nut oil, *Macadamia integrifolia* oil	0.139
Margarine	0.136
Mink oil	0.140
Mustard seed oil	0.123
Mutton tallow, sheep tallow	0.138
Neat's root oil, beef hoof oil	0.141
Olive oil, loccu oil, Florence oil (olium olivate),	0.134
Palm kernel oil, palm butter	0.156
Palm oil	0.141
Peanut oil, earth nut oil	0.136
Pistachio oil	0.135
Poppy seed oil	0.138
Pumpkinseed oil	0.135
Rice bran oil	0.128
Safflower oil	0.136
Sardine oil, Japan fish oil	0.135
Sesame seed oil, gigely oil	0.133
Shea butter, African karite butter	0.128
Sheep fat, sheep tallow	0.138
Sheep wool fat, lanolin	0.074
Shortening, vegetable shortening, hydrogenated vegetable oil	0.136
Soybean oil, Chinese bean oil, *Helianthus annus* oil	0.135
Sunflower seed oil	0.134
Theobroma oil, cocoa butter	0.137
Tung oil, China wood oil, nut oil	0.137
Venison fat, deer fat, venison tallow	0.138
Walnut oil, *Juglans regia* oil	0.136
Whale: baleen whale	0.138
Whale: sperm whale, body, blubber oil	0.092
Whale: sperm whale, head	0.102
Wheat germ oil, *Triticum vulgare* oil	0.132
Wool fat, lanolin	0.074

concentration of the lye solution by comparing the density of the sodium hydroxide to the density of the water. This scale was only a general rule for soapmakers to follow and is no longer used by modern soapmakers.

Modern soapmakers use a formula that considers all the ingredients used in a specific soap recipe. The calculations seem rather complicated to those of us with limited math skills, but I've tried to simplify the water calculation for those more daring to experiment with their own recipes. The calculation must be done in the order listed, **with no exceptions.** It's a good idea to do this calculation even with soap recipes that you find in books and on the Web even if it is just for practice. This is the first trouble-spotting tool you can use when a soap recipe fails.

1. **You must first calculate the amount of sodium hydroxide needed. See the Saponification Chart on page 55.**
2. **You will then calculate the amount of water by dividing the weight of the sodium hydroxide by three-tenths (3/10 or .3). This will give you the total weight of the lye solution (sodium hydroxide and water).**
3. **Subtract the known weight of the sodium hydroxide from #1 and you will have the weight of the water needed for the lye solution.**

This example uses a saponification value for 10 ounces of olive oil. The amount of sodium hydroxide needed is 1.34 ounces.

1.34 ounces sodium hydroxide ÷ .3 = 4.47 (total weight of lye solution) − 1.34 (weight of sodium hydroxide) = 3.13 ounces of water needed.

Shaping Soap

Regardless of which soapmaking method you use, you will eventually need either to pour your soap into a mold or to hand-shape it

Interesting Molds

- Plastic eggs (the kind used at Easter)

- Small plastic drawer organizers

- Small sardine or candy tins

- Microwave cooking containers

- Gelatin molds

- Tart pans

- 2- to 6-inch-wide PVC piping (cut down to 5- to 12-inch sections)

- Flexible candle/wax molds

into balls. To prepare a mold for use, evenly apply a release agent to the inside surface of the mold before pouring soap into it. A variety of commercial soap release agents are sold as aerosols, or you can use any nonstick cooking spray. Petroleum jelly also works well. Some soaps shrink during the drying process, making a release agent unnecessary. For example, when working with melt-and-pour soap base, I found a release agent was not needed except when making glycerin soap. The need for release agents is something you will learn through experience.

Some molds, such as polyvinyl chloride (PVC) tubes, must be sealed at one end before melted soap is poured into them. Use rubber bands to secure plastic bags or plastic cling wrap tightly over the end. For extra support, I place this type of mold in a glass bowl before pouring in the melted soap. Do not pick up this type of mold until you are sure the soap has cooled enough to be firm; otherwise you'll end up with a lump of wet soap. Patience is the key!

Soap needs to remain in a mold for about 24 hours, although the time can vary depending on the type and size of the mold. Remove soap from a mold when it is hard enough to hold its shape but not too hard to cut. If you ever have problems removing soap from a mold, place it in the refrigerator for at least one hour. Then try removing the soap. It should pop right out.

If you choose to hand-shape your soap into balls, either pour the soap batch into a square or rectangular mold or leave it in the top pan of the double boiler and allow it to cool. Melt-and-pour soaps cool very quickly, so do not leave the batch unattended while it's cooling, or it may seize on you. Always wear rubber gloves when hand-shaping cold-process soap. Once the soap is cool to the touch, scoop out a handful and shape it into a ball. Reshape the ball every few hours as the soap dries and settles. Once the soap has the desired shape, leave it to dry and harden. You can polish the ball and remove any residue with a wet towel before use.

If you have difficulty creating nice, round balls with your hands, you can use molds. Round, plastic ornaments or ball-shaped candle molds, which are sold at craft stores, work well for round molds. The plastic tree ornament or mold opens into two halves. Pour the soap into each half of the mold and close. As with any mold, allow the soap to cool and harden before removing.

Handy Hint

Add a release agent, such as petroleum jelly, nonstick cooking spray, or a commercial nonstick release agent, to most molds to make it easier to remove the soap.

Labels and Packaging

If you decide to sell your soap, be aware that labels and packaging are important. According to Federal Department of Agriculture (FDA) rules, as long as you present your handmade soap as "soap" and nothing else, you do not have to include any labeling or list the ingredients used to make it. However, if you make any type of claim about your soap, such as proclaiming that it also acts as a moisturizer or a bug repellant, then you must adhere to FDA labeling regulations.

I surveyed and questioned dozens of soapmakers about labeling and listing ingredients used in their soaps. The majority use labels and list ingredients even though they legally do not have to. According to one response I received over e-mail, "Even when I'm giving the soap as a gift to a friend, I package my soap and include a pretty tag that lists the ingredients. I do this so my friend can see what I've used—you never know if someone might have an allergy to a specific ingredient. Labeling and listing ingredients is a courtesy and also, in a small way, a preventative action. I enjoy creating my own labels, and the packaging and tagging are an added touch to my homemade soap."

Creating Your Own Scent Blends

Although it's not difficult to blend your own scents, the following information will increase your success at formulating your own blends. An important part of blending is to know that scents are categorized according to their main aroma characteristic. You can blend a citrus scent with a spicy scent or an herbal scent. You might like a floral scent with just a touch of fruit or citrus. The combinations are unlimited, but knowing which family each scent belongs to will help you blend the individual scents within the categories. Make sure you note in your soap journal any experimentation with scents.

Citrus

Bergamot	Lime	Sweet orange
Grapefruit	Mandarin	Tangerine
Lemon	Pink grapefruit	

Spicy

Cinnamon	Ginger
Clove	Vanilla

Herbal

Bay	Peppermint	Thyme
Cucumber	Rosemary	Wintergreen
Eucalyptus	Sage	
Marjoram	Spearmint	

Earthy

Amber	Patchouli
Musk	Sandalwood

Floral

Chamomile	Lavender	Violet
Gardenia	Lilac	Ylang-ylang
Geranium	Lily of the Valley	
Jasmine	Rose	

Fruity

Apple	Green apple	Peach
Blackberry	Kiwi	Raspberry
Blueberry	Mango	
Coconut	Melon	

How long the fragrance lasts or can be smelled on your skin is also a category of scent. This classification, which is referred to as the note of a fragrance, is broken into two scent families, with certain "cousins" that fall into both categories. These categories of scents are very subjective. All noses are not made the same. What is

A Different Kind of Therapy

Aromatherapy, an increasingly popular use of fragrances to relax, stimulate, rejuvenate, and even promote healing, is becoming popular in soapmaking as well. Adherents claim that scents can heal, prevent, and remedy many health woes, while other people claim there is no legitimate proof that aromatherapy is of any medical benefit. Aromatherapy isn't a new idea, just a resurgence and rediscovery of a practice used for thousands of years. You will have to be the judge of the value of using aromatherapy in your soapmaking.

overpowering to one individual might go barely noticed by another person.

The first family of scents, referred to as high notes, is fleeting, soft, or airy. High notes are the first aromas your nose detects in a blend. High notes don't have much staying power and fade quickly. I prefer a fleeting scent, but some people like a more steady, strong, or heady scent, which is the second fragrance family. Scents in this category, referred to as low notes, are potent and long-lived. In some reference guides or charts, the scents that fall into both high- and low-note categories are called middle notes.

In the following table of scents, an asterisk marks the scents that fall into both categories. When you blend your own scents, you might want to use this middle-note group of fragrances as at least 50% of your blend.

High Notes

Basil*	Clary sage*	Fennel*
Bergamot	Cypress	Geranium*
Chamomile*	Eucalyptus	Grapefruit

*Middle-note fragrances

Hyssop*
Juniper*
Lavender*
Lemon
Lime
Mandarin
Melissa

Neroli*
Orange
Petitgrain*
Pine*
Rose*
Rosemary*
Rosewood

Sandalwood
Spearmint*
Tangerine*
Tea tree
Thyme*
Wintergreen*

Low Notes

Basil*
Cedarwood
Chamomile*
Clary sage*
Clove
Cypress*
Fennel*
Frankincense
Geranium*
Hyssop*
Jasmine*
Juniper*

Lavender*
Lemongrass
Marjoram
Melissa
Myrrh
Neroli*
Nutmeg
Orange
Patchouli
Peppermint
Petitgran*
Pine*

Rose*
Rosemary*
Sage
Sandalwood
Spearmint*
Tangerine*
Thyme*
Vanilla
Wintergreen*
Ylang-ylang

Let's say I want to mix a blend of lemon, sweet orange, and lime. I look on the list and find out that all three scents are from the high-note category. I really need to find a complementary scent that has more staying power. I find that tangerine is considered a middle note. My blend would look like this: 2 drops each of lemon, sweet orange, and lime plus 10 drops of tangerine. If I find that the scent still evaporates or dissipates very quickly, I add a fixative. Fixatives slow the evaporation process, thus prolonging the scent. Fixatives come in all shapes and textures. Carrier or base oils such as apricot kernel, avocado, coconut, corn, grape seed, jojoba, saf-

*Middle-note fragrances

flower, sunflower, sweet almond, vitamin E, and wheat germ are commonly used as fixatives. Table salt, sea salt, rock salt, ice-cream salt, and Epsom salts can also be used as fixatives, as can any dried flower, plant, or herb. Unscented lotions with no colorants added, which are carried by health food stores or soap suppliers, are also wonderful fixatives.

Infusions

To infuse botanicals means to make a concentrated solution of the herb, flower, or fruit and add this solution to soap. There are two methods for infusing soaps, as described below.

Method One

1. Chop, cut, or powder 1 cup of the botanical.
2. Bring 2 cups of mineral or spring water to a boil.
3. Place botanicals in a container that has an airtight lid.
4. Pour the boiling water into the container and seal it.
5. Allow this combination to set for 8 to 12 hours, then strain to remove all botanical matter.
6. For a stronger solution, repeat the process by boiling the infused water and adding it to a new batch of botanicals.

If you don't plan to use the infusion immediately, you can refrigerate it. Shelf life of an infusion is 24 hours. You can use the infusion as a substitute for the water used to make lye in cold-process soap recipes or as a substitute for the water added to a hand-milled soap during the melting process.

Method Two

1. In the morning, chop, cut, or powder 1 to 2 cups of the botanical.

2. Place the botanicals in a glass container with 2 to 4 cups of mineral or spring water. Seal the container.
3. Place the container outside in full sun or in a window that will get full sun most of the day.
4. Strain the mixture at the end of the day, keeping only the liquid.
5. For a stronger solution, repeat the process the next morning, adding new botanicals to the water.
6. Refrigerate if you don't use it immediately.

Decoctions

If you use the bark or roots of a flower or plant to make a concentrated solution, it's called a decoction rather than an infusion. To make a decoction, follow these steps.

1. Cut, crush, or powder the bark, roots, or seeds to measure 1 cup.
2. Soak the crushed material in 3 cups of cold mineral or spring water for 15 to 30 minutes.
3. Pour the water and material into a saucepan and bring to a boil.
4. Reduce heat and simmer for 10 to 15 minutes.
5. Cover the pan with a tight lid and simmer for another 10 to 15 minutes.
6. Strain the solution into another bowl to remove all the botanical matter. Keep the liquid.

If you don't plan to use the decoction immediately, refrigerate it. The shelf life of a decoction is 24 hours. You can use a decoction as a substitute for the water in cold-process soap batches or as a substitute for the water added to hand-milled soap during the melting process.

Gathering and Drying Botanicals

Gathering and drying your own botanicals is fun and gives you a real sense of contributing to your soap. However, do keep in mind that purchasing dried botanicals is a time saver.

Gathering

You will need a sharp knife or a pair of scissors and plastic bags, preferably with interlocking seals. Place a wet paper towel in each bag.

1. Select and cut botanicals in midmorning or late afternoon to avoid the heat of the day, which will quickly wilt the plants.

2. Place cut botanicals in plastic bags with a wet paper towel. When done collecting plants and flowers, immediately return to the kitchen or work area and prepare the botanicals.

3. If you're going to use the plants or flowers fresh, start your soap batch. If you want to press or dry the botanicals, allow them to air dry before proceeding to your method of drying and preserving.

Drying

To preserve flowers or plants, you'll need silica gel, glycerin, and string or a microwave flower press.

Hanging Method

1. Place flowers or plants in a solution of 50% water and 50% glycerin.
2. After a few days, remove the botanicals and gather them into small groups. Tie string around the stems, and hang the botanicals in a dry, cool area with good ventilation. Allow a drying time of two to six weeks.

Flower Press Method

1. Place the botanicals on a sheet of acid-free paper. Leave space between the plants or flowers. Place another sheet of acid-free paper on top of the plants.
2. Place the paper between two heavy books or in a press. (Flower presses are sold at most craft or garden shops.) Allow two to six weeks for the botanicals to dry.

Silica Gel Method

1. Pour a small amount of silica gel into an airtight container.
2. Place flowers or leaves on top of the silica gel, pour additional silica gel over the botanicals, seal the container with the lid, and allow to dry for one to two weeks.

Microwave Method

1. A microwave flower press allows you to dry flowers and plants in less than a minute.
2. Place a few botanicals on a cloth sheet and cover with a top cloth sheet. Place the sheets between the microwavable plates and snap closed.
3. Microwave as instructed with a low heat setting for 10-second intervals.

One of the incentives I find so charming in soapmaking is the endless possibilities for creativity and expression. Soapmaking has it all—scent, color, texture. It's a craft that uses all your senses. I find myself making all kinds of lists. A list of new essential oils and fragrances I want to track down to add to my treasured stash. A list of herbs and flowers to buy during my next visit to the nursery. Each batch of soap is unique and a joy to create. Speaking of making soap, it's time to turn the page and get down to business!

Creating Your Soap Recipes

▼▼

IT'S TIME TO MAKE SOAP! This chapter describes three methods of soapmaking: cold-process, melt-and-pour, and hand-milled. I've included recipes for each. I always like to start with the easiest, simplest method of a new craft, and I hope you feel the same. If you're an experienced soapmaker, you can skip the general step-by-step instructions for each method and move straight to the recipes, unless you want to enjoy a lively refresher. Up to this point we've looked in detail at all the components of a soap recipe and covered some general how-to information. Now let's put everything together and try our hand at making a batch of soap.

In all recipes and instructions, when cups of soap base, grated soap, and other solids are referred to, use dry measure cups. For all liquid ingredients, use liquid measure cups.

You can use my original soap recipes in this chapter for your own soapmaking pleasure or to make soaps to sell to the public. I tested each recipe in several batches over the course of three months, giving samples of each batch to my friends and family for feedback. It was my goal and dream to create recipes that are simple to follow but that challenge your creativity. Read each recipe entirely before you start making the soap, and review all safety pre-

Motivation to Create

We all face times when we just can't get motivated to start or finish a project or design. The following list of pick-me-ups may help jumpstart your creative juices and get you inspired.

■ Set your goals. List several short-term (day, week, month) and a few long-term (1- to 5-year) goals. Break the goals into steps. Check off the steps and celebrate every goal reached. Calibrate the celebration to the size of the goal.

■ Add something new to your routine. Change materials, color themes, or ingredients of your current work. Step back to view your work. What can be added? What can be changed?

■ Take or teach a class. Acquiring new skills or developing learned ones sheds new light on your craft. Teaching others brings in new perspectives. Students are often our best teachers.

■ Take a walk, visit a park or garden, watch people at a mall. Exercise builds energy, and energy gets you motivated. Nothing inspires like nature, so surround yourself with the sights, colors, smells, motion, and taste of it. People-watching is a joy. Listen to people laughing. Observe what the buyers are browsing.

■ Organize your supplies or rearrange your work area. Think of ways to find your supplies more easily and efficiently. Personalize your space; make it yours. Rearrange your work area to add more light, more color, more stimulation. If you're

cautions as well. See full-color photos of these finished soaps in the center of the book.

You may wonder how I came up with the fun and silly names for each recipe. I tend to see humor in life and enjoy laughter and smiles. I took all the instructions and directions for making soap very seriously but couldn't help myself when it came to naming the soap recipes. I've used the names of my family and friends, who not only helped me write this book but have always had great faith

bored in your work area, you'll be bored in your work. The routine of organizing may also help you relax into creativity.

- Visit gift shops in your area or take a day trip to a nearby city. Schedule a trip to a museum or special exhibit. Invite your friends to a creativity party.

- Pick up a magazine you've never read before, or read a book on your favorite subject. Learn more about your craft and about others who also enjoy your medium. Or read a book about sales, marketing, design, writing skills, or bookkeeping. Update your knowledge with the latest information. New data will refresh you and might inspire new ideas.

- Take time out to play. Experiment each week for an hour or two with your medium. Don't put any pressure on yourself to complete or create anything. Just play. Experiment with scent, color, and texture and get messy. As a soapmaker you'll have a fun time cleaning up too.

- Visit a trade or consumer show. Find out what craft, gift, or consumer shows are coming to your area. If you are a professional crafter, visit at least one trade show every one to two years.

- Take a vacation. It doesn't have to be one where you travel by car, boat, or plane. It can simply be a vacation from your craft or your business. Take a day, two days, or even a week and don't touch, do, or even think crafts. Absence often does make the heart grow fonder. Don't risk burnout! If you are a craft professional, treat yourself to a leisure activity outside of crafting or select a craft to enjoy for fun, not for work or profit.

in my abilities. Without our family and friends, art and crafting wouldn't have the same gentle radiance or satisfaction.

Hand-Milled Soap

The true soap connoisseur might call this step-by-step process of hand-milling soap an imposter, because hand-milled soap is initially made by machines. But this process falls within the broadest definition of hand milling. Machines create very thin sheets from soap base, and the thin sheets are flaked and then re-melted. Additional additives are mixed into the soap, creating a new and very rich soap. We don't have the machinery, but the following step-by-step process is a practical guide to using commercial soap bars to create a unique soap. I don't recommend using a microwave oven to melt a hand-milled soap. The heat of the microwave varies and is difficult to measure accurately. Clear or colored glycerin soaps will explode in a microwave if heated too fast or at too high a temperature.

1. Select a recipe or create your own.

2. Select and buy commercial, unscented, hypoallergenic soap bars. Do not *use* glycerin or clear soaps that have alcohol listed as an ingredient.

3. Grate the soap bars with a hand grater (see step HM-1). The finer the grating, the easier it is to melt.

4. Gather and measure all additional ingredients, including scent and color. Keep each ingredient in a separate container.

5. Clear your work area of anything not used in the recipe.

6. Prepare a mold if you're going to use one.

7. Prepare and heat your double boiler or mock double boiler.

8. Add water to the top pan of the double boiler, then add the soap flakes. Most hand-milled recipes call for one cup of water to every two dry measured cups of soap. Some soapmakers prefer to mix the water with the soap the evening before they melt it.

9. Do not leave the double boiler unattended. As the soap begins to melt, gently stir the mixture until the soap and water are completely mixed. Once mixed, add any colorants at this time and, again, mix completely, producing even color throughout the mixture.

10. When the mixture of soapbase, water, and color has the consistency of sour cream or yogurt, remove from heat and add any additional ingredients. Stir until mixed. Remove from heat.

11. If using a mold, pour the mixture into the prepared mold. If hand-shaping the soap, leave the mixture in the top pot of the double boiler until it cools. Then hand-shape the soap into soap balls.

12. Let the soap in the molds cool for several hours or overnight. Remove the soap from the mold. Allow to dry from 72 hours up to a full week before use.

Step HM-1. Grate the soap bars with a hand grater.

Hand-Milled Recipes and Projects

This set of recipes focuses on hand-shaping soap. You can hand-shape the soap from any of the recipes in this chapter, but the hand-milled recipes will give you some practice.

Marie's Citrus Lavender Soap

Marie Browning is a great friend of mine who lives in Canada. Her book, Beautiful Handmade Natural Soap, *inspired me to learn more about all aspects of soapmaking. Her book includes some great recipes for hand-milled and melt-and-pour soaps. The following recipe yields a soap with gentle exfoliating qualities and a very relaxing, yet rejuvenating, scent.*

Materials

Hand grater/food processor
Measuring cups
Measuring spoons
Double boiler
Wooden spoon

Time

1–2 hours, plus 1 hour cooling time and 24 hours for curing/drying

Ingredients

2 cups grated soap
1/2 cup infused orange water
1/4 teaspoon vitamin E or grapefruit seed extract
1/2 tablespoon ground lemon peel
1/2 tablespoon ground orange peel
1/2 tablespoon crushed or whole lavender buds
10 drops lavender essential oil
10 drops lemon essential oil
10 drops sweet orange essential oil

Instructions

1. Grate the soap and measure out 2 cups. Gather and measure all other ingredients.

2. Prepare the double boiler. Melt the grated soap and infused orange water together.

3. Once the soap is melted, remove from heat, add remaining ingredients, and mix well.

4. Allow the soap to cool and thicken. Once cool to touch, remove a small handful and shape into a ball.

5. Let the soap balls dry for several hours. Repeat hand shaping into tighter, smoother soap balls.

6. Let the soap dry for 24 to 48 hours. Mix a few drops of sweet orange essential oil with 1 to 2 tablespoons of a carrier/base oil, such as almond oil or grape seed oil. Apply a small amount of this oil to your hands. Pick up one soap ball at a time and roll the ball in your hands. The oil on your hands will polish the soap ball. Allow the soap balls to air-dry for another 24 to 48 hours before use.

 ## Nancee Bee's Honey Soap

My friend Nancee Bee McAteer loves to collect bees, in part because of her middle name and in part because her children's high school mascot is the bumblebee. She tested this soap recipe for me and was all abuzz about homemade soaps. This is a hard soap with a lot of lather.

Materials

Hand grater/food processor
Measuring cups

Measuring spoons

Double boiler

Wooden spoon

Time

1–2 hours plus 1 hour cooling time and 24 hours for curing/drying

Ingredients

3 cups grated soap

1 cup water

1/4 cup beeswax chips

3 tablespoons honey

3 tablespoons wheat germ, baby oats, or ground almond

1/4 teaspoon vitamin E or grapefruit seed extract

20 drops lily of the valley or other floral essential oil

Instructions

1. Grate the soap and measure out 3 cups. Gather and measure all other ingredients.

2. Prepare the double boiler. Melt the grated soap and water together.

3. Once the soap has melted, add the beeswax.

4. When the beeswax has melted and been mixed well into the soap mixture, remove from heat, add remaining ingredients, and mix well.

5. Allow the soap to cool and thicken. Once cool to touch, remove a small handful and shape into a ball.

6. Let the soap balls dry for several hours. Repeat hand shaping, forming a tighter, smoother soap ball.

7. Let the soap dry for 24 to 48 hours before use.

Mary Jo's Spice-Is-Nice Soap

My sister-in-law Mary Jo is one of the nicest, smartest people I know. Her Pennsylvania roots inspired the recipe for this soap, which has a long-lasting scent and is very invigorating.

Materials

Hand grater/food processor
Measuring cups
Measuring spoons
Double boiler
Wooden spoon

Time

1–2 hours plus 1 hour cooling time and 24 hours for curing/drying

Ingredients

2 cups grated soap
2/3 cup water
1/2 teaspoon rosemary
1/2 teaspoon thyme
1/2 teaspoon sage
10 drops rosemary essential oil
5 drops cinnamon essential oil

Optional

1/2 disk orange soap colorant
1 tablespoon grape seed oil, California walnut oil,
    or other carrier/base oil

Instructions

1. Grate the soap and measure out 2 cups. Gather and measure all other ingredients.

2. Prepare the double boiler. Melt the grated soap and water together.

3. When the soap has melted, place the colorant and 1 tablespoon of carrier/base oil in a small glass dish. Place the dish in the microwave on a low temperature and heat in 10-second intervals until the colorant is dissolved in the carrier/base oil. Stir and add to the melted soap. Mix well by stirring.

4. Once the colorant is mixed with the soap, remove from heat and add all remaining ingredients. Mix well.

5. Allow the soap to cool and thicken. Once cool to touch, remove small handfuls and shape into balls.

6. Let the soap balls dry for several hours. Repeat hand shaping into tighter, smoother soap balls.

7. Let the soap dry for 24 to 48 hours. Mix 2 drops of cinnamon essential oil with 2 tablespoons of a carrier/base oil, such as almond oil or grape seed oil. Apply a small amount of this oil to your hands. Pick up one soap ball at a time and roll the ball in your hands. The oil on your hands will polish the soap ball. Wash your hands immediately. Allow the soap balls to air dry for 24 to 48 hours before use.

 Tollee's Banana Fun Soap

Tollee is another sister-in-law of mine. She has the most infectious laugh and a radiant smile. As a child, I often visited her and her family on

their farm to enjoy some down-home fun during the summer. This soap has a very soft, smooth lather.

Materials

Hand grater/food processor
Measuring cups
Measuring spoons
Double boiler
Wooden spoon

Time

1–2 hours plus 1 hour cooling time and 24 hours for curing/drying

Ingredients

3 cups grated soap
1 cup water
1/4 cup beeswax chips
1/4 cup pureed banana (must be fresh and ripe with no bruising)
1/4 teaspoon citric acid (or 1 teaspoon lemon juice)
1/2 teaspoon or 20 drops vitamin E or grapefruit seed extract
1/2 cup dried milk
10 drops banana fragrance oil
10 drops coconut essential oil

Optional

1/4 to 1/2 disk yellow soap colorant
1 tablespoon grape seed oil, California walnut oil, or other carrier/base oil

Instructions

1. Grate the soap and measure out 3 cups. Gather and measure all other ingredients.

2. Puree the banana and add the citric acid.

3. Prepare the double boiler. Melt together the grated soap and water.

4. Once the soap has melted, add the beeswax.

5. When the beeswax has melted and been mixed well into the soap mixture, you can add colorant if you desire.

    > Place the colorant and 1 tablespoon of carrier/base oil in a small glass dish.

    > Place in the microwave on a low temperature setting and heat in 10-second intervals until the colorant is dissolved in the carrier/base oil.

    > Stir and add to the melted soap.

    > Mix well by stirring.

6. Remove the soap from the heat, add the remaining ingredients, and mix well.

7. Allow the soap to cool and thicken. Once cool to touch, remove small handfuls and shape into balls.

8. Let the soap balls dry for several hours. Experiment with shapes. For example, flatten the soap ball into a thick, flat shape. Let the soap dry for 24 to 48 hours.

9. Mix a few drops of coconut EO with 1 to 2 tablespoons of carrier/base oil, like almond oil or coconut oil. Apply a small amount of this oil to your hands. Pick up one soap at a time and polish the soap with your hands. Allow the soap to air dry for 24 to 48 hours before use.

Melt-and-Pour Soap

Making melt-and-pour soap is similar to making hand-milled soap, except that you'll be working with soap base rather than commercially produced bars. You don't need to add water to melt this type of soap. Melt-and-pour soap base can be creamy white or clear glycerin and comes in small chunks, one-pound blocks, five-pound blocks, or noodle-shaped nuggets. This soap base can be melted in a microwave if you follow the manufacturer's labeling and product information. You don't *have* to grate the soap base, but you do need to chop large blocks of melt-and-pour soap base into smaller chunks to melt evenly.

1. Select a recipe or create your own.

2. Grate the melt-and-pour soap base with a hand grater or chop the soap base into smaller pieces with a knife or metal chopping blade.

3. Gather and measure all additives and additional ingredients, including scent and color. Keep each ingredient in a separate container.

4. Clear your work area of anything not used in the recipe.

5. Prepare a mold if you're going to use one.

6. Prepare and heat your double boiler or mock double boiler. Or use your microwave to melt the soap. If using a microwave, heat the soap base for one minute at a low setting. Continue to melt soap base in 20-second intervals. If using a double boiler, add the soap base to the top pot of the double boiler. Do not leave the double boiler unattended. Gently stir the soap as it begins to melt. Add any colorant at this time.

7. When the mixture has liquefied (most melt-and-pour soaps melt to a clear liquid even if the original soap was cream colored or white; the soap will cool to the original color or the color you add to it), remove from microwave or from heat and add any additional ingredients. Stir until mixed.

8. Pour the mixture into a prepared mold or leave to cool in the top pot of the double boiler for making hand-shaped soap balls. Melt-and-pour soap cools quickly. In most cases, you can hand shape after just a few minutes of cooling.

9. After pouring the soap into the mold or hand-shaping, allow it to cool for 15 to 45 minutes. Remove from the mold. Allow to dry for one or two days before use.

Melt-and-Pour Recipes and Projects

In the following recipes I used Environmental Technology, Inc., soap bases, which I found the easiest to work with. There are other brands on the market, and you'll have to experiment to find the products you like to work with best. The first four recipes call for a coconut soap base, and the last three use a glycerin soap base. The coconut base is creamy off-white unless a colorant is added. The coconut soap melts to a clear liquid but will cool and dry to the original color. The glycerin is transparent or clear unless a colorant is added. The packaging of the soap base I used gave instructions for melting in a double boiler or the microwave. Use whichever melting method you prefer for the recipes, but be sure you check the instructions on the packaging of the soap base.

 David's Body Scrub Soap

David Fonsen, president of Environmental Technology, Inc., helped me considerably while I was writing this book. His company provided the

soap base, molds, and colorants I used in all my melt-and-pour recipes.
David also patiently explained to me the process of melt-and-pour soaps.
This is one of David's favorite recipes.

Materials

Hand grater/food processor
Measuring cups
Double boiler or microwave
Microwavable glass measuring cup or bowl
    (if using microwave)
Spoon
Mold(s) and mold release

Time

1–2 hours plus 1 hour cooling time and 24 hours for
curing/drying

Ingredients

2 cups grated coconut soap base
1/2 cup finely ground almonds
1/2 disk almond soap fragrance chopped finely or
    20 drops almond essential or fragrance oil

Instructions

1. Grate soap base or chop into small chunks. Gather and
   measure all ingredients.

2. Prepare your mold.

3. Prepare a double boiler or use a microwave.

   ■ *Microwave:* Heat the soap base for one minute at a low set-
     ting. Continue to melt soap base in 20-second intervals.

■ *Double boiler:* Add the soap base to the top pot of the double boiler. Do not leave the double boiler unattended. Gently stir the soap as it begins to melt.

4. Once the soap base is liquefied, remove from microwave or from heat and add remaining ingredients. Stir and mix well.

5. Pour the soap into the mold.

6. Allow the soap to cool for 30 minutes to an hour.

7. Remove the soap from the mold.

8. The soap is ready to use. Conditions may vary, however, and you might want to let the soap set and dry for a few days.

 # Matt's Crazy Coconut Soap

Matt McAteer is a really good sport! He's a teenager who too often is asked to be a test case for my craft ideas. When I asked Matt what kind of soap he'd use, he told me he wanted coconut. How could I turn down such a wonderful friend? Matt raved about this soap and even asked for a sample to give his girlfriend. The sweet smell of coconut stays lightly on the skin, and the soap has a soft, fine lather.

Materials

Hand grater/food processor
Measuring cups
Double boiler or microwave
Microwavable glass measuring cup or bowl
   (if using microwave)
Spoon
Mold(s) and mold release agent

Time

1–2 hours plus 1 hour cooling time and 24 hours for curing/drying

Ingredients

2 cups grated coconut soap base

1/2 cup finely ground coconut (use unsweetened
coconut or fresh coconut)

20 drops coconut essential or fragrance oil or
1/2 coconut fragrance disk, finely chopped

Optional

Several slivers of white candle colorant

Instructions

1. Grate the soap base. Gather and measure all ingredients.

2. Prepare the mold or molds.

3. Prepare the double boiler or use a microwave.

   - *Microwave:* Heat the soap base for one minute at a low
     setting. Continue to melt the soap in 20-second intervals.

   - *Double boiler:* Add the soap base to the top pot of the
     double boiler. Do not leave the double boiler unattended.
     Gently stir the soap as it begins to melt.

4. If adding colorant, do so near the end of the melting process.
   Stir well to mix the colorant and to make sure all of it has
   melted.

5. When the soap is liquefied, pour it into the mold(s).

6. Allow to cool for 30 minutes to an hour.

7. Remove the soap from the mold(s).

8. The soap is ready to use. Conditions vary, however, and
   you might want to let the soap set and dry for a few days.

Bill's Bold and Bodacious Soap

My oldest brother, Bill, has always been a hero to me. Even as a kid, I knew he was a wonderful role model. He's bold and true; he's bodacious and kind. This soap has a high lather, and the mint scent is a real pick-me-up!

Materials

Hand grater/food processor
Measuring cups
Measuring spoons
Double boiler or microwave with
Microwavable glass measuring cup or bowl
(if using microwave)
Spoon
Simple box mold
4-inch PVC mold
Mold release agent
Sharp knife

Time

1–2 hours plus 1 hour cooling time and 24 hours for curing/drying

Ingredients

5 cups grated coconut soap base
1/2 cup dry milk
1/2 to 3/4 disk red soap colorant or slivers of red candle
  colorant melted in 1 tablespoon of carrier oil
15 drops of peppermint essential or fragrance oil
20 drops of spearmint or wintermint essential or
  fragrance oil

Instructions

1. Grate the soap base. Gather and measure all ingredients.

2. Prepare mold or molds.

3. Prepare the double boiler or use a microwave to melt 2 cups of soap base.

    ■ *Microwave:* Heat the soap base for one minute at a low setting. Continue to melt the soap in 20-second intervals.

    ■ *Double boiler:* Add the soap base to the top pot of the double boiler. Do not leave the double boiler unattended. Gently stir the soap as it begins to melt.

4. Add the red colorant and peppermint essential or fragrance oil toward the end of the melting process. Stir and mix well.

5. When the soap is liquefied, pour it into the simple box mold (see step BB-1). Cool for about an hour, remove from the mold, and chop into chunks.

6. Prepare the 4-inch PVC mold.

7. Melt the remaining 3 cups of soap base and add the remaining ingredients. Mix well.

8. Pour a small amount of melted soap into the PVC mold. Drop in a few chunks of the red/peppermint soap. Add more uncolored melted soap to the mold. Repeat until all the soap is used.

9. Allow to cool at least two hours. Check the top of the mold to make sure the soap has firmed. Remove the soap from the mold by gently pushing it. To make removing the soap easier, refrigerate the mold for several hours after it has cooled.

10. The soap will be in a long, rounded loaf. Cut the loaf into 1/2-inch to 1-inch sections (see step BB-2). Place the round

soap bars on a drying rack. (The soap will have pretty red pieces inside the white creamy soap.) Turn occasionally for even drying. Allow the soap to dry for a few days, and then it's ready to use. Conditions vary, however, and you may have to allow more days for drying and hardening.

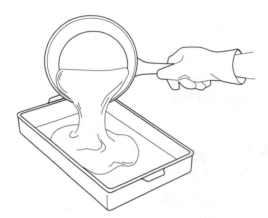

Step BB-1. When the soap is liquefied, pour it into the simple box mold.

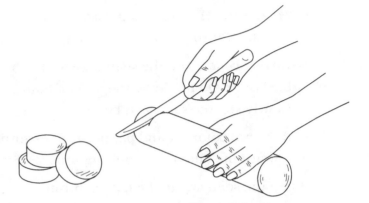

Step BB-2. The soap will be in a long, rounded loaf. Cut the loaf into 1/2-inch to 1-inch sections.

Ron's Refreshing Raspberry Soap

This soap is named after the middle brother in my family. Ron has always been rather regal. When I was a kid, he requested that I call him Ron, the King of Everything. He's still kind of like that now, but as an adult I find him refreshing and honest. This soap's aroma is fleeting but heaven to smell while washing your hands or face. The lather is smooth and silky.

Materials

Hand grater/food processor
Measuring cups

Measuring spoons

Double boiler or microwave

Microwavable glass measuring cup or bowl
(if using microwave)

Spoon

Simple box mold

Mold release agent

Sharp knife

Time

1–2 hours plus 1 hour cooling time and 24 hours for curing/drying

Ingredients

4 cups grated coconut soap base

1/2 to 3/4 disk brown soap colorant or slivers of brown
candle colorant melted in 1 tablespoon carrier oil

10 drops chocolate fragrance oil

15 drops raspberry essential or fragrance oil

5 drops peppermint essential or fragrance oil

Instructions

1. Grate the soap base. Gather and measure all ingredients.

2. Prepare the simple box mold.

3. Prepare the double boiler or use a microwave to melt 2 cups of soap base.

   ■ *Microwave:* Heat the soap base for one minute at a low setting. Continue to melt the soap in 20-second intervals.

   ■ *Double boiler:* Add the soap base to the top pot of the double boiler. Do not leave the double boiler unattended. Gently stir the soap as it begins to melt.

4. Toward the end of the melting process, add the brown colorant and chocolate fragrance oil to the mixture. Stir and mix well.

5. At the same time, melt the other 2 cups of soap base and add the raspberry and peppermint essential or fragrance oils.

6. Pour the uncolored soap mixture into the simple box mold. Now pour small amounts of the brown soap into the mixture already poured in the mold, forming a grid pattern (see step RR-1). Working quickly, use a spoon, knife, or other utensil and swirl the brown soap (see step RR-2). Allow the soap to cool for about an hour, then remove it from the mold.

7. The soap will be in a flat rectangular or square loaf. Cut the loaf to make several manageable bars. Place the soap bars on a drying rack. (The soap will have a marbled look, with brown swirled in the creamy white soap.) Turn occasionally for even drying. Allow the soap to dry for a few days, and then it's ready to use. Conditions vary, however, and you may have to allow more days for drying and hardening.

Step RR-1. Pour small amounts of the brown soap into the mixture already poured in the mold, forming a grid pattern.

Step RR-2. Working quickly, use a spoon or knife and swirl the brown soap.

Jim's Jeweled Jelly Soap

My youngest older brother (that makes me the baby of the family) has a wicked sense of humor, and his laugh is full and robust. This soap is full of laughter, smiles, and fun. The sparkling clear glycerin soap, when cut into smaller bars, shows off all the wonderful colors of the spectrum. It reminds me of looking through the glass of faceted jelly jars. This soap is very delicate and light in aroma.

Materials

Hand grater/food processor

Measuring cups

Double boiler or microwave

Microwavable glass measuring cup or bowl
(if using microwave)

Spoon

4-inch PVC mold or bread-loaf pan

Mold release agent

Sharp knife

Time

1–2 hours plus 1 hour cooling time and 24 hours for curing/drying

Ingredients

4 cups grated glycerin soap base

3 to 4 bars purchased, scented, colorful glycerin soap

Instructions

1. Grate the soap base.

2. Chop and sliver the purchased glycerin soaps.

3. You can use either a 4-inch, round PVC mold or a bread loaf pan as a mold. Whichever you choose, prepare the mold.

4. Prepare the double boiler or use a microwave to melt the soap base.

   ■ *Microwave:* Heat the soap base for one minute at a low setting. Continue to melt the soap in 20-second intervals.

   ■ *Double boiler:* Add the soap base to the top pot of the double boiler. Do not leave the double boiler unattended. Gently stir the soap as it begins to melt. There's no need to add fragrance because the other purchased soaps will be more than fragrant.

5. When soap is liquefied, work quickly following either of these processes:

   ■ Fill the PVC mold about halfway with the sliced, slivered, and chopped purchased soap (see step JJ-1). Pour enough uncolored soap to cover the purchased soap pieces (see step JJ-2). Add the remaining purchased soap to the mold and pour the remaining melted soap. Allow the soap to cool several hours and remove it from the mold. Slice into half-inch to one-inch round soap slices.

   ■ Pour a small amount of uncolored melted soap into the bread loaf pan. Add the purchased soap pieces. Pour the remaining melted soap into the pan. Allow several hours for the soap to cool and then remove it from the mold. Cut into manageable bar soap.

6. Place the soaps on a drying rack and turn occasionally. Allow the soap to dry for a few days, and then it's ready to use. Conditions vary, however, and you may have to allow more days for drying and hardening.

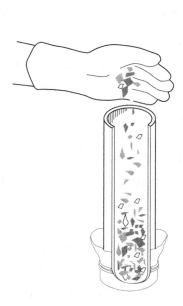 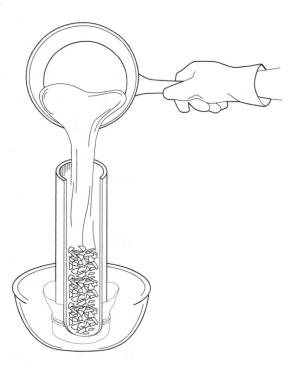

Step JJ-1. Fill the PVC mold about halfway with the sliced, slivered, and chopped purchased soap.

Step JJ-2. Pour enough uncolored soap to cover the purchased soap pieces.

Cold-Process Soap

The cold process is one of the purest forms of soapmaking. There is no softer-feeling lather. The finest-quality hand-milled soaps can't compare to the luxury of cold-process soap.

1. Select a recipe or create your own. (Refer to the saponification table of SAP values of the fats/oils in chapter 4.)

2. Gather and measure all ingredients needed for the recipe. Remember, most cold-process soap recipe ingredients are measured by weight unless otherwise specified. Keep each ingredient in a separate container. Use a glass bowl,

measuring cup, or pitcher to hold the measured amount of water needed to make the lye.

3. Clear your work area of anything not needed for the recipe.

4. Prepare your double boiler.

5. Place fats/oils in the top pot of the double boiler and begin to melt. Keep a thermometer in the pot (see step CP-1).

6. Wearing rubber gloves, appropriate clothing, and eye goggles, slowly add small amounts of the measured sodium hydroxide to the water (see step CP-2). Keep stirring until all the sodium hydroxide is dissolved. Don't stand directly over the lye, and don't breathe any of the fumes. This step can be done outside if you wish. Keep a thermometer in this container to measure the heat of the chemical reaction.

7. When the temperatures of both the melted fats/oils and the lye solution reach between 90 and 130 degrees Fahrenheit, remove the fats/oils from the heat element, and slowly add the lye solution to the melted fats/oils (see step CP-3). Stir slowly and carefully. Don't remove your safety equipment.

8. Stir the soap constantly for the first 15 minutes. (It's a good idea to keep a clock within view.) Then continue to stir every 15 minutes after that until the soap thickens and traces. Never leave the mixture unattended while waiting for the soap to trace. Trace is easy to recognize, so relax. All soap recipes take different amounts of time to trace. Most recipes provide an estimate of the amount of time it takes, but temperature, humidity, and other variables in your work area can change even the most tried recipes. All mixtures will trace eventually.

To identify a trace:

Drip some soap from your spoon back onto the surface of the soap in the stirring bowl. The dripping should leave a trace, or slight mound or shadow, on the surface of the soap mixture (see step CP-4).

Draw a line in the soap with a spoon or rubber spatula. The line should remain for a few seconds before blending back into the soap mixture (see step CP-5).

9. Once the batch has reached trace, add the additional ingredients, such as scent, color, fillers, and additives. Stir until all the ingredients are evenly blended into the soap.

10. Pour the soap into a prepared mold or molds. Insulate the molds by covering them with an old towel or blanket (see step CP-6). The saponification process is still taking place in the soap at this point. Leave the soap insulated to set for 24 hours.

11. After 24 hours have passed, remove the soap from the mold and cut it into bars or hand shape it. Wear rubber gloves when removing the soap from the molds, cutting it into bars, or hand-shaping soap balls. Allow the soap to cure for four to six weeks before using it. Beginners should test soap with a pH strip, which can be found at science stores and pet stores that sell aquarium supplies. Follow the manufacturer's instructions. Basically you place the strip on top of your soap and wait for the strip to react. The strip changes color to indicate the level of pH.

Cold-Process Recipes

These are very simple, small batches of cold-process recipes to make as a beginner. I kept the recipes small so that you won't spend a lot of money and time on a craft you might not enjoy. After you have a few batches under your belt, feel free to double the recipe. The following processes may seem rather complicated for such a small return, but preparing these recipes will give you a feel for the cold-process method. You'll either figure out you don't have much

Step CP-1. Place fats/oils in the top pot of the double boiler and begin to melt. Keep a thermometer in the pot.

Step CP-2. Wearing rubber gloves, appropriate clothing, and eye goggles, slowly add small amounts of the measured sodium hydroxide to the water.

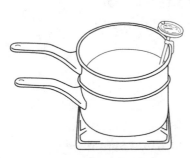

Step CP-3. When the temperatures of both the melted fats/oils and the lye solution reach between 90 and 130 degrees Fahrenheit, remove the fats/oils from the heat element, and slowly add the lye solution to the melted fats/oils.

Step CP-4. Drip some soap from your spoon back onto the surface of the soap in the stirring bowl. The dripping should leave a trace, or slight mound or shadow, on the surface of the soap mixture.

Step CP-5. Draw a line in the soap with a spoon or rubber spatula. The line should remain for a few seconds before blending back into the soap mixture.

Step CP-6. Pour the soap into a prepared mold or molds. Insulate the molds by covering them with an old towel or blanket.

interest in the techniques, or you'll find you can't wait to make a bigger batch!

Ken's Pioneer Days Soap

My husband, Ken, was very brave and helped me make all the cold-process soaps when I was first learning the method. Like a guardian angel, he made me read all the safety and health precautions twice while he read them at least a dozen times to make sure I didn't try to take any shortcuts while preparing the soaps. What can I say—I married a saint!

Materials

Dish towels, paper towels, or sponges
Double boiler
Glass mixing bowls, large

Heat-resistant glass measuring bowls (4- to 8-cup)
Rubber gloves
Accurate scale (food or postage)
2 candy or cake thermometers
Old towels or blanket
Eye protection
Sharp paring knife or potato peeler
Sharp, thin-bodied knife or soap blade
Plain square or rectangular mold
Mold release agent
Wooden spoons or dedicated utensils
Drying rack (wooden or metal)

Time

2–4 hours plus 24 hours in mold; 4–6 weeks curing time

Ingredients

8 ounces rendered beef fat/tallow
1 ounce sodium hydroxide
2.5 ounces water

Instructions

1. Gather and measure all the ingredients. Remember, most cold-process soap recipe ingredients are measured by weight unless otherwise specified. The 2.5 ounces of water needed to make the lye should be in a glass bowl, measuring cup, or pitcher.

2. Prepare the double boiler.

3. Place the rendered beef fat in the top pot of the prepared double boiler and begin to melt. Keep a thermometer in the pot.

4. Wearing rubber gloves, appropriate clothing, and eye protection, slowly add small amounts of the measured sodium hydroxide to the water. Keep stirring until all the sodium hydroxide is dissolved. Don't stand directly over the lye, and don't breathe any of the fumes. This step can be done outside if you wish. Keep a thermometer in this container to measure the heat of the chemical reaction.

5. When the temperatures of both the beef fat and the lye reach between 90 and 130 degrees Fahrenheit, remove the beef fat from the heat source and place on a covered table. Slowly add the lye solution to the melted beef fat. Stir slowly and carefully. Don't remove your safety equipment.

6. Continue to stir intermittently and never leave the mixture unattended while waiting for the trace of the soap. This soap should trace in less than 30 minutes, but temperature, humidity, and other variables in your work area can change the time needed.

7. Once the batch has reached trace, pour the soap into the prepared mold. Insulate the mold by covering with an old towel or blanket. Leave the soap insulated for 24 hours.

8. Wearing rubber gloves, remove the soap from mold. Cut the soap into bars. Place the bars on drying racks and, turning occasionally, allow to cure for four to six weeks before use. Beginners should test soap with a pH strip.

Smooth and Simple Soap

Materials

Dish towels, paper towels, or sponges
Double boiler
Glass mixing bowls, large

Heat-resistant glass measuring bowls (4- to 8-cup)

Rubber gloves

Accurate scale (food or postage)

2 candy or cake thermometers

Old towels or blanket

Eye protection or eye goggles

Sharp paring knife or potato peeler

Sharp, thin-bodied knife or soap blade

Plain square or rectangular mold

Mold release agent

Wooden spoons or dedicated utensils

Drying rack (wooden or metal)

Time

2–4 hours plus 24 hours in mold; 4–6 weeks curing time

Ingredients

8 ounces lard

1 ounce sodium hydroxide

2.5 ounces water

Instructions

1. Gather and measure all the ingredients. Remember, most cold-process soap recipe ingredients are measured by weight unless otherwise specified. The 2.5 ounces of water needed to make the lye should be readied in a glass bowl, measuring cup, or pitcher.

2. Place the lard in the top pan of the double boiler and begin to melt. Keep a thermometer in the pot. Turn off the heat when the fat is completely melted.

3. Wearing rubber gloves, appropriate clothing, and eye goggles, slowly add small amounts of the measured sodium hydroxide to the water. Keep stirring until all the sodium hydroxide is dissolved. Don't stand directly over the lye, and don't breathe any of the fumes. This step can be done outside if you wish. Keep a thermometer in this container to measure the heat of the chemical reaction.

4. When the temperatures of both the melted lard and the lye reach between 90 and 130 degrees Fahrenheit, remove the lard from the heat and place on a covered table. Slowly add the lye solution to the melted lard. Stir slowly and carefully. Don't remove your safety equipment.

5. Continue to stir intermittently and never leave the mixture unattended while waiting for the trace of the soap. This soap should trace within 15 to 30 minutes, but temperature, humidity, and other variables in your work area can change the time needed.

6. Once the batch has reached trace, pour the soap into the prepared mold. Insulate the mold by covering with an old towel or a blanket. Leave the soap insulated for 24 hours.

7. Wearing rubber gloves, remove the soap from the mold. Cut the soap into bars. Place the bars on drying racks and, turning occasionally, allow to dry and cure for four to six weeks before use. Beginners should test soap with a pH strip.

 # Vegetarian Delight*

Materials

Dish towels, paper towels, or sponges
Double boiler

*This soap is not featured in the color insert in the center of the book.

Glass mixing bowls, large
Heat-resistant glass measuring bowls (4- to 8-cup)
Rubber gloves
Accurate scale (food or postage)
2 candy or cake thermometers
Old towels or blanket
Eye protection or eye goggles
Sharp paring knife or potato peeler
Sharp, thin-bodied knife or soap blade
Plain square or rectangular mold
Wooden spoons or dedicated utensils
Drying rack (wooden or metal)

Time

2–4 hours plus 24 hours in mold; 4–6 weeks curing time

Ingredients

8 ounces vegetable shortening
1 ounce sodium hydroxide
2.5 ounces water

Instructions

1. Gather and measure all the ingredients. Remember, most cold-process soap recipe ingredients are measured by weight unless otherwise specified. The 2.5 ounces of water needed to make the lye should be readied in a glass bowl, measuring cup, or pitcher.

2. Prepare the mold.

3. Prepare the double boiler.

4. Place the shortening in the top pan of the double boiler and begin to melt. Keep a thermometer in the pot. Watch for the shortening to reach approximately 130 degrees Fahrenheit. Turn off heat when the shortening is completely melted.

5. Wearing rubber gloves, appropriate clothing, and eye goggles, slowly add small amounts of the measured sodium hydroxide to the water. Keep stirring until all the sodium hydroxide is dissolved. Don't stand directly over the lye, and don't breathe any of the fumes. This step can be done outside if you wish. Keep a thermometer in this container to measure the heat of the chemical reaction.

6. When the temperatures of both the shortening and the lye solutions reach between 90 and 130 degrees Fahrenheit, slowly add the lye solution to the melted vegetable shortening. Stir slowly and carefully. Do not remove your safety equipment.

7. Continue to stir intermittently and never leave the mixture unattended while waiting for the trace of the soap. This soap should trace in one to three hours, but temperature, humidity, and other variables in your work area can change the time needed.

8. Once the batch has reached trace, pour the soap into the prepared mold. Insulate the mold by covering with an old towel or a blanket. Leave the soap insulated for 24 hours.

9. Wearing rubber gloves, remove the soap from the mold. Cut the soap into bars. Place the bars on drying racks and, turning occasionally, allow to dry and cure for four to six weeks before use. Beginners should test soap with a pH strip.

More Adventurous Cold-Process Recipes

 Gardener's Treasure

This is a great soap for gardeners. The soap helps remove dirt stains from hands and removes odors from the skin.

Materials

Measuring spoons
Measuring cups

Time

2–4 hours plus 24 hours in mold; 4–6 weeks curing time

Additives

2 tablespoons ground coffee beans
2 tablespoons wheat germ
1/2 cup dried flower petals or dried herbs (try rosemary, thyme, or parsley)
5 drops lemon essential or fragrance oil
5 drops sweet orange essential or fragrance oil
10 drops lily of the valley or another floral essential or fragrance oil

Instructions

1. Make the recipe for Ken's Pioneer Days Soap, Smooth and Simple Soap, or Vegetarian Delight.

2. At trace, add the additives.

3. Mix well until all additives are blended. Pour the soap into a prepared mold or molds. Cover and insulate for 24 hours.

Remove the soap from the molds and, if necessary, cut the soap into bars. Cure for five weeks, turning occasionally.

 ## Bo's Bubble & Bath

This is my 84-pound basset hound, Bo's, favorite soap. The pennyroyal and citronella are natural bug repellents for an animal's coat, either four legged or two!

Materials

Measuring cups

Time:

2–4 hours plus 24 hours in mold; 4–6 weeks curing time

Additives

1/2 cup dried pennyroyal herb
20 drops lemon eucalyptus or citronella essential or
    fragrance oil

Instructions

1. Make the recipe for Ken's Pioneer Days Soap, Smooth and Simple Soap, or Vegetarian Delight.

2. At trace, add the additives.

3. Mix well until the additives are well blended. Pour into a prepared mold or molds. Allow 24 hours to insulate and remove from mold(s). Cut into bars or shape into balls. Allow to cure for four weeks, turning occasionally.

Rebatching

If you don't like the way a cold-process soap batch turns out, instead of throwing the entire thing away, you may choose to rebatch it. Even if your soap turns out fine, you may choose to rebatch it before including more delicate additives. Saponification is very harsh on essential oils, fragrance oils, herbs, botanicals, and other additives. Adding these items during a rebatch will help preserve their character and can result in brighter colors and stronger fragrances.

Rebatching is similar to making a hand-milled or melt-and-pour soap except that a rebatch uses a soap that has been made from scratch by the soapmaker. Commercial soaps and melt-and-pour soap bases that you buy are regulated so that the soap won't be caustic or harmful. There is no guarantee with a rebatched cold-process soap that all the lye has disappeared. This means that all the safety precautions followed when making the cold-process batch must be followed when rebatching.

1. Cold-process soaps must be allowed to dry and cure at least three weeks before rebatching.

2. Gather and measure any additional ingredients. Keep each ingredient in a separate container.

3. Clear your work area of anything not needed in the recipe.

4. Wearing rubber gloves, grate the cold-process soap batch using a hand grater or a food processor. Whichever type of grater you use, be sure to clean it thoroughly before returning it to food preparation.

5. Weigh out the soap. Set aside 12 ounces of water per pound of grated soap.

6. Prepare a double boiler.

7. Place the water and soap into the top pot of the double boiler. Stir occasionally while the soap begins to melt.

8. Cover the top pot with a lid or a piece of foil.

9. Allow the mixture to simmer but not boil. It may take an hour to an hour and a half for the soap to melt completely. Continue to check the mixture and stir occasionally.

10. When the mixture has melted completely and is of a smooth consistency, remove the mixture from the heat source. Add any additional ingredients. Mix well.

11. Pour the soap into a prepared mold or allow to cool before shaping the soap into balls.

12. Remove from the mold after 24 hours and allow soap to dry for one to two weeks before use.

Rebatched Cold-Process Recipes

 ## Maria's Mint Melody

Materials

Measuring spoons

Time

2–4 hours plus 24 hours in mold; 4–6 weeks curing time

Additives

2 tablespoons each dried peppermint, spearmint, and wintergreen

7 drops each peppermint, spearmint, and wintergreen essential or fragrance oils

Several slivers of green candle colorant or green crayon

Instructions

1. Make the recipe for Ken's Pioneer Days Soap, Smooth and Simple Soap, or Vegetarian Delight.
2. At trace, add the additives.
3. Mix well until blended. Pour the soap into a prepared mold and insulate for 24 hours. Cut into bars and allow to cure for five weeks.
4. After one to two weeks you can grate this soap and rebatch it. Add 1/2 cup water, 1/2 cup superfatting oil of your choice, and a few more drops of each mint essential or fragrance oil.

Chocolate and Coffee Lover's Temptation

Materials

Measuring spoons

Time

2–4 hours plus 24 hours in mold; 4–6 weeks curing time

Additives

2 tablespoons powdered coffee mix
2 tablespoons powdered cocoa mix
2 tablespoons finely ground coffee

Instructions

1. Make the recipe for Ken's Pioneer Days Soap, Smooth and Simple Soap, or Vegetarian Delight.

2. After the soap has cured for one to two weeks, rebatch the soap by grating it into fine slivers, adding 1/2 cup regular milk or goat's milk and 1/2 cup superfatting oil of your choice, and melting this mixture in a double boiler.

3. Once the soap has melted completely, stir in the additives and mix well.

4. Pour into a prepared mold. Allow to cool for 24 hours and remove from the mold and cut into bars. Allow one to two weeks for drying.

 ## A Red, Red Rose

Materials

Measuring spoons

Time

2–4 hours plus 24 hours in mold; 4–6 weeks curing time

Additives

3 tablespoons red rose petals, crushed and dried
15 drops grapefruit seed extract or vitamin E
Several slivers of red wax colorant or red crayon

Instructions

1. Make the recipe for Ken's Pioneer Days Soap, Smooth and Simple Soap, or Vegetarian Delight.

2. After the soap has cured for one to two weeks, rebatch the soap by grating it into fine slivers, adding 1/2 cup pureed

beets and 1/2 cup superfatting oil of your choice, and melting this mixture in a double boiler.

3. Once the soap has melted completely, stir in the additives and mix well.

4. Pour into a prepared mold. Allow 24 hours to cool. Cut into bars or shape into soap balls.

 # Fresh As a Cucumber

Materials

Measuring spoons

Time

2–4 hours plus 24 hours in mold; 4–6 weeks curing time

Additives

3 tablespoons aloe vera gel
Several slivers of white and green wax colorant
15 drops grapefruit seed extract
20 drops cucumber essential or fragrance oil

Instructions

1. Make the recipe for Ken's Pioneer Days Soap, Smooth and Simple Soap, or Vegetarian Delight.

2. After the soap has cured for one to two weeks, rebatch the soap by grating it into fine slivers, adding 1/2 cup pureed cucumber and 1/2 cup superfatting oil of your choice, and melting this mixture in a double boiler.

3. Once the soap has melted completely, stir in the additives and mix well.

4. Pour into a prepared mold. Allow 24 hours to cool. Cut into bars or shape into soap balls. Allow soap to dry for one to two weeks before use.

 # Florida Sunshine Soap

Materials

Measuring cups
Measuring spoons

Time

2–4 hours plus 24 hours in mold; 4–6 weeks curing time

Additives

1/2 cup superfatting oil (optional)
1 tablespoon finely chopped or grated lime rind
1 tablespoon coarsely chopped or grated orange or
    tangerine rind
1 tablespoon coarsely chopped or grated lemon rind
Several slivers of yellow colorant
5 drops lime essential or fragrance oil
5 drops sweet orange essential or fragrance oil
5 drops tangerine essential or fragrance oil
10 drops lemon essential or fragrance oil

Instructions

1. Make the recipe for Ken's Pioneer Days Soap, Smooth and Simple Soap, or Vegetarian Delight.

2. After the soap has cured for one to two weeks, rebatch the soap by grating it into fine slivers, 1/2 cup water and 1/2 cup superfatting oil of your choice, and melting this mixture in a double boiler.

The Language of Nature

Allspice: Compassion

Almond: Indiscretion, hope

Amethyst: Loyalty, admiration

Apple: Temptation

Azalea: Temperance

Basil: Love washed with tears

Bittersweet: Truth

Cactus: Warmth

Chrysanthemum: Truth, friendship, slighted love

Cloves: Dignity

Crocus: Abuse not

Daffodil: High regard

Daisy: Innocence

Fern: Sincerity

Forget-me-not: True love

Gladiolus: Strength of character

Hemlock: "You will be the death of me"

Honeysuckle: Sweetness of disposition

Hyacinth: Sport, play, game, fun

Ivy: Friendship, marriage, fidelity, knowledge

Larkspur: Lightness, levity

Lavender: Undying love, sweetness, cleanliness

3. Once the soap has melted completely, stir in the remaining additives and mix well.

4. Pour into a prepared mold. Allow 24 hours to cool. Cut into bars or shape into soap balls.

Lilac: Love, purity, modesty, innocence
Lily of the valley: Return of happiness
Magnolia: Love of nature
Mint: Spirit, virtue
Narcissus: Egotism
Oak tree: Hospitality
Orange blossoms: Brides, purity equals beauty
Pansy: "You're in my thoughts"
Parsley: Victory, honor, destiny
Peach: Charms unequaled
Pears: Affection
Petunia: Never despair
Pine: Pity
Raspberry: Remorse
Rose: Love, charm, desire, innocence
Rosemary: Remembrance, enduring love, loyalty
Sage: Domestic virtue, immortality, youth
Salvia: "I think of you often," forever love
Sweet basil: Good wishes
Thyme: Activity, courage, elegance, energy
Violet: Modesty, simplicity, honor
Willow: Sorrow
Zinnia: Thoughts of absent friends

With a few batches of soap under your belt, you can begin to formulate your own recipes. For a craft that seems like a science project at times, soapmaking allows you to be creative with the ingredients and additives. When a soap batch doesn't turn out exactly the way you planned, don't fret. In most cases the soap is safe to use even if it doesn't look pretty, and you can almost always rebatch it. Keep notes in your soap journal, and don't lose sight of the greater glory. You're learning a new skill. Your friends are going to love receiving your handmade soaps. And you're sharing in the traditions and craft of our ancestors.

Creative Uses for Essential Oils and Fragrance Oils

- Place a few drops of your favorite essential oil onto a small piece of terrycloth and toss into the clothes dryer while drying.

- Add 5 drops essential oil to 1/4 cup fabric softener or water and place in the center cup of the wash.

- Adding a few drops of essential oil to potpourri that has lost its scent can revive it.

- Add a few drops of oil to water in a spray bottle and use as an air freshener.

- Add a few drops essential oil to a pan of water and simmer on stove or in potpourri pot.

- To enjoy a scented candle, place a drop or two of oil into the hot melted wax as the candle burns.

- To dispel household cooking odors, use a few drops of clove oil in a simmering pan of water.

- For tired aching muscles or arthritis aches, mix 1 part cajeput, sage, and basil oil to 4 parts carrier oil to make a great massage oil.

■ Ease headache pain by rubbing a drop of rosemary or lavender oil plus a drop of a carrier oil onto the back of your neck.

■ To blend your own massage oil, add 3–5 drops of your favorite essential oil to 1 ounce of jojoba or other skin-nourishing carrier oil.

■ Add 10 drops of essential oil to a box of cornstarch or baking soda and mix very well by shaking. Let set for a day or two and then sprinkle over the carpets in your home. Let set for an hour or more, then vacuum.

■ To make a natural flea collar, saturate a short piece of cord or soft rope with pennyroyal or tea tree oil, roll up in a handkerchief, and tie loosely around the animal's neck.

■ Remove odor from shoes by dropping a few drops of geranium essential oil directly into the shoes or by placing a cotton ball dabbed with a few drops of lemon oil into the shoes.

■ Put a few drops of your favorite essential oil on a cotton ball and place it in your vacuum cleaner bag. Lemon and pine are nice. Rose geranium helps with animal odors.

■ To fragrance your kitchen cabinets and drawers, place a food scent dabbed on a cotton ball in an inconspicuous corner.

■ Are mice a problem? Place several drops of peppermint oil on cotton balls and place them at problem locations.

■ The bathroom is easily scented by placing oil-scented cotton balls in inconspicuous places or by sprinkling oils directly onto silk or dried flower arrangements or wreaths.

■ Apply true lavender oil and tea tree oil directly to cuts, scrapes, or scratches. One or two drops promote healing.

■ Handmade sachets are more fragrant when essential oils are blended with the flowers and herbs.

■ An essential oil dropped on a radiator, scent ring, or light bulb will not only fill the room with a wonderful fragrance, but also will set a mood. Don't put essential oil in the socket.

- Place a few drops of your favorite oil or blend in the rinse water of your hand-washables.

- Fishermen have used anise oil for years. Use a drop or two on the fingertips and hands before baiting up. Anise covers up the human scent that scares the fish away.

- Essential oils or blends make wonderful perfumes. Create your own personal essence. Add 25 drops to 1 ounce of perfume alcohol. Let age two weeks before using.

- To dispel mosquitoes and other picnic or barbecue pests, drop a few drops of citronella oil in the melted wax of candle or place a few drops on the barbecue hot coals.

- Rosemary promotes alertness and stimulates memory. Inhale occasionally during long car trips and while reading or studying.

- Selling your home? Fragrance sells! Fill the kitchen area with the aroma of spices such as clove, cinnamon, and vanilla by simmering a few drops of the essential oils on the stove.

- Geranium oil sprinkled throughout the home creates a warm, cheerful, inviting mood.

- Add cinnamon oil to furniture polish and wipe down the wood.

- Add essential oils to papier-mâché paste. The result is a lovely aromatic art piece.

- Infuse bookmarks and stationery with essential oils. Place drops of oil on paper and put them in a plastic bag. Leave overnight to infuse the aroma.

- Neck pillows and padded decorative hangers make more memorable gifts simply by putting a couple of drops of essential oil on them before giving.

- Overindulge last night? Essential oils of juniper, cedarwood, grapefruit, lavender, carrot, fennel, rosemary, and lemon help soften the effects of a hangover. Make your own blend of these oils and use 6 to 8 drops in a bath.

- Cypress, atlas cedarwood, frankincense, and myrrh all make wonderful firewood oils. Drop 2 to 3 drops of oil or blend of your choice on a dried log and allow the oil to soak in before putting the log on the fire.

■ Flies and moths dislike lavender oil. Sprinkle it on the outside of your window frames.

■ When moving into a new home, first use a water spray containing your favorite essential oils and change the odorous environment to your own. Do this for several days until it begins to feel like your space.

■ Ideal scents for the bedroom are roman chamomile, geranium, lavender, or lemon.

■ A drop of lemon essential oil on a soft cloth will polish copper with gentle buffing.

■ When washing out the fridge, freezer, or oven, add 1 drop of lemon, lime, grapefruit, bergamot, mandarin, or orange essential oil to the final rinse water.

■ Use 1 drop of chamomile oil on a washcloth wrapped around an ice cube to relieve teething pain in children.

■ Add 6 to 8 drops of eucalyptus oil to bath water to cool the body in summer and to protect skin in winter.

■ Add 1 drop of geranium oil to your facial moisturizer to bring out a radiant glow in your skin.

■ Place 1 or 2 drops of rosemary oil on your hair brush.

■ When the flu is going around, add a few drops of thyme to your diffuser or simmer in a pan on the stove.

■ To bring fever down, sponge the body with cool water with 1 drop each of eucalyptus, peppermint, and lavender oils.

■ The blend of lavender and grapefruit oil is good for the office. Lavender creates a calm tranquil atmosphere while grapefruit stimulates the senses and clears up stale air.

Your Crafts Vision

▼▼

FOR ME, SOAPMAKING IS LIKE cooking. I feel like the greatest chef when a batch turns out well—it looks appealing, suds abound, and it feels soft and slick when used. There is a peaceful feeling when creating something soothing and reassuring. A very basic need—to be clean and fresh—has been filled with wholesome delight and a touch of care. Scent and aroma fill the home and bring with them smiles and happy memories. Homemade soap is a nourishing gift.

Has the soapmaking bug bitten you? Are you enjoying the pleasures of mixing ingredients and discovering new recipes? Do you want to expand your skills and creativity? Selling the soaps you create to bring in income to support your hobby or increase household cash flow is an achievable goal and dream.

There are many opportunities to sell, market, and merchandise your soaps. You'll explore and find out more about those opportunities in Part 2. But before getting into the details, take some time with this chapter and the Dreams and Goals questionnaire on page 121. The questionnaire will help you focus on the areas that you need more information about. You will really think about what steps you want to take toward selling your handcrafted soap.

It didn't take me long to come up with the fifty questions in the questionnaire. After more than a decade of making and selling just about every craft imaginable, I know what questions I wish I'd thought about before diving headfirst into an unknown lake. Exploring uncharted territories entails taking risks, but those risks can be tempered and refined with careful thought. Making a plan is important to achieve your goals.

One of my favorite sayings is "When you lose or don't succeed, don't lose the lesson too." The one thing to which I attribute my long-term success is that I keep a written personal and business plan that I constantly review and adjust. Never be so rigid in your hopes and dreams that you forget that sometimes the best-made plans need a backup plan B, C, and D.

Handy Hint

At a craft show, bag sold items in a see-through plastic bag. Customers will walk around the show, "advertising" your product to others.

Many years ago, when I first started to exhibit at craft shows, I was very concerned that my prices be reasonable. It was important that everyone could afford my crafts. Yet even after a decade of selling crafts, it's still difficult for me to sell to my friends. My first reaction is to give the craft to my friend as a gift. But I wouldn't be in business very long if I gave my crafts away all the time, and Uncle Sam and the IRS wouldn't find it charming or sweet. So I came up with a compromise. I sell to friends at a discount of 10%. I feel better, and my friends recognize that my crafting is more than a hobby. It's a business.

There will always be a marketplace for handmade, handcrafted, and down-to-earth product lines. Somehow calling homemade soap a product seems to commercialize it. But to succeed in business, you must conform, to a degree, to the jargon of the business world. That won't take away from the wholesome ingredients of your soap, diminish the care and dedication you put into your soap, or reduce your creative and artistic talents and skills.

It's somewhat ironic that a creative person must learn how to be a logical, left-brained, practical businessperson. Creative people tend to be the opposite of order and calm. We're free spirited and sensory driven. We want everyone to be happy. We don't look forward to writing receipts and invoices in a company cash ledger, and we don't like following an exact schedule to the minute.

We especially don't like being told we can't do something the way we want to do it. Most of us don't even want to take the time to read and answer the Dreams and Goals questionnaire. But you must think about these questions to develop a solid business foundation. The questionnaire will help you understand that you have many options in this endeavor. You may not be able to answer all the questions in one sitting, so take your time and put your best effort into it. Consider it a challenge from one soapmaker to another!

To Thine Own Self Be True

1. List the five reasons you like to make soap.
2. Why do you want to make soap and sell it?
3. List at least five skills, talents, and assets you can bring to this endeavor as an artist.
4. List any weakness, liabilities, or obstacles you have to overcome.
5. Do you have the motivation and determination to work on your own? Do you have the time management skills to schedule your workday and your personal life?
6. Will your family support your efforts? Will your friends?
7. Which additives, ingredients, and recipes are your favorites?
8. Do you want to make only one-of-a-kind or special-order soaps? Or will you make multiples? Do want to keep adding new soaps to your inventory or only make a few varieties?

KIM'S STORY

Kim Anderson began making soap when she moved to North Idaho in 1994. She had seen some handmade soaps and thought "I can do that and maybe even do it better." Kim's daughter also had some skin problems and soap seemed like a good way to help her.

Now Kim's soapmaking has turned into Anderson Country Products, a very nice business. She had made so much soap when she started that she was giving it away to family and friends, who began asking for more, which initiated the idea in her head. "In August of 1998, I flew home for a family reunion and my brother, who is a marketer, told me that he wanted to put my soaps in his stores. From there, my business grew. A big thanks for my success goes to my brother, John. His belief in my product did so much for my business confidence. But I can't ever thank the storeowners or my customers enough for having faith in me and my company.

9. What aspects of soapmaking do you find most interesting or challenging?

10. If there were no obstacles in your way, what would your goal be in soapmaking? In selling your soap?

11. What obstacles do you see that prevent you from reaching this goal?

12. Are there ways to overcome the obstacles? Does someone have the knowledge or skill you need? Can you get the information to educate yourself? Can you change directions and still meet your dream or goal?

"It's the small, independent soapmakers who really make a difference. I've made some wonderful friendships since I started making soap. A small group of us from all over the country have gotten to know each other via the Internet. We shared stories about our first craft fairs, new recipe experiences, building Web sites, and so much more. Together we faced the good, the bad, and all the in-betweens.

"My best advice to other soapmakers is to read everything you can get your hands on and do lots of research. Most important, never be afraid to ask questions."

Getting Started

1. What is your number one goal? Can it be measured? Is there a finish line or a way to know when you've accomplished this goal?
2. How will you define success? By creative achievement? By financial bottom line? By the freedom of working for yourself? By growth of market? By the reaction of your family and friends?
3. Will the money from soapmaking be used to support your hobby? To earn extra household income? To earn extra

leisure spending money? Or do you want to work at soapmaking full-time?

4. How much time can you realistically dedicate to your craft? To your business?

5. What other responsibilities do you have? Rank these responsibilities in order of priority to you. Rank them in order of priority to your family and friends. How do the rankings compare? How do you feel about the comparison?

Business Is Business

1. List at least five skills, talents, and assets that you can bring to this endeavor as a businessperson.

2. Do you want to be a sole proprietor? Form a partnership? Incorporate?

3. Do you have starting capital? Can you create a company budget? A five-year plan?

4. Do you have a system of accounting?

5. Do you want employees? Will you hire your family or friends?

6. Do you want to work from your home?

Day to Day, Year to Year

1. If you had to come up with a business name for your endeavor, what would it be? Does the name limit you? Is the name self-explanatory? Will a customer remember you by your business name?

2. What do you wish to accomplish during a day, a week, a month, and a year of soapmaking?

3. Do you have room in your home to dedicate space to your work?

4. Will your local area have enough business opportunities to help you earn the income you desire? Will you have to market outside your local area? Do you want to do that?

5. What does your city, county, or state require from you in terms of paperwork or licenses to start a business? Do you understand all the city, county, and state regulations and laws? Do you need to consult an attorney?

Profit and Bottom Line

1. What business records do you need to keep, and how will you keep them?

2. How will you price your soap? Do you know how similar items are priced in the marketplace? How does your pricing compare?

3. Do you need to consult an accountant or a CPA?

4. Do you understand all the federal income tax forms required of you for the extra income? Are you willing to keep all your receipts and invoices in order, filed, and understandable?

5. Do you want to set up a business checking account? Can you keep your personal and business finances separate?

6. Does your area support arts and crafts?

To Sell Your Soap

1. What makes your soap unique? What are the selling points?

2. How must the work be displayed? Does your item need explanation, or does it sell on its own merits?

3. Will you need to package your work? Is the work fragile, or does it need special handling?

4. Is there a market for your soap? Are people showing an interest in what you make?

5. What selling markets are available in your local area? Craft co-op? Craft mall? Bath shop? Health food store or natural goods co-op? Annual art and craft shows?
6. Do you want to sell directly to the consumer?
7. Do you want to wholesale your work? Sell through a sales representative?
8. Do you want to mail order your work? Do you have space to handle the packaging and shipping supplies needed? How will you cover the costs of handling and shipping?
9. Do you want to sell on the World Wide Web? Will you create or maintain a Web site for sales? Or will you be part of a large Web site?

Teaching and Demonstrating

1. Do you want to teach others how to do your craft?
2. Are there places for you to teach? Out of your home? At a retail craft store? At a local art museum? At a health food store?
3. Do you want to sell the soap recipe (written instructions) to a magazine or book publisher?
4. How will you keep current on trends, colors, textures, motifs, techniques, lifestyles, and consumers?

Reality Check and Planning for the Future

1. Where do you want to be a year from now in terms of dreams, goals, personal affairs, and business?
2. Where do you want to be five years from now in terms of dreams, goals, personal affairs, and business?
3. Where do you want to be 10 years from now in terms of dreams, goals, personal affairs, and business?
4. In your heart and mind, do you think that there's nothing you want to do more than reach your dream or goal? Can you

make the sacrifices? Do you have a clear vision of what you hope to accomplish? Can you keep motivated? Can you keep positive?

Successful artists and craftspeople learn to balance the wants and needs of creativity with the bigger picture of long-term business growth and prosperity. You can do the same. I'm living proof that even the most unorganized, unanalytical person can learn to follow sound business practices with some creative adjustment. The questions listed above didn't just pop into my head. I've spent 15 years learning the answers to those questions for my own company. There are no right or wrong answers. Each individual will find what works for him- or herself and for the company.

The first step is to look closely at what your dreams, hopes, and goals are in your soapmaking. The questionnaire will help you do this just as the first part of this book helped you discover the joy and pleasure of soapmaking. Take all that you've learned and focus that creativity in part 2 of this book. The chapters ahead will fill in all the blanks you may have about starting a business and selling your wares. The journey begins with the first step forward.

Handy Hint

Always put a business card into each bag of sold merchandise so customers can conveniently purchase or order more of your soap.

Part Two

For Profit

Profiting from Your Talents

▼▼▼

I WROTE THIS BOOK BECAUSE I have a strong interest in soapmaking as an art-and-craft discipline. When I used the first bar of my own handmade soap, I knew, without a doubt, that handmade soap was very different from commercially manufactured soap. There is a real difference in the feel and lather of a homemade soap. The aroma of homemade soap can be personalized to please any nose. Homemade soap is visually pleasing and it can pamper any type of skin. The many options of soapmaking appeal to the artist, crafter, and writer in me. I'm guessing that you will catch the same passion as you begin to create your own unique, salubrious soaps—and hopefully use these attributes to make a product you can sell.

We're often in such a hurry that we don't take time to review all the options available to us as creative individuals. By taking time to read this book, you'll gain much of the knowledge needed to explore these options. Above all else, it's important to remember that no matter how much information you gather, read, and study, the road to selling your work will be unique. Remain flexible and open-minded about your options.

Creative people share several common traits. We are always thinking about creativity in one form or another. Our creative minds rarely shut off, even when we're busy doing things other than crafting. We're also strongly driven to be perfect. We often believe that items we make can be done better the next time. Don't let this universal need for perfection take the joy out of your creativity. Too much perfection leads to burnout. The idea of selling soap for profit means you can have a job you love. No one could ask for more from an occupation.

▼▼▼▼▼▼▼▼▼▼▼▼▼▼▼▼▼▼▼▼▼▼▼▼▼

Did you know???

One of the most common errors made by novice creative businesses is to underestimate the time involved in creating a product.

▲▲▲▲▲▲▲▲▲▲▲▲▲▲▲▲▲▲▲▲▲▲▲▲▲

There are many ways to profit from soapmaking, and not all of them have to do with selling directly to the public. Perhaps you know yourself well enough to know that you would become bored producing the same soap batches or recipes over and over and over again. If so, consider other options, such as selling your recipes to publishers or teaching or demonstrating soapmaking skills to others. These options are addressed in more detail in chapter 9.

The first year I sold my work, I did so only as a hobby. Before committing myself to a full-time career as a professional crafter, I wanted to make sure I really did enjoy the occupation. I also needed to find out if I could earn a profit for my efforts. I reported the money I earned that first year as extra income on our household tax forms. I had only limited deductions from my supply costs. After taxes, I had a healthy profit for my efforts. I used the profit from that first year to educate myself about the crafting and business principles I needed to operate as a sole proprietorship. I could have stopped right there and been very happy just crafting as a hobby, as it's wonderful to have a hobby pay for itself. But I decided to make a career out of my newfound skills and talents. You might consider this option to introduce yourself slowly to the business world.

Hobbyist or Professional?

The broadest definition of a craft or art professional includes teachers, product or craft demonstrators, and designers. Most professionals who fall into these categories don't purchase large amounts of supplies. Instead they use a large variety of materials, making it difficult for them to qualify for the minimum purchasing orders of wholesale supplies. Therefore, craft manufacturers have set up programs that help teachers, demonstrators, and designers obtain supplies at discount prices. Or they offer endorsement programs that reward the individual monetarily for using a specific brand.

There are no official studies or surveys in the craft industry that explore the ways of the professional crafter or artisan, let alone those of professional soapmakers. Industry trade journals, however, state that professional crafters spend a little more than $2 billion on raw supplies each year. Put that fact in the big picture of the $10 billion spent on raw supplies each year in the craft industry and you'll see that the professional artisan plays an important role. Unless you meet the requirements of being a professional crafter, you can't qualify to purchase raw supplies wholesale (from a distributor or manufacturer). (See chapter 11 for details on how to form an official business that qualifies for wholesale purchases.)

Declaring yourself a professional soapmaker isn't the only step required to turn your hobby into a moneymaking situation. You'll have to prepare yourself and your family and friends for the transition. You'll need their support to make a success of your business. These might be the same people who have received your soap as gifts. Change on any level isn't easy. That same human nature that gives us creativity and enthusiasm is the same human nature that likes to keep the world steady. The crafter who feels uneasy about self-promotion and selling is now becoming the crafter who is trying to establish a business. It's not easy. It's not simple. And it's not

Selling Designs to a Manufacturer

1. You've found a product that you love to work with and your designs are great, if you do say so yourself. You may be able to work with the manufacturer of the product. There is always a need for photographs of finished designs for ads, exhibit displays, and project sheets. Prepare your best designs as finished samples. Quality of work counts.

2. Photograph your work. Your photograph doesn't require a professional photographer. Simply use plenty of light (outdoor light is best). Use a gray or light blue sheet or towel as a backdrop. Avoid creases in the backdrop. If the work is small, have a ruler or other measure in the photograph to give perspective. Take several shots from several angles. Have the film developed, and select one or two of the best shots. Write your name and address on the back of each photo.

3. Write a brief summary of the design piece. Include all materials used, basic steps, time involved, skill level, and total expense. Include your name and address on the summary. It's also a good idea to title the design.

going to happen overnight. You'll have to work on giving the same confident message to your family, friends, and community: *I am in business*. Part 2 gives the direction and guidance you need to establish this message in a professional manner.

Figure out what is important to you to see yourself as an authentic business. Don't listen to those who don't understand what you do for a living. Use your own goals and business plan to measure your success. Professional crafting doesn't fit a brief job description. It is an occupation that may perpetually be a round peg that doesn't fit smoothly into society's square hole. But you're creative enough to come up with your own answer for the question "What do you do for a living?" Your attitude toward your business efforts

4. Write a cover or query letter to the manufacturer. It's best to take the time to contact the manufacturer in advance. Find out who the contact person is for design submission. A design sent to a specific contact person will be responded to faster than a general posted letter.

5. If the manufacturer is interested in your design, you'll be contacted with a contract. Read it carefully and fully understand it before signing. This is also the time to ask if the manufacturer has a demonstrator's or designer's program that you can get involved with.

6. If the design is rejected, don't take it personally. It might not meet the needs of the manufacturer at the current time. Feel free to ask the contact if the manufacturer is looking for designs and, if so, what types of designs is the manufacturer interested in. Remember to be polite and professional.

7. Fees paid for designs do vary from manufacturer to manufacturer. It depends on how the manufacturer is going to use the design. Average fees range from $50 to $150.

will be the keystone for how others react to you. If you take yourself seriously, if you approach all challenges as a professional, if you outwardly glow with confidence and determination, the rest of the world will soon follow suit. There's only one exception: Never take yourself or your business so seriously that you can't, every once in a while, have a good laugh at yourself or your business. Don't be so serious that you forget that your work should be a positive influence on your life, your family, and your community. It's tough to keep smiling sometimes when facing deadlines, preparing for a big craft show, or sending off a design to a new publisher (when the last publisher turned you down), but in the long run that smile will give you the energy you need to keep trying.

Take Pride in Your Work

I wish I could tell you that crafting is considered an important and highly respected profession. But that impression might lead you to stumble. I have a résumé that contains seven pages of published work listing my more than 500 designs in print and my own television segment on a national cable network. But when I tell people I'm a professional crafter, nine out of 10 respond by saying, "How cute. Must be nice to sit home all day, making crafts." And my husband and family wonder why I don't have a big ego. If you hear comments like this often enough, you'll want to pull your hair, hold your breath until you turn blue, and pitch a temper tantrum. So much for professionalism! I've learned over the years to smile and tell all who are listening that indeed I have the best of all worlds as a sole proprietor. I'm a small-business owner who has the freedom of creativity and expression while earning an income from my crafting.

Did Someone Say Something About Organization?

Once you make the decision to take your enjoyment of soapmaking into the business world, you'll be making a commitment to become an efficient, well-organized business owner. You'll learn to shop for supplies while mentally calculating what prices are the best for your business. You'll learn to keep records of supplies, inventory, invoices, and cost of goods until all the paperwork becomes second nature. You'll learn to schedule, plan, and orchestrate your time. But don't think that just because you now have to consider a profit-and-loss statement, balance your business checking account, and keep an inventory of soap on hand for sales that the joy and fun of soapmaking has to disappear. At times all the needs and concerns of your business will seem overwhelming (even to the most organized of small-business people), but it's these challenges that motivate us and keep us on our toes. While learning all the dos and don'ts, do not forget that this is all about independence and success.

Selling Your Work for Profit

Some creative spirits find the thought of giving or selling their crafts to family, friends, or strangers (the buying public) a terrifying idea. Creative people put such a sincere effort into their craft. The thought that others might not like the work is enough to start a mild anxiety attack. This book is about soapmaking for fun *and for profit*. The profit made from your hobby will include the process of you becoming a salesperson.

Few products (including soap) sell themselves without a little help from a salesperson. The consumer buys items and products that he or she needs or desires. Part of your responsibility as a business owner is to make sure you offer a soap that meets these needs and desires.

Value Added

A lesson I learned early in my career as a doll maker is that consumers don't just buy the doll. They also buy a small piece of the artist or craftsperson. It's human nature to be curious about the artist behind the work. It's also human nature to want those we know to be successful. In the business world this is called value added.

After several years of selling my work at outdoor craft shows, I began to really understand that my customers wanted to buy from *me*. They didn't like it if I sent my husband or a friend to a show in my place when my schedule became hectic. Often the customers would good-naturedly tell my husband that they sincerely hoped I

Tips for Staying Organized

One of the most difficult tasks in crafting is organizing your supplies. Here are a few tips to make organizing a little easier. The amount of space you have does make a difference, but large or small, use your space wisely.

- Keep a running list of all your supplies and inventory. When you are running low or are out of a specific supply, make a note of it as soon as you think about it. Keep the list handy for ordering or for when you go to the store.

- Label everything. It is best to use see-through containers for storage. If this is not an option, make sure all storage containers are clearly, concisely labeled.

- Organize your supplies the way you think they should be organized. If you can find supplies by storing them alphabetically, do so. Or consider storing supplies by category. Organization should be easy, not something you have to think about.

- If you use a lot of small items, such as beads and buttons, consider the utility-drawer cabinets sold at craft or hardware stores. These cabinets can have 30 to 60 small see-through drawers.

wasn't getting so busy with my career that I couldn't find time to come to a show and talk with them. I got the message loud and clear. The customer wants to see the human face behind the work. Being able to purchase directly from the artist, artisan, or craftsperson is considered an added value to the product line.

Another important value to add to your items is an explanation of your craft. Fern LaFurjah, an artist who paints designs on slate, called me from her New England home. She said her work was selling well, but she wanted to raise her prices to increase her income, but she had a hard time justifying the price increase. Because I didn't have a clue about why painting on slate was different from painting on something like wood, I asked her to explain the special

- Place the items you use frequently or daily in easy-access areas. Store seldom used or seasonal items (when out of season) out of reach.

- Color-coordinate your files, calendar, and labels. Use the colored dot stickers available at office supply stores, and select a different color for each category of your craft or business. For example, red for orders, green for supplies, and blue for craft shows. Or red for herbs, green for colorants, and blue for essential oils.

- If you like to craft when traveling, keep a separate container with all the supplies you need. At a moment's notice, you can grab the container without having to worry about gathering everything you need.

- Use your supplies as part of your workroom or home decor. Put dried herbs in decorative glass containers. Store oils in a rainbow of dark-colored glass jars.

- Avoid clutter. Keep supplies off the floor, and put supplies away when not in use. The few seconds it takes to clean up will save you hours of trying to find the supplies when you need them later.

or unique qualities of her designs. I learned that she uses slate from the roof of a church that had been built in the early 1900s and that had recently been torn down. She knew the history of the church and even of the town where the slate had been mined. The history was fascinating, so I asked if she had written any of the history to package with the paintings. I heard silence on the other end of the phone, then she hesitantly asked why anyone would want to know the history of the slate. That was simple to answer: human curiosity and the fact that we love stories, histories, and trivia.

The first step in sales is never to assume your potential customer knows anything about what you do. It's too easy for a potential customer to assume that it was effortless to create your soap.

Keep tucked away in your memory the history, traditions, and other interesting facts behind your soapmaking techniques and ingredients. Explain how an item is made. Tell how you select the ingredients for your soap recipes. Talk about the differences between melt-and-pour and cold-process soap recipes. Describe how you decide which scents to use. This may seem like simply talking about your craft, but it is also a form of sales.

Do you grow your own herbs for your soap? Are your ingredients free of chemicals? Do you use water from a specific spring-fed lake? Do you render your own fats for a soap recipe? Are your recipes original? Is there a story behind why you make soap? These are all selling points. Make sure you label your soap with all its unique or fresh ingredients. Show your customers the difference between a store-bought bar and the hand-molded or hand-cut soap bars you're offering. Instead of seeing a list of chemicals that they can't even pronounce, your customers will read a label that boasts of wholesome, simple ingredients. Play up the differences. Play up the time and care you put into a soap batch. Start bragging.

How to Sell Yourself

For anyone who is feeling a little shy about selling soap, here is some advice that has worked for hundreds of hobbyists and professionals. Take a deep breath, and for just one minute close your eyes and pretend your mother or best friend made the soap you want to give as a gift or sell. Make a mental list of all the reasons why someone would and should value or purchase this item, which your dear mom or your best buddy made. Now, start writing down each positive element you thought of. Is the quality of work superior? Does the product make you smile? Are the colors cool? Does the soap help chapped skin? Did you grow your own herbs? You're writing a list of the selling points of your soap. Next turn this list into a mini sales presentation.

Once you remove your own feelings and emotions of rejection or insecurity about selling your craft, you can see your soapmaking skills in a clearer, less personal light and tackle the reasons why a customer should buy your design. Too often we're our own worst critics, brutally nit-picking and finding fault with our creations. It's easier to come up with a list of values and selling points for a craft when you aren't personally and emotionally involved. Most of us have learned it's better to be humble than be perceived as big-headed or boastful. Self-promotion and promoting your crafts has little to do with modesty. It has much to do with recognizing the quality you put into the soap craft. You wouldn't make a soap that wasn't worth using. Be prepared to share that pride with your customers.

The Next Big Step

There are so many possibilities and opportunities to profit from your soapmaking. As you continue reading the chapters in part 2, you'll learn about all the markets where you'll be able to sell your soap—craft shows, craft malls, retail gift shops, co-ops, catalog sales, Web sites, or any combination of these. You'll also learn to be creative in your packaging, merchandising, and displays.

To earn a profit from soapmaking, you need to learn about a few legalities and paperwork. All of this is covered in chapter 11, written by Barbara Brabec. Barbara has been writing about craft, cottage, and home businesses for 25 years. She's one of the most recognized writers in this area. When I first decided to turn my hobby into a business, I read her books with a passion, and I use her books for handy reference. There's no one I can think of who has more knowledge of or background on the challenges and joys of using creative talents as an occupation.

Handy Hint

Practice a brief, one- to three-minute sales presentation in front of a mirror, your children, or a good friend. Ask for feedback. Adjust the presentation and get comfortable with it.

Success in Selling Original Designs

- Make the commitment to become a business. You may choose to start small or part-time, but understand that the goal of business is to grow and make a profit.

- Put it all in writing. Write a business plan and keep it with your business records. If you don't know what a business plan is, read a book on starting a business (see Resources for many book suggestions). Your plan should include short-term and long-term goals.

- Know your talents and skills. Know your assets and liabilities. The way to succeed is to show off your best. Stay in focus.

- Know your markets. Investigate. Make your work shine by placing your best work in the markets.

- Educate yourself, not only in the business of design, but also in the business of anything on the consumer's or manufacturer's mind. Always trust your own instincts.

- Keep an updated résumé and portfolio. Don't assume others know who you are or what you do. A business card in your pocket could mean a job!

- Grow in your talents and your craft. Experiment and have fun every once in awhile. Change is part of the business. You're not the same person today as you were five years ago, trust me.

- Share your talents in your community. Volunteer. Network with your industry. Once or twice a year, give your soap away for free.

- Believe in yourself and your abilities. If you don't believe in yourself, no one else will. Self-promotion is not bragging.

- Enjoy your work. Rest often. Daydream every day. And go for it!

In soapmaking we must watch carefully for the trace. The following chapters are the trace of making a profit from soapmaking. You already understand the pleasure of succeeding with a batch of soap. Now get ready to feel the pleasure of succeeding in earning some money for your efforts.

Who's Selling Soap?

To get an overview of who's selling soap, I interviewed 12 soapmakers from several Internet news groups, mailing lists, and chat rooms. I randomly selected soapmakers until I reached the count of 12. This sampling was done anonymously since most using the Internet/World Wide Web have screen names or nicknames. The interviewees knew who I was; however, I didn't ask for real names in hopes of gathering the most current and accurate information from each individual.

How many years have you been selling your soaps?

Years	Number of Soapmakers
1–2	6
3–4	3
5–6	1
10	2

Is your sale of soap additional family income, a part-time job, or a full-time occupation?

Additional family income	5
Part-time job	4
Full-time occupation	3

How many hours do you put into soapmaking each week?

Hours	Number of Soapmakers
Under 10	3
11–20	5
21–40	4

What is your yearly income from selling your soaps?

Yearly Income	Number of Soapmakers
Under $3,000	2
$4,000–$5,000	3
$8,000–12,000	3
$14,000–$18,000	2
$20,000	1
$35,000+	1

Do you work primarily from your home?

Yes: 12

No: 0

Where do you sell your soaps?
(Some crafters gave more than one answer.)

Word of mouth to family and friends	12
Farmers' markets/flea markets	9
Art and craft shows (indoor and outdoor)	8
Web sites	8
Directly to retailers	7
Craft mall or craft co-op	4
Catalog or mail order	4
Garage sales	3
Home shows	2
Directly to wholesale/distributor	2
Sales representatives	1

What is the average cost of an item you sell?

Cost	Number of Soapmakers
Under $5.00	3
$5.50–$8.00	7
$8.50–$10.00	2

What is your best-selling item?

Soap made from mainly mild ingredients	3
Decorative soap (swirls, decorative mold, bright colors)	2
Soap with skin-softening qualities	2
Soap with almond as an ingredient and scent	1
Glycerin soap (melt and pour)	1
Floral-scented soaps	1
Soap with natural exfoliants	1
Hot-process soap made from rendered fat	1

What do you consider the best aspect of selling your soaps?

Working for yourself/independence/being your own boss	5
Being able to work and still be home with the children	4
Creativity and new challenges	2
Being able to work with a disability/physical challenge	1

What advice would you give someone who wants to start selling soaps?

"Learn everything you can about ingredients and different soapmaking techniques."

"List all your ingredients on your soap labeling. And don't be afraid of providing samples to customers. Once they try handmade soap, they're sold for life!"

"Experiment with recipes and ingredients. Try to make your soap unique. Don't add anything that doesn't give your soap a better quality. Have fun with it."

Pricing
Your Soap

▼▼

CRAFTING IS CONSIDERED A SHARING, caring activity. Many crafters initially feel a little guilty for selling their crafts. They would rather give their craft designs to others than sell to customers. But professional crafters are providing products as well as a service, and it's only fair that they earn a wage or salary. As professional crafters, we must evaluate how each product is received, how well it sells, and *most* importantly, whether it makes a profit. To keep customers, as well as our bank account, happy, we must keep our items fresh and appealing.

Pricing your work will be one of the most difficult aspects of profiting from your soapmaking skills. It's never easy to put a value or price tag on an item you made with your own hands. As a businessperson, however, you need to treat the pricing of your soap just as carefully as you, the creative craftsperson, treat the selection of the ingredients for the soap. To build your pricing confidence, consider these questions: Did you provide your best work? Did you use quality supplies to make your craft? Did you put your sincere care (and love of soapmaking) into each piece of work you created? Each time you answer yes to a question, you are proving to yourself that you, as a professional, deserve fair payment for your soapmaking

147

efforts. Fair and reasonable pricing means that you, the crafter, and your customer are satisfied with the final selling price.

You may find that some soap recipes aren't suitable for selling in the marketplace because costly ingredients raise the price you'll have to charge to make a profit. For example, I love to work with paper casting. I could spend hours making the paper pulp, placing it in the molds, allowing the item to dry, painting the piece with a colorful paint wash, and then adding little details of glitter and lace. The final price for a 3-by-3-inch paper casting was around $15. I priced myself out of the market. I knew this because not one piece sold after several shows. I looked in galleries and art catalogues and found that the price range for similar work was between $5 and $10. I could not match or beat this range; however, I've discovered that selling the instructions and designs to magazines and publishers pays for the hobby. So I paper cast for fun, and keep track of materials used and steps followed for profit.

> ### Handy Hint
>
> Relax. Remember that prices aren't set in stone. Feel free to adjust them up or down according to your needs and the needs of your customers.

The bottom line is that you feel comfortable with the price tag you put on your work. Don't be afraid to let a high-ticket item sit on the shelf. Would you rather give the design away or wait until the right customer comes along who is willing to pay for a quality design? It's not a personal rejection if a potential customer doesn't buy your work. That customer could have a dozen reasons for not buying your soap, none of which has anything to do with you personally or your work.

Cost of Goods, Labor, and Overhead

Sometimes a manufacturer seems to pull a price out of thin air like a magician pulls a rabbit out of a hat, but chances are the price of the product is based on very specific information. This information is based on the cost of goods, supplies, and materials; the cost of your labor and time; and the cost of any overhead used to make a design.

I use Mary Jo's Spice-Is-Nice Soap recipe from chapter 5 (see page 77) as an example for determining the price of soap. This is a small batch of soap that yields four 2-ounce bars of soap.

Cost of Goods, Materials, and Supplies

The first step is to list all the components of your soap. I recommend making this list as you gather the ingredients for a soap recipe. Take time to note even the smallest amount of an ingredient, from a quarter teaspoon of spice to three drops of an essential oil. To determine exactly how much it costs to make a soap batch, break down the overall cost of each item (a 2-ounce bottle of essential oil) into smaller units (drops per 2 ounces). You can estimate essential oils and fragrance oils by using water instead of the scents to measure out smaller increments. For example, fill an empty essential oil container with water. Extract the number of drops for a batch, continuing on a batch-by-batch basis until the container is empty. This tells you the number of batches per bottle.

This list shows not only how much of each ingredient is used in the recipe but also how much it costs to use the specified amount of ingredient.

2 cups grated soap base = $3.00
 1 pound (4 cups grated) soap base costs $6.00
 ($6.00 ÷ 4 cups = $1.50 per cup of grated soap base)

2/3 cup spring water costs $0.07 ($0.14 if rounded up)*
 1 gallon (8 cups) of spring water costs $1.15
 ($1.15 ÷ by 8 cups = $0.14 per cup)

1/2 teaspoon of rosemary = $0.06 ($0.13 if rounded up)*
 Jar of dried rosemary (18 teaspoons) costs $2.29
 ($2.29 ÷ 18 teaspoons = $0.13 per teaspoon)

continues

1/2 teaspoon of thyme = $0.055 ($0.11 if rounded up)*
Jar of dried thyme (18 teaspoons) costs $1.98
($1.98 ÷ 18 teaspoons = $0.11 per teaspoon)

1/2 teaspoon of sage = $0.07 ($0.14 if rounded up)*
Jar of dried sage (18 teaspoons) costs $2.59
($2.59 ÷ 18 teaspoons = $0.14 per teaspoon)

10 drops of rosemary EO = $1.20
Bottle of rosemary EO (50 drops) costs $5.98
($5.98 ÷ 50 drops = $0.12 per drop)

5 drops of cinnamon EO = $0.60
Bottle of cinnamon EO (50 drops) costs $5.98
($5.98 ÷ 50 drops = $0.12 per drop)

Total cost of ingredients: $3.00 + $0.14 + $0.13 + $0.11 + $0.14 + $1.20 + $0.60 = $5.32

Total bars made: 4

Price Per Bar: $5.32 ÷ 4 bars = $1.33 per bar of soap

Cost of goods: $1.33

Labor Cost

The next step is to add a labor cost. Labor is what you pay yourself for your efforts and time. Most crafters and artisans grossly underestimate the time involved in making a finished design. To avoid this, track the time that it takes to complete each step in the soap-making process on several different occasions. Then average the results to determine just how much time you put into a batch of soap. The following shows the amount of time to complete each step in making Mary Jo's Spice-Is-Nice soap. Remember, this batch yields 4 bars of soap.

To increase profits, round up the price depending on measurement. For example, in the soap base section above I have rounded 2/3 cup spring water up to 1 cup, making it the same price as 1 cup spring water. This works for all formulas.

Clockwise from Top: Florida Sunshine; Jim's Jeweled Jelly;
Ken's Pioneer Days; Matt's Crazy Coconut

Clockwise from Top: Tollee's Banana Fun; Bo's Bubble & Bath;
Ron's Refreshing Raspberry; Marie's Citrus Lavender; Maria's Mint Melody

Clockwise from Top: Mary Jo's Spice-Is-Nice; David's Body Scrub; Smooth and Simple; Bill's Bold and Bodacious

Clockwise from Top: Fresh As a Cucumber; Chocolate and Coffee Lover's Temptation; Gardener's Treasure; A Red, Red Rose; Nancy Bee's Honey

Shopping for supplies or ingredients:

1 hour for 10 batches of soap

(60 minutes ÷ 10 batches = 6 minutes per batch)

Ordering and unpacking shipments of supplies:

2 hours for 10 batches of soap

(120 minutes ÷ 10 batches = 12 minutes per batch)

Gathering supplies to work area:

15 minutes per batch

Preparing molds:

15 minutes per batch

Making soap and pouring into molds:

60 minutes per batch

Unmolding or cutting soap:

15 minutes per batch

Packaging and pricing soap:

5 minutes per bar

4 bars per batch (5 minutes × 4 bars equals 20 minutes)

Total time spent per batch: 6 + 12 + 15 + 15 + 60 + 15 + 20 = 143 minutes (rounded up to 150 minutes to make even); 150 minutes ÷ 60 = 2 1/2 hours

Total time per bar: 150 minutes ÷ 4 bars = 37. 5 minutes per bar (rounded up to 38)

A labor rate can be paid by the hour or by the piece. If you choose to be paid by the hour, set a rate that is fair and reasonable. Most of us would be tickled to earn $25, $50, or $100 per hour for our efforts, but a reality check will tell you that your new business venture can't afford your services. You are working for yourself, so avoid caps or ceilings on your income. Consider the national minimum wage as a starting point for your own labor rate. As your skills and talents grow, your labor rate per hour can be increased to include your efficiency and acumen. The following example shows the labor rate for a batch of soap paid on an hourly basis.

Hourly Basis

> Hourly labor rate for a batch of soap: $8.00 per hour (this is just an example. Depending on where you live, a good way to figure your hourly labor rate is to add a couple dollars to the minimum wage in your state).

Selecting the way you price your labor is very subjective. Personally, I'd rather pay myself by the piece because I'm very quick and efficient when crafting. You might prefer to use an hourly rate. Calculate the different ways you can apply a labor rate to see what works best for you. You can reevaluate and adjust your labor rate at any time, based on your needs and your skills.

Overhead

The final consideration in pricing is referred to as *overhead*. It's a catchall category for anything outside of the cost of materials and labor. You may not think of it, but you're using electricity as you make soap, you're occupying space in your home for business rather than personal needs, and most soap sold needs some type of packaging, including price tags and receipts for the purchaser of the item. You may have supplies that don't directly become part of the item you're selling but that are needed to make the item. Overhead includes supplies that are reused and wear out in less than a year. For example, equipment and depreciable items like pots, pans, molds, storage containers, cooling racks, thermometers, computer or office equipment, cameras, phone, travel, shipping and postage, show fees, display costs, packaging, and insurance are used indirectly to make your finished product.

Overhead is calculated as a percentage of cost of goods and labor. Where does this magical percentage used to figure out overhead come from? Millions of pages of books explain overhead, but for a businessperson selling handmade items, I'm almost positive that using precious memory cells to store such data leads to an inevitable breakdown of the artistic nervous system. All you need to know, as a businessperson, is that overhead must be proportionate to cost of goods and labor. The cottage industry standard overhead percentage is 25 to 35%. Soapmaking is not overhead intense, so I opted to take the middle ground of 30% for my pricing formulas.

I have received feedback over the years from peers and experts who state that this percentage is way too low. I stick to my guns. Fortune 500 companies who need to cut costs often look first at overhead costs. Do you want to cut your labor rate? Do you want to use inferior or cheaper materials in your piece? Take a look at your overhead, and don't let it get out of control.

Just a Few More Things to Consider when Pricing

In addition to cost of goods, labor, and overhead, you must also take into consideration other factors, including competition, the economy, supply and demand, and turnover. You need to consider how much competition you have for a sale to a customer. How many other artists or craftspeople in your area are selling work with similar motifs, media, techniques, style, or form? Look for and keep a running total of how many other artists or craftspeople are making soap. Is your work unique? Is your craft a standout, or can you put everyone's work side by side and not see any differences? Your only real difference may come down to the price tag. Can you still make a profit and keep competitive?

You need a well-rounded knowledge of how items similar to yours are priced in the marketplace. Visit bath shops, cosmetic areas of department stores, gift shops, and any other retail establishments that sell soap. Look at catalogs and magazine advertisements for soap. By comparing your price with your competitors' prices, you are able to gauge the reasonableness of your prices. You can determine if you are underpricing, overpricing, or getting it just right. Underpricing means you're paying your customers to purchase your work; you are essentially devaluing the item. Overpricing means you'll be sitting on the inventory or end up with a low turnover rate, causing cash flow problems.

Consider the economy of the area where you'll be selling. Certain areas or communities fare better than others in terms of economics. I live in an area that is deeply affected by the space industry. When times are good, people spend their money freely, but when rumors start flying about budget cuts, the family budget is watched carefully. When I travel to another part of the state, where my customers aren't as dependent on one industry, I can sell at almost twice my asking price. In my hometown area I have decided not to sell directly to customers because it isn't cost-effective. Instead, I sell only through a local craft co-op that caters to tourists.

There's no surefire formula for determining supply and demand. If you think the market will bear a higher price than you've calculated with a pricing formula, it's better to trust your instincts. If you think that a new design will attract more attention from loyal customers, increase the retail price to take advantage of this higher demand. This will also help maintain inventory. If costs are too low for a product with a high demand, will you be able to keep the item in stock?

Another consideration is turnover. Do you want to pack up and take home products after each show? Do you want items to sit week after week at a craft mall, gathering dust? Every time the items are packed and unpacked, you risk damage and loss of product quality. Consider pricing items to move.

Handy Hint

Review or take some time to study the theory of supply and demand, which can be found in a basic high school or college economics book.

Pricing Formulas

Now that you have determined cost of goods, labor, and overhead and have researched all other factors in determining prices, it's time to take a look at pricing formulas. I developed the following three pricing formulas after interviewing and talking with soapmakers. The majority of soapmakers price their work using these formulas. Don't let numbers confuse you, and don't be intimidated. Pricing formulas are designed to make it easier to understand what goes into the selling price of your soap.

Cost Plus Markup

The first way to price is a very basic formula often referred to as *cost plus markup*.

Total all the costs incurred to make one item and multiply by a markup factor of anywhere from 2 to 8 depending on competition, your community's economy, and your experience.

Cost of materials × markup factor = Retail price

The following shows the cost plus markup price for Mary Jo's Spice-Is-Nice soap.

Cost plus markup = $1.33 × 3 (markup)* = $3.93 per bar

Standard Retail Pricing:

Another formula used for pricing is referred to as *standard retail pricing*. This formula uses the percentage of overhead plus the cost of goods and labor. Using this method provides an accurate accounting of all expenses plus a standard wage.

*I use a 3× factor which was derived from industry data on the average price for handmade soap.

(Cost of materials + labor rate) × overhead = Retail price

The following example, based on Mary Jo's Spice-Is-Nice formula, shows how to use this formula with an hourly labor rate.

(Cost of goods + labor rate) × overhead = Retail price

Cost of goods = $1.33

Hourly labor rate = $8.00 per hour

Overhead: $0.30

($1.33 + $8.00) = $9.33 × $0.30 = $2.80 per bar of soap

Standard Retail Price = $1.33 + $8.00 + $2.80
= $12.13 per bar of soap

Going Rate

The *going rate* pricing formula for pricing soap is pretty straightforward. Simply compare the prices of similar soaps already on the market. This pricing strategy works well when your goal is to be competitive with other soapmakers. I found soaps similar to mine in a mail order catalog ($5.99 plus shipping and handling), at a gift shop ($6.95), and on the Web ($6.50 plus shipping and handling). It's important to use more than one source when researching the going rate because you will take the average using the average formula. The average cost to the consumer for a bar of handmade soap is $6.48 per bar.

$5.99 (price from mail order catalog) + $6.95 (price from gift shop) + $6.50 (price from Web) ÷ 3 prices = $6.48 per bar.

It's time to compare the prices for each pricing formula to determine the best price for you to charge.

Cost plus markup = $3.93 per bar

Standard retail pricing = $12.13 per bar (labor rate)

Going rate = $6.48 per bar

The price given by the standard retail rate using hourly labor rates seems out of proportion in comparison with the prices calculated from the other pricing formulas. In this case, the standard retail rate is not helpful; however, in other cases, this rate may be the most accurate, so sometimes it is good to use this formula. All the other prices fall into the same basic price range. Add to the formula a good healthy economy, a high demand for the product, and few competitors marketing handmade soaps. What would you price the bar of soap?

I'd start my pricing at $4.50 or $4.95 because this would make a good profit for my efforts but keep the item under $5. From experience I know that I'll average two bars of soap per customer if I keep the price under $5.00. If sales are brisk, I might consider pricing the soap higher next time. If sales are slow, I'll review the price and see if it's possible to lower the cost without severely cutting into my profit. Most likely I'd look at my soap packaging. The more attractive and eye-catching my packaging and the overall display of the soap, the more value will be added to the item for potential customers.

Industry retail buying studies for pricing indicate that adding cent numbers that end in 5 or 9 are the most easily accepted by a consumer. In a random testing, a consumer would pick the item priced $5.95 over one priced at $6.00 and even preferred the price of $5.99 over the same item priced at $6.00. It may seem deceptive or silly to use this information, but consider the lost sales over what amounts to one penny or five cents. Granted, consumers are savvy and react negatively to being patronized, but I have found that pricing my own work at 25, 50, and 75 cents instead of the next dollar amount did increase my multiple sales of same-item purchases.

Industry studies also indicate that consumers consider purchases under $10 to be casual purchases—impulse buys with no post-purchase consumer guilt. The average amount spent purchasing a gift item for a family member or friend averages around $20. Gift

▼▼

Raising Your Prices

Prices can easily come down in a customer's eye, but most customers don't react positively to price *increases*. It may feel like you are sitting on product at an art and craft show, or like your soap is just collecting dust at a boutique, but it's not the end of the world. With patience and some restraint, you can adjust your prices to your marketplace. The general rule is to lower a price rather than suddenly raise prices, but what happens if you do need to raise prices? Either orally or with a simple flyer/card, explain why ingredient prices have risen or why shipping costs have increased. Let your customer know that you thought carefully before asking them to help share in the increased expenses.

▲▲

items purchased for work associates, children's teachers, and other service providers should be priced from $5 to $7. High-ticket gifts are priced from $25 to $75.

I stopped pricing my work a few years ago. I grew frustrated with some customers telling me my prices were way too high while others snatched up my work and told me how reasonable my items were. I asked my husband, Ken, to take over the pricing. I gave him all the information on material costs and labor time, and I let him set the overhead percentage. In some cases, he doubled my prices. And guess what? Most of my customers didn't even bat an eye.

Once you've learned to price your soap and understand that the price must allow you to earn a profit for your efforts, you'll have accomplished one of the most difficult tasks for any small-business person. The next task is to find a market, or combination of markets, in which to sell your soap. The costs of getting your soap to market are covered in the overhead part of your pricing formula. Although it may not seem logical, we must establish prices for our goods before researching the markets where will sell them. In the next chapter I discuss how to find a marketplace for your soap.

Selling Your Soap

▼▼

FOR THE PAST DECADE OR TWO, most professional crafters sold their handmade items in one of two ways. The first was simply to set up a business in the home and sell directly to a market of family and friends, who in turn would give the item as a gifts to another party. A savvy artisan would include with each item sold at least one business card with all the important contact information, such as name, address, and phone number. Over time, a business clientele would grow by word of mouth. Word of mouth is still the best form of advertising that a professional artist; craftsperson, or artisan can invest in. A good word-of-mouth reputation is built by consistently providing a quality product or service with good customer service.

The second marketplace for the professional crafter was the art and craft show, which could be anything from local community events to church bazaars to elaborate craft show productions operated by professional promoters. These shows would often be outdoors. The atmosphere would range from flea market to high-scale gallery. The original outdoor craft show had a festive, carnival feel—service groups sold hot dogs and popcorn and local talent,

CHRISTIN'S STORY

Christin Ocasio created Wyndham Soapworks because store-bought soap made her skin dry and itchy. After coming down with a horrible rash from scalp to toes, she went to a dermatologist and was diagnosed with eczema. The doctor gave her steroid shots and recommended that she take cool showers and rub down with heavy mineral oil before toweling off. But the eczema never disappeared, and showers always left her skin uncomfortably dry, itchy, and tight.

"I wanted to treat my skin better and prevent further discomfort," says Christin. "I bought a computer and started hanging around the America Online soapmaking bulletin boards. A kind person I met online gave me a bar of handcrafted goatmilk soap. Using the handmade soap made showering a joy rather than a test of endurance."

From then on, Christin decided to learn the alchemy of turning fats and oils into soap. "I bought just about every book on soapmaking. I prac-

such as dancers, singers, and poets, entertained from morning until closing.

The appeal of handmade craft or art items seems to have peaks and valleys, just like that of any other retail product. It's trite but true that everything old is, at some point, new again. Since the mid-1980s a steady buying cycle of consumers has wanted to purchase homemade designs. Because of this trend hundreds of art and craft shows have been organized annually, biannually, quarterly, and even monthly. On any given day, there are at least a dozen craft shows being held somewhere in the United States.

ticed and experimented until I came up with the perfect recipe to suit my taste. I began giving bars away at family gatherings and at some places where I volunteer. Finally, someone close to me urged me to start selling it and Wyndham Soapworks was born."

Wyndham is a small, family-owned and -operated cottage business and a home school that "manufactures" their soaps in small batches right in Christin's kitchen. The "distribution" center is her family's dining room table. Christin's six-year-old daughter helps with labels and sample bags, and her daughter's own handmade bookmarks are included in the outgoing packages. The soaps are in several local shops and mail-order catalogs across the globe. "At some point in the future, we'd like to branch out and sell supplies and hold classes," says Christin.

So where do professional crafters go today to sell handmade items? Where will you sell your soap? You may decide to sell directly to the final user, the consumer (retail sales), or an intermediate buyer, placing your product in the hands of a wholesaler. Or you may opt to combine retail with wholesale to boost year-round income. Basically few real differences exist between the retail and wholesale markets, with the exception of pricing and category. No matter which marketplace you choose for selling your wares, you must find the market, build your inventory, create a display, and get soap to the customer.

Soap is an item needed year-round, so soapmakers have the advantage (over craftspeople who sell seasonal products) of being able to increase recipe batches to handle additional sales. Keep in mind that if you choose to sell cold-process soaps, you'll have at least a four-week wait (to allow the soap to cure) before you can sell the batch.

This chapter takes a close look at the many marketing options, choices, and venues available to you as a professional soapmaker. Selecting the right marketplace for you and your soap is just as important as selecting quality ingredients or figuring out the right price for your soap. As you read about the markets available to you, ask yourself some serious questions: How involved do you wish to be in the selling of your soap? How large of a geographical area do you wish to cover? How much soap can you make to fill the needs of your marketplace selections?

Retail Craft Shows

Most of us think of retail shows as art and craft shows, but they can also include seasonal boutiques, church and community bazaars, indoor or outdoor markets, and any type of program where you display your own work to sell directly to the end user—your consumer or buyer. The outdoor craft show is probably one of the oldest markets in our industry, and it started the professional craft and artisan industry as we know it today. In modern times many of these shows have moved indoors at shopping malls and convention centers. It remains one of the most popular and profitable marketplaces for those selling handmade works.

If you look around your town or city, you'll find that there is at least one retail craft show each weekend. The show may be outdoors or indoors, with or without a professional promoter. To participate in the craft show, you need to apply to the show, set up a display in which to showcase your work, and in most cases, free up your weekends to participate (most craft shows are scheduled for Saturday and Sunday).

At the craft show, you sell retail, so rarely is a commission taken from your sales. The show gives you a chance to meet and learn from your customers, who can be a great source of information. Talk to customers about what they are looking for, what colors appeal to them, and what they would like to see on your shelves and tables. Thirteen years ago a customer asked me to make rag dolls. I hesitated at first because I didn't make dolls and had no desire to make them. The customer persisted, so I made the dolls for her. Not only did I enjoy this type of craft, it became my best seller at shows. Many times since then I've added different items to my product line because of customer interest.

The down side to shows, especially outdoor shows, can be the weather. Shelters or canopies are a must for the outdoor marketplace. Wind, sun, and rain can take a toll on the best of us. You are essentially a store on wheels, so all the concerns of travel must be considered. Displays must be compact. They should be designed for ease of travel, setup, and breakdown. For each show, pack change boxes, folding chairs, tables, table coverings, and a good attitude.

One of the first questions many new craft professionals ask is, What is the difference between a juried and a non-juried art and craft show? The most basic difference is that acceptance to a non-juried show is based on first come, first serve. A potential crafter fills out an application and pays a show fee. Once the show spaces are filled, no more applications are taken. Acceptance to a juried show is based on the decision of a judge or jury. You are often required to submit slides or photos of your work or booth. In addition to the application and show fee, you may be required to pay a separate, nonrefundable jurying fee, which pays for the judges' time. The jurying process ensures quality of work and, in some cases, limits the number of crafts in a specific medium. For example, a juried show with a hundred spaces may allow 20% for decorative painting, 20% for stained glass, 20% for needle arts, 20% for ceramics, and 20% for mixed media. The idea is to keep variety in the show place and to spread the competition for the consumer's dollar.

Wholesale Craft Shows

Wholesaling provides the artisan or craftsperson with an outlet for selling goods in volume to a specific buyer at a specific time at a specific price. You have a certain amount of control over this marketplace. You can establish minimum buys by quantity (for example, the product must be purchased by the half dozen, dozen, or gross) or by dollar value (for example, a minimum purchase of $250). Set your prices so that you and the wholesaler can make a profit. Keep in mind that wholesalers mark up the goods. This provides the craft professional with a good way to manage cash flow and inventory. Wholesale selling is normally done at a trade show or gift market. These shows and markets are located throughout the country, with some of the largest taking place in Atlanta, Miami, Dallas, Los Angles, San Francisco, Chicago, Columbus, and New York City. To become a part of a gift show, you must contact the specific gift market for an exhibitor package, which includes information about exhibit fees, space allowances, display requirements, and other information for putting your exhibit or booth together.

Handy Hint

Not all craft shows are created the same. Take time to learn as much as possible about a craft show before investing in the show fee.

Finding the Shows

Whether your marketplace is retail or wholesale, there are some basic requirements to participate in any show. The first is to locate the shows. Wholesale shows can be found through calendars and advertisements in industry trade journals, such as *Craftrends, Country Business,* and *Gift and Stationery News.* Find out about retail or consumer shows by networking with fellow professionals, calling your local chamber of commerce, or reading show guide periodicals. The many regional show guides can be found by searching in the directory of periodicals at your local library. The Web sites for *Sunshine Artist Magazine* (www.sunshineartist.com) and The American Craft Malls (www.procrafter.com) list hundreds of craft shows throughout the United States. (See Resources for more detailed information about these sources.)

There are no guarantees that even the most successful annual craft shows won't have a bad year, but the more you find out about a show, the better your odds are of finding the shows that are right for your soap or product lines. The following list provides some things to consider and some questions to ask the show's contact person.

Information Needed Before Applying to Any Show

- Show fee/cost of space (How do these fees compare with the cost of other shows?)
- Cost of travel to show
- Date of show and show hours
- Annual or first-time event?
- Group, community, or promoter-organized event?
- Contact information to request a show application
- Deadline for submitting application
- Slides or photos required for entry?
- Are there specific categories or media allowed?
- Total number of exhibitors or booths at the show
- Refund policy/rain dates
- Indoor or outdoor exhibit
- Specific display requirements for participating

- Booth space size, in exact measurements
- Electrical outlets if applicable. Charge for electricity?
- Last year's show attendance
- How the show is promoted and advertised

Once you are accepted to a show, you need to prepare for selling at it—a hectic experience even for the seasoned professional. If you've never done a show before, it can be downright chaotic. Over the past 15 years, I developed the following checklist of what to take to shows. I keep a copy of the list for each show I participate in and check off each item as I pack my vehicle. Keep the list handy for when you break down your booth, too. You'll find you won't forget to pack and return home with each item you brought to the show.

Items Needed at a Show

- All display items: tables, table covers, shelves, crates, tools needed for assembling the display, chairs, and ice chest/cooler (if allowed)
- Inventory/products: priced, packaged, and ready to display
- Guest book: Used to build a mailing list
- Cash box, receipt book, plenty of coins and small bills, calculator, charge card imprinter, credit card charge slips, and a state sales tax table (if applicable)
- Needed extras: Pens for writing checks, extra price tags
- Business cards, brochures, any signs or other paper-good items
- Special order forms (if applicable)
- Copy of your state sales tax license to post in full view of consumers (if applicable)
- A handcart to carry items (if needed)
- Bring some items to demonstrate during slow selling times.
- Repair kit: Scissors, glue, tape, and small quantities of any craft supply needed to make small repairs at the show

- Snacks and beverages plus weather gear if outside: Visor, hat, change of clothing, sunscreen, and comfortable shoes
- Attitude: Positive thinking, high energy, enthusiastic sales presentation, and a smile
- Leave at home: Small children, books, TV, radio, and pets (Most potential customers find sales help who read during selling hours to be rude and will not ask for help.)

If possible, schedule relief times for yourself during the show by asking for help from friends and family. You can pay your relief team an hourly wage, a commission of sales, or free product for time. If all else fails, ask your closest neighbor at the show to exchange a break time with you.

A Home Show

A craft home show is like a Tupperware or Mary Kay home party for crafts. There are two ways for the craft professionals to use the home show or home party. The first is to use the home show as the main avenue for selling your soap. To earn income this way, you must book new home shows continually in various individuals' homes. The second use for the home show is to bring in additional income. To do this, you schedule home shows in your own home on an annual, biannual, or quarterly basis.

If you use home shows as the main source of income, you must continually and consistently promote your product to increase your sales area. Many professional artisans often hire others to book, prepare, and sell at home shows. They pay the additional sales help a straight fee or a commission based on total sales. If you use the home show to bring in additional income, you can probably manage an annual or a quarterly show without additional sales help.

Whether you use home shows for additional income or as your sole income, contact the city or county where the home show will be held to make sure no city or county statutes prohibit the exchange of money in a private home for business reasons. The rules in every state, city, and country vary. Note: Most municipalities equate an annual or quarterly home show with a garage or an estate sale but with some zoning and sales tax considerations. (See chapter 11 for more information on this topic.) Most states require that sales tax be collected. Often the city or county's main concern is that the neighborhood is not disturbed by the additional traffic flow of the invited guests. Plan ahead for parking and notify your neighbors about when the event will take place. Also keep track of all expenses, including travel and business deductions. Record and file mileage and expenses for each show, and report this information to the IRS.

When preparing for a home show, advance planning pays. Think about location, date, hours, inventory, invitations, and advertising. This marketplace allows you to display your work as it can be used by your potential buyer. Literally transform the rooms in the house into a sales showroom. Remove all personal property from the rooms where items will be sold. Set up an area for money exchange and bagging purchased supplies. (When an item is purchased, replace it immediately.) Consider inviting other professionals from noncompeting media to join you. This will broaden the craft appeal, provide a way to share expenses, and expand your guest list.

Christmas boutiques are the most popular and successful home shows. Play holiday music, light scented candles, decorate a tree with lights, serve punch and cookies, and hire a babysitter for the customers' kids so mom or dad can browse without distractions. In the invitation, suggest that customers bring a gift shopping list. Offer gift-wrapping and handmade gift tags. Have an area of lower-priced items so children can purchase gifts for their parents. For any buyer who brings a new guest for your mailing list, offer a prize, such as a free soap ball or percentage off an item. Personalize items on site. Teach bow making or another small craft. Home shows can be fun and enjoyable celebrations of crafting and of being a professional, so get creative and show off. If held at the end of your fiscal year, there's the added bonus of reducing your inventory, making it much easier to handle in the tax time ahead of you.

A Few More Thoughts about Shows

If you are prepared, well rested, and enthusiastic about doing a show, the results will be positive and profitable. Many professional crafters feel they aren't good salespeople. If you feel you are not cut out to sell your own work, hire someone to do it for you. The extra cost of hiring someone who enjoys selling may be worth the peace of mind it brings you not to have to it yourself. And remember that everyone has a bad show every once in awhile. Bad weather, poor advertising, and regional economics can directly effect sales. Don't get discouraged. Chalk it up to experience and get ready for the next show.

The show business of arts and crafts keeps you in touch with the buyer. Enjoy your time with your customers, and take every opportunity to network with your peers.

Pay attention to the body language of browsers. If the potential buyer is with a friend, you may need to sell to the friend just as much as to the interested browser. Place your craft in the buyer's hand so he or she can touch it and take control of it. Watch your own body language. Smile and interact with everyone in your booth. Make eye contact and lean closer when you talk to customers. Talk about your craft with pride and enthusiasm, and be sure to ask questions to find out what your customers want. Share what you love about soapmaking. Remember, most buyers aren't just buying your soap; they're buying a small piece of your personality, too.

The craft show is the perfect place to become a showperson. Participating in a show can bring you new markets and customers.

> ## Handy Hint
>
> Be courteous not only to your customers, but also to your fellow exhibitors. For example, avoid loud music or strong scents.

So relax. Put your best foot forward at all times, even with rude or impatient customers. And trust me, you'll meet every kind of temperament and personality while selling at a show. When struggling with a difficult customer, remember that the situation is only temporary.

Have ample inventory for each show.

Arrive early and be prepared to unload your inventory and supplies quickly. Parking is often limited at shows. Usually you will be allowed only a short time to unload and reload near the exhibit area and then you will have to remove your vehicle.

Evaluate any show you do soon after the show. Some items to note include total sales, total inventory count before and after, weather, traffic in the booth, and ease of setting up. The following evaluation form is a sample you can use to fill out after each show. These evaluations are valuable when scheduling future shows.

▼▼▼▼▼▼▼▼▼▼▼▼▼▼▼▼▼▼

Handy Hint

Don't stay up half the night before a show trying to prepare more inventory; it's never worth the lost sleep. You're better off feeling rested and refreshed at show time.

▲▲▲▲▲▲▲▲▲▲▲▲▲▲▲▲▲▲

Sample of a Show Evaluation

Show Name _____

Sponsor _____

Date of Show _____

Show Fee _____

Location _____

Annual Event? _____ Number of Shows to Date _____

Parking for Vendors   Good   Poor

Parking for Customers   Good   Poor

Customer Turnout   Excellent Good Fair Below Average Poor

Buyers or browsers?

Customers   Men Women Children Teenagers Seniors Other

Publicity   Good   Fair   Poor

Space Provided   Good   Fair   Poor

Is there a better space for increased buyer traffic? _____

Is there a better way to set up booth for buyer traffic? _____

Space Number _____

Total Exhibitors _____

Direct Competitors _____

Sponsor's Attitude _____

Other Exhibitors' Attitude _____

Shoppers' Attitude _____

Weather and Environmental Conditions _____

Food Available   Good   Poor

Does the sales tax differ from home base? _____

Total Sales _____

Total Expenses _____

Comments _____

_____

_____

_____

_____

Craft Malls

Craft malls, which are found across the country, are like shopping malls that sell crafts. Most malls require a signed contract allowing you a set period to occupy a set amount of space. A contract of six months or one year is normal. Craft malls don't require that you spend any time in the mall other than the time you spend stocking your space or changing your display. The display space can vary from a single shelf to a large open floor space. You are responsible for setting the price of items to be sold and for keeping the display stocked. The mall management is responsible for the actual selling, collecting of sales tax, and providing the vendor with a detailed sales report.

Important Documentation of Your Business

To work in any marketplace, you need proof that you have a legitimate, credible small business. Before doing business with you, most suppliers, craft malls, retailers, trade associations, and other professional organizations require you to show at least three to four of the following. You may not need everything listed here.

- State, city, or country licenses, if applicable: A state sales tax license must be displayed where sales are accepted or where money changes hands for goods. Most trade shows require a copy of your business licenses for admittance.

- Résumé: Include name; contact address; contact numbers like phone, fax, e-mail; photo of self and photo of work; shows and other markets participated in; company mission statement. This is your advertisement, your foot in the door; it introduces you to potential buyers.

- Portfolio: Picture book of your work, accomplishments, awards, and items for sale. Photos don't need to be professionally done; they just need to be clear. Include pictures that show different angles of the craft. Include measurements if photos don't show proportions.

- Business cards: Make your card unique to your company. Your card must have the business name, your name, a contact address, and a phone number. If you have an e-mail address or Web site, always list this information on all business materials.

- Letterhead: Should match the business card. A must for all business and professional correspondence.

- Business checking account: There is *no* business without one. I highly recommend that you have a business savings account. Consult your accountant, lawyer, bank, or savings institution on all small-business matters. Never mix personal and business money. Never borrow out of the business for a personal reason unless it's truly an emergency.

Imagine, starting a new industry just to help some friends sell crafts. This is what Rufus Coomer, a retired IBM executive, did in 1988 when he founded Coomer's Craft Mall, the first organization to open a large-scale craft mall. The original Coomer's Craft Mall was a

2,500-square-foot retail store with an opening day gross of $4,500 in the town of Azle, Texas. Within 10 years Coomer's has grown to more than 40,000 square feet of retail space in nine states. An estimated 1.5 million buying customers have visited the thirty retail stores since 1988, generating more than $20,000,000 in sales for more than 25,000 professional artisans and crafters displaying their work.

Coomer's Craft Malls quickly became the leader in providing new customers for the professional crafter and artisan. According to a Coomer's representative,

> Our tenth anniversary was as much a comment on the growing acceptance and success of craft malls as a retail concept as it was about the success our company has enjoyed as the originator of this segment of the industry. We continue to promote the benefits of craft malls to craftspeople. We have an understanding of the historical perspective of the industry with an exciting look at the future of this industry.

Part of that future involves using new technology, such as bar coding and Internet dealer sales (programs that the crafter/artists sells on the Coomer web site to give professional crafters easier ways to manage retail sites and to operate business). "Our purpose in introducing state-of-the-art technology into what is generally considered to be a low-tech, hands-on artistic industry is to help artisans and crafters minimize the time they spend on retail operations, such as inventory and sales, giving them more time to concentrate on what they know and love best—creating their crafts," continued the Coomer's representative. "Coomer's was built one crafter at a time. Many of our initial crafters are still with us in their original locations, while others have expanded into more markets as we opened new stores."

Coomer's has shared its success every step of the way with its professional crafters. Rufus Coomer has shown all of us that helping promote our friends and American handicrafts is a winning and profitable idea. Rufus Coomer will be the first to tell you that the reason Coomer's has thrived and grown is because the people who "run our stores and the crafters who fill our shelves are the finest and most dedicated people" in the world.

Although there is no official directory of craft malls in the United States, many do advertise in show guides and supply source magazines. You can also check your local yellow pages under Arts and Crafts to find a craft mall near you. The Professional Crafter Web Site (www.procrafter.com) is another good resource for finding craft malls.

Exhibiting in a craft mall is a legal agreement. Before you sign the dotted line, research the mall where you want to set up shop. I found the following list of questions and considerations at The Professional Crafter Web Site. It's a great list of questions for any type of market in which you aren't selling directly to your customer. The list is provided courtesy of Phillip Coomer, the owner of The American Craft Malls.

Considerations for Selecting a Craft Mall

Appearance

Does the store look clean?
Are booths straightened?
Are booths well stocked?
Is the front counter cluttered?
Does the store have visual appeal?

Sales Staff

Does the staff seem helpful?
Did the staff greet you as you entered the store?
Does the staff talk to customers?
Are staff members smiling?

Does the staff seem positive and easy to talk to?

Can you talk to the manager easily? The owner?

Customer Service

Does the staff know the answers to your questions?

How does the staff handle customer/crafter problems?

If the staff does not know the answer, will someone find out
  for you?

Jury for Quality

Does the store allow anything in?

Will it allow imports?

Will it allow factory-made or mass-produced items?

Spaces

Does the store have a complete floor plan, with sizes and
  space names marked?

Is there more than one size of booth?

Can you change booths, upsize or downsize without penalty?

Do traffic patterns take customers to your booth?

Signage

Can the store and sign be seen easily from the main road?

Can you tell it's a craft mall?

Is the sign lit at night?

Location

Is the location in a high-traffic area?

What is the demographic profile of the area around the store?

Are there plenty of cars in the parking lot?

Are there complementary businesses nearby, such as
  antiques malls or women's stores?

Hours

Are they open seven days a week?

Are they closed more than four or five days of the year?

Are they open during the standard retail hours of the rest of the shopping center?

Are they open when it will be convenient for you to stock your shelves?

Crafter Resources

Does the mall have a resource center?

Does it have wholesaler catalogs for your use?

Does the management keep you informed of trends?

Crafter Development

Will they help you with displays? Pricing? New ideas?

Legal

Does the store inform you of required legal requirements? Licenses?

Will management help protect your copyrights?

Does the store allow others to violate copyrights in the store?

Information

Does the mall produce an informative newsletter?

Are the newsletter articles interesting?

Will management tell you sales levels for the store?
How much income the store generates from sales compared to income generated by space rentals?

Does management keep you informed of store events?

Do they advise you of or show you specific advertising?

Do they constantly have promotional events going on?

Are the ads for your individual store?

Do the ads affect the area immediately around the store?
Do the ads look great? Good? Boring?

Sales

Does the store allow layaways on any item?
Will the store coordinate special orders or is the store
   hands-off?
Does the store protect you from check and credit card fraud?
Does the store accept major credit cards?
Can you check sales for all the stores within the chain?

Remote Service

Does the mall provide a remote service for out-of-state
   or out-of-city vendors?
Will the mall accept shipments of crafts?
Will your products be set up and displayed with care?
Is there an additional fee charged for the remote service?
How many remote vendors are in the mall?

Terms of the Contract

Read all contracts carefully several times because of the legal
   commitments. Ask questions.
Understand exactly what is expected of you as a vendor.
Understand what you expect from the mall management.
How long must you agree to display your goods according
   to the contract? Six months? A year?
Get an opinion from a lawyer on the contract.

Payment and Money

Does the mall pay frequently? Every two weeks?
   End of the month?
Is the time from closeout of the time period short between
   sales (bimonthly, 130 days) to the actual "check in the

mail" date, or do you have to wait 10, 15, or 30+ days for payment?

Can you pick up your check? Is direct deposit available?

Can you call any time to get a summary of your sales?

Costs

Does the store pay sales taxes or do you?

Does the store take a commission? If so, how much?

Is the rent above or below average?

Does a space at the front counter cost as much as one
in the back of the store?

When is rent due? Can you pay at the store?

Security

How does the store prevent shoplifting?

If there is an electronic system, what do tags cost?

Can the tags be concealed?

Does the staff check containers on the way out?

Sales and Merchandising

Does the manager or staff have a booth at the store?

Can you pick your crafter identification number,
or is one assigned to you? (You'll remember
the number easier if you choose it yourself.)

Do you have to buy the store's price tags?

Are you required to use bar codes?

Are you required to work at the store?

Are you allowed to decorate your booth?

The Business

Has the store been around for a long time?
Will it still be around tomorrow?

Who is the competition?

Does the store consistently pay on time?

Does the store have more than one location?

Can you get discounts?

What are the benefits of a remote program?

Does the store have sales on a regular basis?

Does the mall have crafter gatherings on a regular basis?

Is the mall a credible risk? What makes it one?

What are other crafters saying?

Have you checked for complaints against the company?

Does the mall compete in any way with crafters?

Craft Cooperative

The main difference between a co-op and a craft mall is that the individuals who make up the co-op own it. A craft mall is run and operated by an owner or a manager in conjunction with a paid sales staff. In a co-op, however, each vendor is expected to spend a certain amount of time working in the shop as a member of the sales staff. Another difference between a craft mall and a cooperative is that a co-op is normally juried. You submit finished samples of your work for review by a committee of co-op members. The work is judged quality of work and originality. In most cases a competitor of a current co-op member won't be allowed in the co-op. One of the great advantages of a co-op is that it limits the number of arts or crafts in different media.

You may also have a bigger voice in the management and policies in a co-op. Because you have control over the look of your display, change the theme and motifs frequently to keep regular customers interested. Low-ticket items (from $5 to $15) sell quickest and will more than likely cover rent and commission expenses. Make unique price tags and keep a good supply of business cards in your display.

If you have the option to work in the shop once or twice a month, take advantage of the opportunity. Working on site will keep you in contact with your buyer, show you how a business with a storefront operates, and allow you to add inventory to your display. The same set of questions asked when deciding on a craft mall can be applied for considering the craft cooperative (see page 174).

Consignment

Consignment sales are different from those at a craft mall or co-op. In simple terms, the craft professional allows a retailer to display the work, and when a sale is made, the craft professional is paid. In most cases the retailer adds a percentage to the price of an item to make the shop's profit. The retail consignment shop doesn't claim ownership of the crafts, but it should be responsible for damage or theft. At all times during a consignment agreement, the professional holds all ownership rights to the product. Yet in most cases the artisan or craftsperson has no control over the final selling price, how the work will be displayed, or how well the items will be explained or highlighted. This category of sales is one of the most controversial, with horror stories of shops closing over night and wonderful stories of very successful sales. Do your homework. Talk to other consignees within the shop.

There are good reasons to go into consignment sales. First, it's better to have your work on display somewhere rather than just sitting in inventory. Second, to sell through consignment requires no up-front investment as in other markets where rent, time, or other expenditures must be made in advance. Finally, in many cases a shop will buy outright if the crafts are selling well to the consumer. Make sure there's a contract that states what is expected of both par-

Handy Hint

Post a brief bio and photo of yourself within your display to give customers a chance to find out more about you, even when you are not there.

ties, even if you must write the contract yourself. Make frequent calls to the shop to ensure that you have enough inventory on the shelves to make this market worth the effort. Always tag the product with your company information so that future sales will come directly to you.

The Internet

The Web may be the greatest business tool the craft professional has in the current business market. Participating in a new craft mall can be a gamble if the management team isn't business savvy.

Our communities can get overrun with craft show after craft show that compete and saturate for the same gift dollar. Artisans and craftspeople are increasingly competing against imports, which are sold so cheaply the artist is tempted to buy the imports and sell them rather than put labor into original, handcrafted items. How do we stay current and compete with an ever-increasing consumer base? Check out a cyber craft show on the Web.

The first and largest craft show on the Web is CraftMark (www.craftmark.com), which was the idea of Phillip Coomer, owner of The American Craft Malls. In addition to CraftMark, which opened for business in January 1995, Phillip Coomer also provided a free information service for craft professionals (www.procrafter.com). Coomer said he "always knew the craft industry would play a big part in the World Wide Web. When I first started to create my Web sites, there were no craft industry Web sites at all." Within the first month of being online, the original dozen professionals had increased to hundreds of artisans showing their wares at the site. Today, with more than 250 handcrafted businesses on CraftMark,

> ### Did you know???
> Over 50% of craft malls close their doors before celebrating their first anniversary?

Tips for Selling on the Web

Phillip Coomer recommends several key tips for placing your work on the Web:

1. Be a part of a large site. It's tempting to want your own domain, but to key into buyers, you need to be part of a larger site, where your buyer can find you quicker and easier.

2. Be creative and change your site periodically. Add different products to sell.

3. Be ready for orders. Think out payment plans and shipping needs in advance.

4. Check out other vendors and sites. Be different. Stand out.

5. Ask about how the site advertises. Ask about the marketing plans for the site.

6. Do your research and study the contracts. Be aware of what you're being offered in services. Find out if each service is an additional charge or part of the monthly fee.

7. Because you're on the World Wide Web, your customer may not use American currency. Consider money exchanges and services fees.

8. Keywords are important for search engines. What keywords will help your customer find you? Search engines search words not graphics. Be descriptive of your product. Tell your buyers exactly what they are buying, including materials used and dimensions.

the site boasts more than 5,000 pages of handmade American crafts for buyers to choose from.

In numbers, CraftMark is twice the size of its largest competitor. It continues to lead the way for several reasons. Most important to its success is the marketing plan that Phillip implemented, which included heavy advertising to get the word out both to vendors and to craft/gift buyers. The second reason for CraftMark's success, in my opinion, is that Phillip Coomer provides easy-to-follow guidelines for getting on the Web, so that creative, but not high-tech, artisans and craftspeople can get on the Web in a hurry. CraftMark offers services like digital photography and Web page design as part of the vending contract. For only $10 per month, and no set-up fees, CraftMark can put a crafter on-line with full-color photos.

Fern LeFurjah of Bent Oak Farms in King George, Virginia, was the second craft professional to sign on with CraftMark. Here's what she had to say about the experience:

> I was actually afraid of putting things on the Internet at first. The first week my friends would call up using silly accents and say, "I saw your work on the World Wide Web." I thought my first order was just another prank by my friends! When the caller asked to place an order, I responded in a less than professional manner. Luckily the customer had a great sense of humor. I've had to cut back on the larger wholesale orders I was getting, but my pages on CraftMark have been wonderful for business. . . . It's important to give some information to each person who spends time on your pages or your site. . . . If you make soap, offer a list of qualities to look for when buying handmade soaps. Or have a calendar on your page that lists all the upcoming holidays. It's customer service, Internet style. Value added is just as important online as it is in a storefront. We have to know the craft consumer as well as the gift consumer. As a businessperson, the artisan and craftsperson is always trying to get a new customer.

Research the Internet, as you would any potential marketplace. Take time to find and view established Web sites as each has a unique way of presenting the work of art and craft professionals. Some sites have up to 1,000 visitors a day from all over the globe. To become part of a Web site showcase or gallery, you will have to make two investments: programming time to set up your page at the site, which is normally an hourly charge, and a rental fee per month to maintain the page. Shop around because pricing for both programming and Web site page rental varies greatly. It's also very helpful if you have an e-mail address for inquiries, which means you should (and must) become Internet savvy—a task that really isn't that difficult or time consuming. To participate with e-mail, your business must have a computer, a modem, and an online service. To sell on the Internet, you don't need to access it, but the more involved you are with your selling tools, the better informed you'll be. Many artists and craftspeople have been very successful online. Many use the Internet as a tool to expand customer base, build a mailing list, and increase yearly sales. Catalogs, new product information, and newsletters can all be sent very inexpensively via e-mail. It's also an excellent idea to participate in bulletin board services (areas where notes are posted, usually within an online service) and newsgroups (areas where notes are posted from all over the world about specific topics, such as soapmaking, holiday crafts, quilting, pottery, or doll making). Some commercial bulletin board services sell products directly through the board.

The most successful craft professionals keep an eye on the future, stay aware of new marketplaces and marketing tools, and take risks every once in a while. The Internet is the future. Whether to network with fellow professionals or to sell your wares, keep up to date with what's happening on the Web.

Wholesale Sales Representative

Many professional crafters sell their products only in the wholesale marketplace. Rather than selling their crafts at trade shows or gift marts, they choose to have a sales representative market and merchandise for them. A sales representative may be independent or part of a larger service; the sales representative's marketplace may be regional, national, or international.

To find a sales rep, ask your peers, look in trade magazine classifieds, ask a local gift shop or boutique for a referral, or consult one of the trade organizations in the hobby, gift, or toy industries. A sales rep usually works for a commission or a percentage of the total goods sold. Commissions vary, so shop around before hiring anyone. Read the contract carefully or prepare your own. Most craft professionals require a sales representative to prepay or pay COD the first order delivered. The sales rep won't receive the commission fee until the new account's payment clears. It's also a good idea to make shipping and handling costs a separate fee from cost of products. Make sure that a minimum per unit or minimum dollar total is well established. Some wholesale establishments do charge a separate fee if the total amount of an invoice falls below the minimum order requirements. This type of fee varies from $10 to $25.

It's important that you fully understand that in this type of market, you may be asked to produce hundreds to thousands of items in a short time. This market is really for the true production artist or craftsperson. The cost of supplies, labor, and overhead must be carefully calculated to keep expenses low and profit high. Additional expenses of employees, packaging, labeling, and shipping often must be added to the pricing formula. The trade-off is that there are no long show hours, no restocking at a gallery or mall, and no worries if an item does or does not sell well. The greatest benefit of this market is that the item you make has been sold in advance through the sales representative's order.

Selling for Publication

Before I jump into the who, how, and why of selling your designs to a publisher, let me be very clear about what is considered an original design. Every designer, professional crafter, and hobbyist must be very careful not to infringe on the copyrights of another individual or publisher. For years I've heard the rumor that if you change 10% or three parts of a design, you may claim it as your own. As is the case with most rumors, however, there's no foundation for this thinking. An original design is one you create on your own merits or skills. Motifs may be used by many. An example of a popular motif is a rose, a heart, or an angel. But you may not directly copy the style of another person or business.

Be familiar with copyright laws, both as a hobbyist and as a professional, because there may come a time when you want to copyright a design or group of designs. One of the reasons I'm so adamant about hobbyists and professionals knowing the law is that litigated disputes over copyrights and infringements are becoming commonplace. The only way to protect your interests and have a hope of winning is to be well documented and prepared. Details about copyrights can be found in Brabec's chapter 11.

> **Handy Hint**
>
> Take clear photographs of each new design you create and store these in your journal.

There are several ways to document and keep records of your design work. It's easy to forget just how much you've created over time. It's important to keep a journal of your work and make notes about supplies used, successful ingredients, and so on.

These notes and photographs may help jog your memory when you decide to publish a recipe or soapmaking instructions years later.

As a professional crafter, I usually sell a finished item to the public for at least one to three years before I attempt to sell the work and written instructions to a publisher. As a soapmaker you won't need so much lead time from selling to the public to selling the recipe to a publisher because you are selling the rights of the written instructions for your soap recipe. You may continue to sell the soap without worrying about infringing on the copyrights of the publisher. You might also create a soap that you decide not to sell to the public because it costs too much or takes too much effort to make. But this soap might be perfect for publication.

These notes can also be used to send to an editor for consideration. Before deciding to publish your designs, take an honest look at your ability to communicate. Designing for publication takes practice, discipline, and patience. Writing may not be your forte or a skill that you wish to develop. A healthy dose of self-esteem comes in handy, as even the best designers receive rejection letters. But, if you'd like to see your name in print and get paid for the effort, follow these basic steps:

1. Find a publisher who matches your style or work. The easiest way is to select your favorite craft magazine. If your design is quick or easy to do, submit your work to something like *Quick and Easy Crafts Magazine.* Be sure to match your craft to the subject of the magazine. For example, a soap recipe and design would be of no interest to a quilting magazine, just as a proposal for a book of soap recipes would be useless to a publisher of business textbooks. It seems a no-brainer, but you'd be surprised at how often people don't take the time to research where they are submitting designs. Take a look at all the art, craft, and home decor magazines. Or check out a periodical guide, which lists magazines by category.

2. Write a brief letter to the editor, asking for the magazine's writer's guidelines. Even if you are submitting to two magazines published by the same company, be sure to get writer's guidelines for each publication. The name of the editor and the magazine's address are usually listed near the front of the magazine. Also, ask for a copy of the magazine's editorial calendar, which shows what the magazine will be looking for in future issues and includes deadline information.

3. Send a query letter to the editor, describing your design, and include a sketch or clear photograph of your work.

4. Allow time for the editor to review your submission. After four to six weeks, if you haven't heard from the editor, follow up with a phone call or letter.

5. If your design is accepted, find out about your deadlines. If you haven't written instructions, do so immediately. Ship a sample and the instructions to the editor.

6. You will be signing a contract, so be sure to read it carefully and understand it thoroughly. If you don't understand details of the contract, ask questions. Most contracts ask for all rights, but you can always negotiate this with the publisher. Don't be intimidated by the legal language.

7. If your design is rejected, don't take it personally. It may not fit the magazine's current needs, so try a different magazine.

Teaching and Demonstrating

Teaching and demonstrating your soapmaking skills to others is yet another marketplace. You can volunteer, form a class, or have demonstration. Teaching can be very rewarding to the soapmaker. It's a great opportunity to interact with others and to help them enjoy a skill in which you have expertise. Teaching requires a class plan. You will have to create a project; write an outline, including the soap recipe; prepare a list of class materials that each student must bring; and coordinate how the class lesson will flow. Ask yourself how much time you will need to teach your class, and determine whether the students will leave with a finished soap. If you decide to have students make the soap as part of the class, be sure to choose a recipe that can be taught and made within the time and space allotted. Also, check the room where the class or demonstration will be given to be sure there is enough ventilation.

Preparation is the key to teaching success. Check out the location of the class. Is there enough space to move about safely while teaching? Does the room have everything you need, such as run-

Great Places to Teach or Demonstrate

Adult education programs	Family gatherings/reunions
Art supply stores	Hardware/do-it-yourself shops
Bookstores	High schools
Children's after-school care	Home shows or home parties
Churches	Libraries
City parks	Local chapters of associations
City recreational centers	Middle schools
Civic club lunches or meetings	Museums
Community colleges	Nursing homes
Community festivals	Scouting groups
Craft retail stores	Senior centers
Craft shows	Trade schools
Cultural associations	Trade shows
Day care	Universities
Elementary schools	Zoos

ning water and good lighting? How many students can fit in the room without crowding? What do you have to bring to the classroom in terms of equipment (pots, pans, a heating element, table protection)? What will the storeowner or organizer provide? Some problems can be solved easily, while others might have to be worked around by making adjustments to your lesson plan.

Learn as much as you can about the students. What is the age group and gender? Are students beginners, with no knowledge of soapmaking at all? Although to a certain degree you can set the standard for the students you want to teach, be prepared for anything!

The final consideration for you is the cost of the class. Determining the price of your class or demonstration is like pricing your soap. Research the going rate of other teacher's fees and determine what the regional economy can afford. You can set a flat fee or you can charge by the hour. Whichever you choose, consider the cost of preparing samples, of goods used during the class, and of any transportation costs to and from the class. Carefully write down all your expenses. Make sure that your bottom line is in the black, not in the red.

The more experience you get as a teacher, the higher your class fee can be. When I started teaching, my class fee was about $10 per hour of teaching. I often supplied my own materials for students to use in class. I still supply materials for my classes, but my average class fee is now $20 per hour of class. At trade shows I often earn up to $200 for an hour class because the planning and preparation time are much more intense than for a local class.

Demonstrating your skills does not require the same amount of preparation as teaching it does because you'll only be showing others how to make soap. Although the entire audience will never actually make the soap you demonstrate, it is still a good idea to provide handouts or flyers with a list supplies and instructions for making the soap.

Most demonstrations are set up at a table where you can stand or sit while demonstrating. If your demonstration lasts several hours be sure to take breaks. As a demonstrator, you may be paid an hourly rate or a flat day rate or whatever you set up with the organizer of the demonstration. The fee usually does not include setup or breakdown time, but you may arrange to have reimbursement for travel expenses. The industry average is about $60 for a four- to five-hour day.

Whether you approach a store or organization as a teacher or demonstrator, it's important to provide them with a résumé and portfolio. A portfolio is a visual display of your work that can be as simple as a three-ring binder or as elaborate as a professional portfolio case (which you can find at office supply or art stores). The portfolio can include extensive illustrations, basic drawings, published work, awards, personal and work references, and photos. The objective of the résumé and portfolio is to show the potential client that you are professional, motivated, prepared, and ready to take on any assignment given to you. Be creative, but be honest.

Displaying Your Work

I recommended visiting several trade or retail shows before preparing for your first craft display. Look at the different products, displays, props, and pricing. Note what catches your eye or brings you into a booth. Record your reaction to prices and sales staff. Then determine what you want your display to accomplish. Displays can include anything from simple to elaborate shelving, decorated tables, informational signs, and useful props.

Use the time you have with customers wisely by putting together an eye-catching display of your work. The average retail customer spends less than 30 minutes shopping in a retail gift shop, like a craft mall or craft co-op. So, you still have only about six seconds to grab the attention of that buyer. But this time you aren't even there to help promote your craft. Therefore you must have a display that works as a top-notch sales force.

An eye-catching display has several components. Your display should have a general or specific theme that pulls together your work. The theme can be based on your craft. As a soapmaker you might want to build a theme around being clean, having soft skin, or the fun of taking a bath. This small touch brings continuity to your

> **Did you know???**
>
> Some professional demonstrators earn up to $25 to $50 per hour for their expertise.

visual presentation. Many artisans use seasonal or holiday themes to create a buying mood—colored lights, garlands of evergreen or fall leaves, or bright spring flowers. This can work well for selling soap. Soap is a great gift for Mother's Day, birthdays, Christmas stocking stuffers, and Easter basket goodies. Better yet, soap can be included in a gift basket for a new mother or bride. Give your customers ideas by displaying soap in these clever packages.

Props can be more than just decoration. They can also be demonstrations of your craft. Consider including some pretty or unique soap holders or bath sponges in your soap display. Don't just lay items flat on a table. Instead give the display texture and detail by adding things like gift-wrapped boxes, bricks, peach crates, terra-cotta pots, or plastic or ceramic risers. Placing soaps on these types of props brings the product to the buyer's eye level. Other clever props include an old-fashioned basin tub or some washcloths folded neatly to the side of the soap, as would be done in a bathroom. Place your soaps in baskets or small wood crates. Fill a large ceramic washing bowl with water so customers can try your soaps. Leave some soap unwrapped so customers can see, feel, and smell the soaps. Using your imagination invites customers in to browse and discover your craft.

Use color to carry a theme. Color catches the eye. With the right selections, the color will accent and complement your work. Choose a color that enhances and brings attention to, rather than detracts from or overwhelms, your pieces. Experiment with color choices. Use contrasting colors so that your work pops from the display rather than fading into it. Colors can set a tone. Bright, bold colors are festive. Pastel, soft colors are comforting. Country colors with gray undertones are rustic and relaxing. Black and white is

Did you know???

The average retail customer spends an average of one hour at a craft show. If the show you participate in has 100 exhibitors, you have approximately six seconds of that potential buyer's time.

stark but builds confidence. Red or yellow means caution, slow down, and yield. Color is also very important in the packaging you use, especially when this packaging is placed against the backdrop of your display. Don't get lazy or careless when selecting your colors.

Signs within displays are important for explaining certain soaps. Never assume that your potential customer knows what your product is and how to use it. You may know that soap with coconut oil softens the skin, but your customer might be clueless. You may know that wheat germ, ground almonds, or lavender buds help gently exfoliate the skin, but the customer might not. Tell your customer that your ingredients are natural, with no harsh colorants or perfumes. Easy-to-read, concise printed signs teach the uneducated buyer about your product. Use small signs to remind your buyer of upcoming special days, such as Mother's Day or Secretary's Day. These little reminders can add more sales to your day. When making signs, follow retail guidelines: never to use more than three to four words per line and use no morge than three lines of words.

Another element of your display is lighting. Make sure the details and workmanship of your products can be clearly seen by a buyer. Avoid shadows within the exhibit. For an indoor show you may have to invest in some spotlights for times when you are placed in dark corners. Outdoors, lighting is rarely a problem except if a canopy top distorts the true coloring of your work. Most artists find that off-white or beige canopy tops cause the least amount of distortion of light, allowing natural sunlight to enhance the color of their items.

Last but not least, give the buyer plenty of room to move within and around your display.

Most booth spaces are approximately 10-by-10 feet, so use every available nook and cranny in your display efficiently. Also remember that you will have to transport, set up, and break down your display many, many times. Try to make your display items only a quarter of your available transportation space in a vehicle or when shipping.

Conclusion

There are so many different markets for the craft professional's work that an entire book could be written on any one of them. In this chapter I've highlighted a few of the most popular and easy-to-access markets. Other markets include selling directly to a retailer; selling wholesale to a catalog sales outlet; organizing a craft fair; selling on television shopping channels or through direct mail; showing at galleries; or opening a storefront.

Part of growing a business is to keep searching for new, exciting markets to promote and sell your unique crafts. Sometimes this growth means taking a risk into an unknown market place, but most markets can be researched with the help of the Small Business Administration or other business-consulting organization.

Have a firm idea of how you expect to be paid for your items. In most cases at any type of craft show, you'll be dealing with cash, check, or charge. If you decide to accept credit cards, you must contact a local bank or a financial institution that works with small businesses or non-storefronts. Research carefully and compare start-up investments and charges. More information about credit card sales can be found in chapter 11. Talk with other professionals in your area who accept credit cards to get some one-on-one feedback about credit card sales. Ask your local bank for advice on accepting personal checks from customers. Most banks have a checklist of what information you must record in case the check bounces.

▼▼▼▼▼▼▼▼▼▼▼▼▼▼▼▼▼

Handy Hint

Keep traffic flow in mind when designing your booth. Use a U- or an L-shape layout of tables, which are both favored by most professional crafters.

▲▲▲▲▲▲▲▲▲▲▲▲▲▲▲▲▲

If you sell wholesale, you may find that this clientele prefers to be allowed 10, 15, or 30 days net, meaning they want credit extended for 10, 15, or 30 days, after which they'll send in payment with an invoice. Consider how allowing your customers this service will affect your own cash flow. Believe it or not, sometimes saying no to new business is the best thing possible for your business. A general rule of thumb is to ask for payment in full for the first wholesale order from a customer and then allow for invoicing that provides 10 to 30 days for payment.

I hope you feel the same excitement that I do when thinking about the different markets that sell handmade goods. Markets change and grow, but there's always a market for quality handmade items. You may decide to sell your soap only in a craft mall or you may choose to use a combination of craft shows, direct-mail catalogs, and a Web site to reach your customers. There's no right or wrong market for the professional. Your goals should complement your market selection. As your business grows, your interests and goals may change too. The marketplace is flexible enough to bend and turn with your business needs.

Marketing Your Soap

▼▼

I'LL NEVER FORGET MY FIRST DAY at the College of Journalism at the University of Florida. I had dreams of getting a degree in journalism, but I didn't meet the college's typing standard of 24 words per minute without typos. So I had to switch my major to advertising. I wasn't thrilled, as I'd had high hopes of winning a Pulitzer Prize. But such is life. In the school of advertising, they didn't care how fast you typed, and there were rumors that the advertising professors never took points off your test for misspelled words. So it sounded like the perfect major for me.

On that first day, I was sitting in a class of 500 students who were also enrolled in Intro to Advertising 101. The professor was well into his lecture about advertising when I noticed that most of the other students in the class were yawning and trying to stay awake. It seemed ironic that the head of the advertising department couldn't keep our attention. However, I gathered three important facts about advertising that day: (1) Advertising is part of a company's overall marketing plan. (2) Public relations is part of the advertising plan of any company or business. (3) All you need to start an advertising agency (or any other business, for that matter) is a business card.

Public Relations

It's free advertising! Advertising your craft business may be hard on your budget, but there are some simple, free ways to publicize your work and business.

- Visit a scout group and teach a craft. Plenty of the parents involved are potential customers.

- Offer to set up a display of your work at a school's teachers' lounge. Teachers have little time to shop craft shows and malls. Bring your crafts to them. Small items are best for this group.

- Get involved with a fundraiser.

- When exciting events happen within your business (for example, getting a new wholesale account, donating to a fundraiser, winning a ribbon at a show, adding a new craft mall), write a press release for the newspaper.

- A press release is simple. Type your name, company name, address, and phone number across the top of a sheet of paper. Just below this, type "FOR IMMEDIATE

Without advertising, businesses would have to rely solely on word of mouth to spread the news that a product or service exists or hope that a customer would stumble on the product or service. At the time I wasn't too sure that advertising was the right major for me. But today I know, without a shadow of a doubt, that everything I learned to earn that BS in advertising (that's bachelor of science) helped me promote and expand my business from selling work at a local craft show to getting my first book into the bookstores. Advertising in any form is important to your company. Many professionals take the attitude that products will sell themselves, but that's a very wrong assumption. All successful companies have an advertising plan to inform and educate the consumer about the products the company sells. Inventory can sit unsold if the public doesn't know where to purchase the goods. Advertising can be a

RELEASE." Then write the information for the press. Send the press release to the community, local, or business section editor, unless the newspaper indicates otherwise.

- Have plenty of inexpensive black-and-white or color photographs of yourself and your work to send with press releases.

- Contact a local television station and volunteer to go on air to talk about crafting, demo a simple craft, or show samples of your work.

- Join any local guild, crafting group, or art association. Network and be an active member to learn of upcoming opportunities. Join national guilds, societies, and associations. Keep on top of trends, events, and activities.

- If you're involved in a charitable activity involving crafting or if you make a very unique item, contact a craft magazine. Many consumer craft magazines have regular columns featuring crafters. Many also spotlight individual artists. Write your story and send it in. Many cover pieces are from individual artists and craftspeople. Also include a clear photo or slide of your work.

creative extension of your company, so have fun with it. Do your homework and check out all the opportunities available before making commitments or spending your advertising budget. The many excellent books that have been written about advertising, marketing, merchandising, and public relations can give you even more detail. (See Resources for a list of recommended books.) Don't ignore your responsibility to get the word out about your soaps.

Business Cards

The most basic tool for your company's promotion and advertising is a business card. This calling card has three essential elements. The first is a company name. Some soapmakers choose to use their own names as their company name, but I strongly recommend using a true company name that symbolizes your business. The company name should be easy to remember and easy to spell and should communicate your expertise to the customer. Your company name will be used on all company information, including brochures, package labeling, letterhead, a Web site, and invoices.

When I started to sell my work to the public, I used By Maria as my company name. Within two years, however, I felt that this company name didn't reflect my work and that my customers didn't remember it. Around that time I was getting a new dining room set from the Virginia House furniture manufacturing company. I liked that company name because it sounded strong and solid. Although you might not guess it was a furniture manufacturer by the name, it was a name you could trust—easy to remember, easy to spell, and

Creating Your Business Cards

A business card should include:

> Company name
>
> Contact person within the company
>
> Phone number
>
> Mailing address
>
> Company logo or appropriate clip art

And, if applicable:

> Fax number
>
> E-mail address
>
> Web site address

memorable. Thus Nerius House was born. But I didn't want to limit my possibilities (always think of the big picture), so I added to my company name *& Companies*. Once I decided on Nerius House & Co. as my company name, consumer recognition doubled.

You can't simply add *incorporated, limited, unlimited,* or other legal terms to your company name unless you take the legal steps to use such terms. (See chapter 11 for a full discussion of the rules and regulations for selecting a business name.) A fictitious name (the company name) is not a trademarked name, nor does it give you sole rights to use the name. Your state may require you to file a fictitious name so the community will know that you "do business as" or you are "also know as" the business name you have selected.

The second element of a business card is your company's contact information. Contact information includes the name of the contact person (which, in most cases, is you) and a company address for correspondence. You may use your home address or rent a post office box. If it's convenient to rent a post office box in your community, I strongly advise you to consider the additional expense. Otherwise, you may risk innocent misunderstandings with customers who assume you own a retail storefront. I've had people stop by while in the neighborhood to visit my "store." A visit out of the blue like that can inconvenience your workdays or evenings. Contact information should also include a phone number. Since you're a business, it's best if you don't allow children to answer the phone during set business hours (for example, 8:00 A.M. to 5:00 P.M.). Although your customers might find it charming to hear your child's voice yelling for you, a supplier or other business associate might not be so thrilled. Use an answering machine during the day if you don't want phone interruptions as you work. At all times, you must be professional and businesslike in your work.

We all must show our very polished business side to the rest of the world. The caller need not know you're in your pajamas or in a splatter apron, but your attitude of professionalism will shine if you're prepared. Other important contact information to include on a business card, if applicable, are an e-mail address, a Web site address, business hours, job title, and selling slogan or trademark.

The final ingredient to a business card is a logo. Many professionals use clip art that is copyright-free. If you have artistic abilities, create your own logo. For my logo, I turned to a graphic artist recommended by my printing company. Just as with your company name, your logo should convey a strong image of what your company is about. My original logo was a clip art doll. I'm a doll maker and felt that the clip art would help people remember what I do. Once I started making enough money to budget for a graphic artist, I hired one to create an illustration of my own doll, which was unique, with wild jute hair and a simple, sweet face. I was thrilled with the image and used it immediately on all my business papers, from business cards to letterhead to invoices. My callbacks from customers increased 200% that year. The most amazing thing to me is that, even to this day, I have customers who pull out my well-worn business cards from their wallets and say, "Remember when I first bought from you?"

The key elements of your business card can be transferred to all parts of your company. Use the information on all your correspondence and communications. Use the logo on all printed materials. Include your e-mail and Web site address on every piece of promotional information. Be consistent: Repetition is what makes people remember information. Reinforce your name, company name, and contact information whenever possible. Tag all your designs and products with this basic contact information. Insert a business flyer in all designs you bag, ship, or package. Take every opportunity to promote and advertise your talents, skills, products, and designs.

Other Promotional Tools

We've all heard the saying, "There's no such thing as a free lunch." But some free promotion is available to you. The first area to explore is the press release. This is a simple document that tells the world about your business, your talents, or any other newsworthy event that happens to your company. You submit a press release to any media in your area or community. Take a good look at your local newspaper. Is there a section dedicated to business? Are there regular weekly feature articles on businesses or activities in your neighborhood? If you can't find such sections, then call the newspaper and ask.

Call local radio and televisions stations as well and ask the same question. You might be surprised at how eager your local media are to spotlight hometown talent. A press release is good, free advertising for your company. It's a part of your advertising plan that will never make a hole in your advertising budget. You never know who might be reading the newspaper or watching television.

Include in the press release all contact information so that the person receiving it can call for confirmation or to ask questions. Use simple language and be brief. A concise, interesting press release will be read and used over more complicated, novel-length releases. Don't be afraid to follow up a press release with a phone call to the media contact. Allow one to two weeks for the press release to be received and read.

Another cost-free tool is word-of-mouth advertising. Your customers can be your biggest billboard and bring in new customers to buy your goods. Word of mouth is mostly based on how good your customer service is and how happy your customers are with your products. Treat your customers with respect and a smile, and they'll tell others about your company. Use customer incentives. Consider

Sample Press Release

Here's an example of a press release. Note the following key points of information: Heading (immediate release or stated date for release of information), contact information, body of release, and end of release (with ##END##, the standard symbol that ends the text).

For Immediate Release
November 2, 1999
Contact:
Maria Nerius
Nerius House & Co.
407-951-3929
Fax: 407-725-0792
E-mail: NeriusM@aol.com
Web: www.procrafter.com

Nerius House celebrates its fifteenth anniversary by adding handmade soap to its product line. Established in 1984, Nerius House manufactures quality handmade goods for the consumer, ranging from folk dolls to holiday decor for any season.

"Consumer demand for handmade soap has been strong, and Nerius House owes its success to its customers," said Nerius. "We pay attention to consumer comments and look for any opportunity to meet our customers' needs."

Maria Nerius is available for interviews and demonstrations. The new soap line, called Sweet Bubbles, is available at The American Craft Malls or can be ordered at the company's Web site: www.craftmark.com.

##END##

giving a 5 to 10% discount on a purchase for every new customer that a loyal customer brings to your businesses. Or offer a discount for every $100 purchase. Or, as a token of customer appreciation, give a free soap ball packaged with netting or lace after six or ten purchases. These are small but effective incentives that spread goodwill between you and your customer base.

Keep a mailing list of all your customers. Use a guest book or a sign-up sheet for a mailing list wherever you sell your work. Mail a postcard to alert customers of upcoming events, such as an open house, a show, or when you add new designs to your line. Offer a small discount or special bar of soap if the customer brings the postcard back to you. I keep a list of all customers who spend more than $100 on a purchase, and I mail a note shortly after the purchase, thanking them for their business. This small task has paid for itself many times over by keeping my loyal customers happy and coming back for more.

You might consider placing a small ad in a local newspaper to advertise a show you'll be participating in or to advertise your business.

Many magazines have the same target market of readers as you have for your soap products. Consider running a classified ad in such national magazines and see what kind of response you get from the ad. If you're well received, consider placing a larger ad in the magazine. This will help you spend your advertising money effectively. Many shows and events have flyers or programs that are handed out to the attendees. This is a great place to advertise. Always have several business cards when you go out. There's always an opportunity to tell someone new about your work and your business. Handing out a business card reinforces your message.

If mail order is your marketplace, design brochures or flyers that you can send to interested consumers. Many professionals learn to make advertising pay for itself. When offering a catalog of your products, request a small token price for the catalog ($1 to $5) that will be refunded on the customer's first order. Another great advertising gimmick is to demonstrate your craft at a local health food store, art/craft retailer, or community center. You don't have to give away your recipes or product, just demonstrate what you do; people love to watch demonstrations. Or you can make small samples and give them to interested customers. Hand out your flyer or company catalog at the event and offer your soaps for sale while demonstrating. This type of promotion can also lead to teaching classes. Most likely, however, the individuals watching you demonstrate will want to buy soap directly from you rather than make it at home.

Self-Promotion

Self-promotion has already been discussed in chapter 7, but it bears repeating. None of us wants to become a bigheaded, egotistical person, but to survive in a very competitive world, we must let others know what we're doing.

No matter what you call it—a bio sheet, publicity release, self-promotion brochure, or bragging papers—everyone in the field of creative businesses needs to write a 100 to 300 word document describing who they are and what they do. This prose should be attached to press releases, new retail or wholesale customer contacts, supplier credit forms, and any other situation where you need to let the other person know what your company is about. This very important tool can help open doors to you and get others to notice your efforts. The bio sheet is a form of introduction. A real bonus is to include a photo of yourself with your designs. Ask your local printer about how to incorporate a photo into a one-page bio sheet. This cost is well worth the price of having customers recognize not only your company but also you and your design line.

It's not easy to sit down and come up with a few hundred words that describe you and your business. But you're doing something that is not only for others to read. Writing your bio sheet is an effective way to promote yourself to others as well as to yourself. The bio sheet can help you focus and concentrate on your goals. It may seem morbid, but I think of my bio sheet as my own eulogy, one that I get to write. If you find yourself struggling to find the right words, write your bio sheet in the third person (as if you were writing about someone you admire). Add interest to the bio sheet by adding the flair, creativity, and imagination of your own personality.

Sample Bio Sheet

A great way to write a bio sheet is to open with a mission statement. In one or two sentences, write your goals or hopes for the business. This concise, concentrated sentence(s) will lead the way for the other tidbits and facts needed in a bio sheet. Can you guess what companies might have the following mission statements? (I made up four of these examples, but the message gets across. One mission statement is real and is used by Nerius House & Co.)

1. **To clean up the world while cleaning up on sales.**
2. **Let's whip the competition and float our boat!**
3. **To promote and preserve the pioneer traditions of soapmaking while teaching a new generation the qualities of handmade soap.**
4. **Crafting can express the care and love of our community. And the world is our community. Let us be the first to make a difference.**
5. **Good clean fun with all natural ingredients: We strive for perfect bars.**

A. Nerius House & Co.

B. Molly's Cleanup Soap Factory

C. Ivory Soap

D. Bo's Old-Fashioned Soap Company

E. Bubbles and More, Inc.

1-B
2-C
3-D
4-A
5-E

Use these examples of bio sheets to help create your own. Remember to bring your own personality to the written word. Don't be afraid and think you're not a good writer. The most important part of bio sheets is informing your customer about you and your company. Always proofread or have a family member or friend proofread the finished bio sheet for you before you have it printed.

Nerius House & Co.

Maria Nerius established Nerius House & Co in 1985 in the city of Palm Bay in central Florida. Her unique folk wood dolls have been treasured by customers and have decorated homes for many a holiday ever since. As the company grew, Maria branched out into design publication and has more than 500 designs in published magazines from *Good Housekeeping* to *Craftworks*. Currently she has four national consumer and trade magazine columns, which reach more than one million readers.

In 1996 Maria was honored as Designer of the Year by the craft industry and was given her own regular weekly television segment on Aleene's Creative Living. "Many opportunities have come my way, and I enjoy the variety of work available to me. Creating holiday folk dolls is still my first love, however, and that love is so strong, I don't think I'll ever retire."

The Soap Opera

If rebels stick with something long enough, even they become part of the establishment. Soap Opera proprietors Chuck Bauer and Chuck Beckwith began selling soaps and toiletries out of an old wooden dresser strapped onto roller skates and covered with a chintz canopy. The drawers made handy storage cubbies, but the noise they made clanking down the streets was enough to wake the dead. Still, it was a way for the two art student graduates to keep their independence and, better yet, to avoid cutting their hair and interviewing for "establishment" jobs.

Today the duo is considered one of State Street's anchor tenants and fiercest supporters. Recently they celebrated the twenty-fifth anniversary of their company, The Soap Opera. Bauer's self-described upbringing as an army brat in Europe, where small *parfumeurs* are commonplace, and Beckwith's simple desire to find a decent hairbrush for his long, wavy hair led to one of the most successful business ventures in the state of Wisconsin.

"When we started, there wasn't much if you wanted to buy personal products, and they weren't very interesting," Bauer said. "So many people wanted an alternative to mass-produced things, and we hand bottle and label to this day. We connected with freelance chemists and manufacturers right at the beginning because we started our own products. It's one of our strengths today. We're still the kind of store where the customers know our name and we know their names. If a couple comes in, we know what the wife likes and what shaving cream her husband shaves with. It's an old-fashioned thing. But it's very much needed. The more high tech we get, the more high touch we need to be."

You're on Your Own

This chapter concludes my writing for this book. Barbara Brabec, the author of chapter 11, will present to you the basics for small businesses. It's my greatest hope that this book will give you the foundation and confidence to continue to learn more about the process of soapmaking. I learned early in my own soapmaking adventures that a desire and passion to learn will get you the perfect color, the perfect scent, the perfect combination of ingredients. But don't let that perfection stand in the way of having fun while making soap. It's much easier to give in to the fact that you're hooked, a newborn aficionado of handmade soaps, than to fight it. Trust me, I know. I was spellbound with the first batch I attempted.

▼▼▼▼▼▼▼▼▼▼▼▼▼▼▼▼▼▼▼▼▼▼▼▼

Did you know???

More than 45 million Americans work full time from home businesses and home offices.

▲▲▲▲▲▲▲▲▲▲▲▲▲▲▲▲▲▲▲▲▲▲▲▲

Use all the resources available to you—this book, the Internet, libraries, retail or catalog staffs—and do your fair share of exchanging information too. I found while interviewing soapmakers that many felt they couldn't share information because they had only been making soap for six months or a year. Time is not a factor when it comes to exchanging thoughts, opinions, and experiences; it's how much effort you put into knowing the process of soapmaking. I'd never call myself an expert on soapmaking or any other topic, but that doesn't stop me from wanting to learn more from others and to let others know what I've learned. A very smart teacher once told me that the only dumb question was the one you were too afraid to ask for fear of looking foolish or silly. I believe that statement with all my heart. Ask questions. And don't forget to answer some along the way.

Any art or craft can bring together a diversity of people in a safe, fun, and creative environment. It's one of my favorite aspects of having a career in crafting. Crafting helped me get involved and active in my own community, where I had the pleasure of meeting the most interesting and caring people. Soapmaking is considered both an art and a craft. I like the fact that it is something that can't be placed in just one category. It's a practical art with a colorful craft application. My best wishes to you as you make and create your own soap. May all your bubbles be big and sparkle in laughter. And may all your little rubber duckies be happy!

A Mini-Course in Crafts-Business Basics

by Barbara Brabec

▼▼▼

THIS SECTION OF THE BOOK will familiarize you with important areas of legal and financial concern and enable you to ask the right questions if and when it is necessary to consult with an attorney, accountant, or other business adviser. Although the tax and legal information included here has been carefully researched by the author and is accurate to the best of her knowledge, it is not the business of either the author or publisher to render professional services in the area of business law, taxes, or accounting. Readers should therefore use their own good judgment in determining when the services of a lawyer or other professional would be appropriate to their needs.

Information presented applies specifically to businesses in the United States. However, because many U.S. and Canadian laws are similar, Canadian readers can certainly use the following information as a start-up business plan and guide to questions they need to ask their own local, provincial, or federal authorities.

Contents

7. **Insurance Tips**

Homeowner's or Renter's Insurance
Liability Insurance
Insurance on Crafts Merchandise
Auto Insurance

8. **Important Regulations Affecting Artists and Craftspeople**

Consumer Safety Laws
Labels Required by Law
The Bedding and Upholstered Furniture Law
FTC Rule for Mail-Order Sellers

9. **Protecting Your Intellectual Property**

Perspective on Patents
What a Trademark Protects
What Copyrights Protect
Copyright Registration Tips
Respecting the Copyrights of Others
Using Commercial Patterns and Designs

10. **To Keep Growing, Keep Learning**

Motivational Tips

A "Things to Do" Checklist with Related Resources

Business Start-Up Checklist
Government Agencies
Crafts and Home-Business Organizations
Recommended Craft Business Periodicals
Other Services and Suppliers
Recommended Business Books
Helpful Library Directories

1. Starting Right

In preceding chapters of this book, you learned the techniques of a particular art or craft and realized its potential for profit. You learned what kind of products are likely to sell, how to price them, and how and where you might sell them.

Now that you've seen how much fun a crafts business can be (and how profitable it might be if you were to get serious about selling what you make!) you need to learn about some of the "nitty-gritty stuff" that goes hand-in-hand with even the smallest business based at home. It's easy to start selling what you make and it's satisfying when you earn enough money to make your hobby self-supporting. Many crafters go this far and no further, which is fine. But even a hobby seller must be concerned about taxes and local, state, and federal laws. And if your goal is to build a part- or full-time business at home, you must pay even greater attention to the topics discussed in this section of the book.

Everyone loves to make money . . . but actually starting a business frightens some people because they don't understand what's involved. It's easy to come up with excuses for why we don't do certain things in life; close inspection of those excuses usually boils down to fear of the unknown. We get the shivers when we step out of our comfort zone and try something we've never done before. The simple solution to this problem lies in having the right information at the right time. As someone once said, "Knowledge is the antidote to fear."

The quickest and surest way to dispel fear is to inform yourself about the topics that frighten you. With knowledge comes a sense of power, and that power enables you to move. Whether your goal is merely to earn extra income from your crafts hobby or launch a genuine home-based business, reading the following information will help you get started on the right legal foot, avoid financial pitfalls, and move forward with confidence.

When you're ready to learn more about art or crafts marketing or the operation of a home-based crafts business, a visit to your library or bookstore will turn up many interesting titles. In addition to the special resources listed by this book's author, you will find my list of recommended business books, organizations, periodicals, and other helpful resources in section 10 of this chapter. This information is arranged in a checklist you can use as a plan to get your business up and running.

Before you read my "Mini-Course in Crafts-Business Basics," be assured that I understand where you're coming from because I was once there myself.

For a while I sold my craft work, and this experience led me to write my first book, *Creative Cash*. Now, twenty years later, this crafts-business classic ("my baby") has reached its 6th edition. Few of those who are totally involved in a crafts business today started out with a business in mind. Like me, most began as hobbyists looking for something interesting to do in their spare time, and one thing naturally led to another. I never imagined those many years

Social Security Taxes

When your craft business earnings are more than $400 (net), you must file a Self Employment Tax form (Schedule SE) and pay into your personal Social Security account. This could be quite beneficial for individuals who have some previous work experience but have been out of the workplace for a while. Your re-entry into the business world as a self-employed worker, and the additional contributions to your Social Security account, could result in increased benefits upon retirement.

Because so many senior citizens are starting home-based businesses these days, it should be noted that there is a limit on the amount you can earn before losing Social Security benefits. The good news is that this dollar limit increases every year, and once you are past the age of 70, you can earn any amount of income and still receive full benefits. For more information, contact your nearest Social Security office.

ago when I got serious about my crafts hobby that I was putting myself on the road to a full-time career as a crafts writer, publisher, author, and speaker. Since I and thousands of others have progressed from hobbyists to professionals, I won't be at all surprised if someday you, too, have a similar adventure.

2. Taxes and Record Keeping

"Ambition in America is still rewarded . . . with high taxes," the comics quip. Don't you long for the good old days when Uncle Sam lived within his income and without most of yours?

Seriously, taxes are one of the first things you must be concerned about as a new business owner, no matter how small your endeavor. This section offers a brief overview of your tax responsibilities as a sole proprietor.

Is Your Activity a "Hobby" or a "Business?"

Whether you are selling what you make only to get the cost of your supplies back, or actually trying to build a profitable business, you need to understand the legal difference between a profitable hobby and a business, and how each is related to your annual tax return.

The IRS defines a hobby as "an activity engaged in primarily for pleasure, not for profit." Making a profit from a hobby does not automatically place you "in business" in the eyes of the Internal Revenue Service, but the activity will be *presumed* to have been engaged in for profit if it results in a profit in at least three years out of five. Or, to put it another way, a "hobby business" automatically becomes a "real business" in the eyes of the IRS at the point where you can state that you are (1) trying to make a profit, (2) making regular business transactions, and (3) have made a profit three years out of five.

As you know, all income must be reported on your annual tax return. How it's reported, however, has everything to do with the amount of taxes you must pay on this income. If hobby income is under $400, it must be entered on the 1040 tax form, with taxes payable accordingly. If the amount is greater than this, you must file a Schedule C form with your 1040 tax form. This is to your advantage, however, since taxes are due only on your *net profit*. Since you can deduct expenses up to the amount of your hobby income, there may be little or no tax at all on your hobby income.

Self-Employment Taxes

Whereas a hobby cannot show a loss on a Schedule C form, a business can. Business owners must pay not only state and federal income taxes on their profits, but self-employment taxes as well. (See sidebar, "Social Security Taxes," page 243.) Because self-employed people pay Social Security taxes at twice the level of regular, salaried workers, you should strive to lower your annual gross profit figure on the Schedule C form through every legal means possible. One way to do this is through careful record keeping of all expenses related to the operation of your business. To quote IRS publications, expenses are deductible if they are "ordinary, necessary, and somehow connected with the operation and potential profit of your business." In addition to being able to deduct all expenses related to the making and selling of their products, business owners can also depreciate the cost of tools and equipment, deduct the overhead costs of operating a home-based office or studio (called the Home Office Deduction), and hire their spouse or children.

Given the complexity of our tax laws and the fact that they are changing all the time, a detailed discussion of all the tax deductions currently available to small business owners cannot be included in a book of this nature. Learning, however, is as easy as reading a book such as *Small Time Operator* by Bernard Kamoroff (my favorite tax and accounting guide), visiting the IRS Web site, or consulting your regular tax adviser.

You can also get answers to specific tax questions twenty-four hours a day by calling the National Association of Enrolled Agents (NAEA). Enrolled agents (EAs) are licensed by the Treasury Department to represent taxpayers before the IRS. Their rates for doing tax returns are often less than what you would pay for an accountant or CPA. (See my checklist for NAEA's toll-free number you can call to ask for a referral to an EA in your area.)

An important concept to remember is that even the smallest business is entitled to deduct expenses related to its business, and the same tax-saving strategies used by "the big guys" can be used by small business owners. Your business may be small now or still in the dreaming stage, but it could be larger next year and surprisingly profitable a few years from now. Therefore it is in your best interest always to prepare for growth, profit, and taxes by learning all you

Keeping Tax Records

Once you're in business, you must keep accurate records of all income and expenses, but the IRS does not require any special kind of bookkeeping system. Its primary concern is that you use a system that clearly and accurately shows true income and expenses. For the sole proprietor, a simple system consisting of a checkbook, a cash receipts journal, a cash disbursements ledger, and a petty cash fund is quite adequate. Post expenses and income regularly to avoid year-end pile-up and panic.

If you plan to keep manual records, check your local office supply store or catalogs for the *Dome* series of record-keeping books, or use the handy ledger sheets and worksheets included in *Small Time Operator.* (This classic tax and accounting guide by CPA Bernard Kamoroff includes details on how to keep good records and prepare financial reports.) If you have a computer, there are a number of accounting software programs available, such as Intuit Quicken, MYOB (Mind Your Own Business) Accounting, and Intuit Quick-

can about the tax laws and deductions applicable to your business. (See also sidebar, "Keeping Tax Records.")

Sales Tax Is Serious Business

If you live in a state that has a sales tax (all but five states do), and sell products directly to consumers, you are required by law to register with your state's Department of Revenue (Sales Tax division) for a resale tax number. The fee for this in most states ranges from $5 to $25, with some states requiring a bond or deposit of up to $150.

Depending on where you live, this tax number may also be called a Retailer's Occupation Tax Registration Number, resale license, or use tax permit. Also, depending on where you live, the place you must call to obtain this number will have different names. In California, for example, you would contact the State Board of Equalization; in Texas, it's called the State Comptroller's Office.

Books, the latter of which is one of the most popular and best bookkeeping systems for small businesses. The great advantage of computerized accounting is that financial statements can be created at the press of a key after accounting entries have been made.

Regardless which system you use, always get a receipt for everything and file receipts in a monthly envelope. If you don't want to establish a petty cash fund, spindle all of your cash receipts, tally them at month's end, and reimburse your personal outlay of cash with a check written on your business account. On your checkbook stub, document the individual purchases covered by this check.

At year's end, bundle your monthly tax receipt envelopes and file them for future reference, if needed. Since the IRS can audit a return for up to three years after a tax return has been filed, all accounting and tax records should be kept at least this long, but six years is better. Personally, I believe you should keep all your tax returns, journals, and ledgers throughout the life of your business.

Within your state's revenue department, the tax division may have a name such as Sales and Use Tax Division or Department of Taxation and Finance. Generally speaking, if you check your telephone book under "Government," and look for whatever listing comes closest to "Revenue," you can find the right office.

If your state has no sales tax, you will still need a reseller's permit or tax exemption certificate to buy supplies and materials at wholesale prices from manufacturers, wholesalers, or distributors. Note that this tax number is only for supplies and materials used to make your products, not for things purchased at the retail level or for general office supplies.

Once registered with the state, you will begin to collect and remit sales and use tax (monthly, quarterly, or annually, as determined by your state) on all *taxable sales*. This does not mean *all* of your gross income. Different states tax different things. Some states put a sales tax on certain services, but generally you will never have to pay sales tax on income from articles sold to magazines, on teaching or consulting fees, or subscription income (if you happen to publish a newsletter). In addition, sales taxes are not applicable to:

- items sold on consignment through a charitable organization, shop, or other retail outlet, including craft malls and rent-a-space shops (because the party who sells directly to the consumer is the one who must collect and pay sales tax.)

- products you wholesale to others who will be reselling them to consumers. (Be sure to get their tax-exemption ID number for your own files, however, in case you are ever questioned as to why you did not collect taxes on those sales.)

As you sell throughout the year, your record-keeping system must be set up so you can tell which income is taxable and which is tax-exempt for reporting on your sales tax return.

Collecting Sales Tax at Craft Shows

States are getting very aggressive about collecting sales tax, and agents are showing up everywhere these day, especially at the larger craft fairs, festivals, and small business conferences. As I was writing this chapter, a post on the Internet stated that in New Jersey the sales tax department is routinely contacting show promoters about a month before the show date to get the names and addresses of exhibitors. It is expected that other states will soon be following suit. For this reason, you should always take your resale or tax collection certificate with you to shows.

Although you must always collect sales tax at a show when you sell in a state that has a sales tax, how and when the tax is paid to the state can vary. When selling at shows in other states, you may find that the show promoter has obtained an umbrella sales tax certificate, in which case vendors would be asked to give management a check for sales tax at the end of the show for turning over to a tax agent. Or you may have to obtain a temporary sales tax certificate for a show, as advised by the show promoter. Some sellers who regularly do shows in two or three states say it's easier to get a tax ID number from each state and file an annual return instead of doing taxes on a show-by-show basis. (See sidebar, "Including Tax in the Retail Price," page 224.)

Collecting Sales Tax at a Holiday Boutique

If you're involved in a holiday boutique where several sellers are offering goods to the public, each individual seller will be responsible for collecting and remitting his or her own sales tax. (This means someone has to keep very good records during the sale so each seller receives a record of the sale and the amount of tax on that sale.) A reader who regularly has home boutiques told me that in her community she must also post a sign at her "cash station" stating that sales tax is being collected on all sales, just as craft fair sellers must do in some states. Again, it's important that you get complete details from your own state about its sales tax policies.

Collecting Tax on Internet Sales

Anything you sell that is taxable in your state is also taxable on the Internet. This is simply another method of selling, like craft fairs or mail-order sales. You don't have to break out Internet sales separately; simply include them in your total taxable sales.

3. The Legal Forms of Business

Every business must take one of four legal forms:

Sole Proprietorship
Partnership
LLC (Limited Liability Company)
Corporation

Including Tax in the Retail Price

Is it okay to incorporate the amount of sales tax into the retail price of items being sold directly to consumers? I don't know for sure because each state's sales tax law is different.

Crafters like to use round-figure prices at fairs because this encourages cash sales and eliminates the need for taking coins to make change. Some crafters tell their customers that sales tax has been included in their rounded-off prices, but you should not do this until you check with your state. In some states, this is illegal; in others, you may find that you are required to inform your customers, by means of a sign, that sales tax has been included in your price. Your may also have to print this information on customer receipts as well.

If you make such a statement and collect taxes on cash sales, be sure to report those cash sales as taxable income and remit the tax money to the state accordingly. Failure

As a hobby seller, you automatically become a sole proprietor when you start selling what you make. Although most professional crafters remain sole proprietors throughout the life of their business, some do form craft partnerships or corporations when their business begins to generate serious money, or if it happens to involve other members of their family. You don't need a lawyer to start a sole proprietorship, but it would be folly to enter into a partnership, corporation, or LLC without legal guidance. Here is a brief look at the main advantages and disadvantages of each type of legal business structure.

Sole Proprietorship

No legal formalities are involved in starting or ending a sole proprietorship. You're your own boss here, and the business starts when you say it does and ends automatically when you stop running it. As discussed earlier, income is reported annually on a Schedule C form

to do this would be a violation of the law, and it's easy to get caught these days when sales tax agents are showing up at craft fairs across the country.

Even if rounding off the price and including the tax within that figure turns out to be legal in your state, it will definitely complicate your bookkeeping. For example, if you normally sell an item for $5 or some other round figure, you must have a firm retail price on which to calculate sales tax to begin with. Adding tax to a round figure makes it uneven. Then you must either raise it or lower the price, and if you lower it, what you're really doing is paying the sales tax for your customer out of your profits. This is no way to do business.

I suggest that you set your retail prices based on the pricing formulas given in this book, calculate the sales tax accordingly, and give your customers change if they pay in cash. You will be perceived as a professional when you operate this way, whereas crafters who insist always on "cash only" sales are sending signals to buyers that they don't intend to report this income to tax authorities.

and taxed at the personal level. The sole proprietor is fully liable for all business debts and actions. In the event of a lawsuit, personal assets are not protected.

Partnership

There are two kinds of partnerships: General and Limited

A *General Partnership* is easy to start, with no federal requirements involved. Income is taxed at the personal level and the partnership ends as soon as either partner withdraws from the business. Liability is unlimited. The most financially dangerous thing about a partnership is that the debts incurred by one partner must be assumed by all other partners. Before signing a partnership agreement, make sure the tax obligations of your partner are current.

In a *Limited Partnership,* the business is run by general partners and financed by silent (limited) partners who have no liability beyond an investment of money in the business. This kind of partnership is more complicated to establish, has special tax withholding regulations, and requires the filing of a legal contract with the state.

LLC (Limited Liability Company)

This legal form of business reportedly combines the best attributes of other small business forms while offering a better tax advantage than a limited partnership. It also affords personal liability protection similar to that of a corporation. To date, few craft businesses appear to be using this business form.

Corporation

A corporation is the most complicated and expensive legal form of business and not recommended for any business whose earnings are less than $25,000 a year. If and when your business reaches this point, you should study some books on this topic to fully understand the pros and cons of a corporation. Also consult an accountant or attorney for guidance on the type of corporation you should select—a "C" (general corporation) or an "S" (subchapter S corporation). One book that offers good perspective on this topic is *INC Yourself—How to Profit by Setting Up Your Own Corporation*.

The main disadvantage of incorporation for the small business owner is that profits are taxed twice: first as corporate income and again when they are distributed to the owner-shareholders as dividends. For this reason, many small businesses elect to incorporate as subchapter S corporations, which allows profits to be taxed at owners' regular individual rates. (See sidebar, "The Limited Legal Protection of a Corporation," below.)

The Limited Legal Protection of a Corporation

Business novices often think that by incorporating their business they can protect their personal assets in the event of a lawsuit. This is true if you have employees who do something wrong and cause your business to be sued. As the business owner, however, if you personally do something wrong and are sued as a result, you might in some cases be held legally responsible, and the "corporation door" will offer no legal protection for your personal assets.

Or, as CPA Bernard Kamoroff explains in *Small Time Operator,* "A corporation will not shield you from personal liability that you normally should be responsible for, such as not having car insurance or acting with gross negligence. If you plan to incorporate solely or primarily with the intention of limiting your legal liability, I suggest you find out first exactly how limited the liability really is for your particular venture. Hire a knowledgeable lawyer to give you a written opinion." (See section 7, "Insurance Tips.")

4. Local and State Laws and Regulations

This section will acquaint you with laws and regulations that affect the average art or crafts business based at home. If you've unknowingly broken one of these laws, don't panic. It may not be as bad as you think. It is often possible to get back on the straight and narrow merely by filling out a required form or by paying a small fee of some kind. What's important is that you take steps now to comply with the laws that pertain to your particular business. Often, the fear of being caught when you're breaking a law is often much worse than doing whatever needs to be done to set the matter straight. In the end, it's usually what you don't know that is most likely to cause legal or financial problems, so never hesitate to ask questions about things you don't understand.

Even when you think you know the answers, it can pay to "act dumb." It is said that Napoleon used to attend meetings and pretend to know nothing about a topic, asking many probing questions. By feigning ignorance, he was able to draw valuable information and insight out of everyone around him. This strategy is often used by today's small business owners, too.

Business Name Registration

If you're a sole proprietor doing business under any name other than your own full name, you are required by law to register it on both the local and state level. In this case, you are said to be using an "assumed," "fictitious," or "trade" name. What registration does is enable authorities to connect an assumed name to an individual who can be held responsible for the actions of a business. If you're doing business under your own name, such as Kay Jones, you don't have to register your business name on either the local or state level. If your name is part of a longer name, however (for example, Kay Jones Designs), you should check to see if your county or state requires registration.

Local Registration

To register your name, contact your city or county clerk, who will explain what you need to do to officially register your business on the local level. At the same time, ask if you need any special municipal or county licenses or permits to operate within the law. (See next section, "Licenses and Permits.") This office can also tell you how and where to write to register your name at the state level. If you've been operating under an assumed name for a while and are worried because you didn't register the name earlier, just register it now, as if the business were new.

Registration involves filling out a simple form and paying a small fee, usually around $10 to $25. At the time you register, you will get details about a classified ad you must run in a general-circulation newspaper in your county. This will notify the public at large that you are now operating a business under an assumed name. (If you don't want your neighbors to know what you're doing, simply run the ad in a newspaper somewhere else in the county.) After publication of this ad, you will receive a Fictitious Name Statement that you must send to the County Clerk, who in turn will file it with your registration form to make your business completely legitimate. This name statement or certificate may also be referred to as your DBA ("doing business as") form. In some areas, you cannot open a business checking account if you don't have this form to show your bank.

State Registration

Once you've registered locally, contact your Secretary of State to register your business name with the state. This will prevent its use by a corporate entity. At the same time, find out if you must

▼▼▼

Picking a Good Business Name

If you haven't done it already, think up a great name for your new business. You want something that will be memorable—catchy, but not too cute. Many crafters select a simple name that is attached to their first name, such as "Mary's Quilts" or "Tom's Woodcrafts." This is fine for a hobby business, but if your goal is to build a full-time business at home, you may wish to choose a more professional-sounding name that omits your personal name. If a name sounds like a hobby business, you may have difficulty getting wholesale suppliers to take you seriously. A more professional name may also enable you to get higher prices for your products. For example, the above names might be changed to "Quilted Treasures" or "Wooden Wonders."

Don't print business cards or stationery until you find out if someone else is already using the name you've chosen. To find out if the name has already been registered, you

▲▲▲

obtain any kind of state license. Generally, home-based craft businesses will not need a license from the state, but there are always exceptions. An artist who built an open-to-the-public art studio on his property reported that the fine in his state for operating this kind of business without a license was $50 a day. In short, it always pays to ask questions to make sure you're operating legally and safely.

Federal Registration

The only way to protect a name on the federal level is with a trademark, discussed in section 8.

Licenses and Permits

A "license" is a certificate granted by a municipal or county agency that gives you permission to engage in a business occupation. A "permit" is similar, except that it is granted by local authorities. Until recently, few craft businesses had to have a license or permit

can perform a trademark search through a search company or hire an attorney who specializes in trademak law to conduct the search for you. And if you are planning to eventually set up a Web site, you might want to do a search to see if that domain name is still available on the Internet. Go to www.networksolutions.com to do this search. Business names have to be registered on the Internet, too, and they can be "parked" for a fee until you're ready to design your Web site.

It's great if your business name and Web site name can be the same, but this is not always possible. A crafter told me recently she had to come up with 25 names before she found a domain name that hadn't already been taken. (Web entrepreneurs are grabbing every good name they can find. Imagine my surprise when I did a search and found that two different individuals had set up Web sites using the titles of my two best-known books, *Creative Cash* and *Homemade Money*.)

of any kind, but a growing number of communities now have new laws on their books that require home-based business owners to obtain a "home occupation permit." Annual fees for such permits may range from $15 to $200 a year. For details about the law in your particular community or county, call your city or country clerk (depending on whether you live within or outside city limits).

Use of Personal Phone for Business

Although every business writer stresses the importance of having a business telephone number, craftspeople generally ignore this advice and do business on their home telephone. While it's okay to use a home phone to make outgoing business calls, you cannot advertise a home telephone number as your business phone number without being in violation of local telephone regulations. That means you cannot legally put your home telephone number on a business card or business stationery or advertise it on your Web site.

That said, let me also state that most craftspeople totally ignore this law and do it anyway. (I don't know what the penalty for breaking this law is in your state; you'll have to call your telephone company for that information and decide if this is something you want to do.) Some phone companies might give you a slap on the wrist and tell you to stop, while others might start charging you business line telephone rates if they discover you are advertising your personal phone number.

The primary reason to have a separate phone line for your business is that it enables you to freely advertise your telephone number to solicit new business and invite credit card sales, custom order inquiries, and the like. Further, you can deduct 100 percent of the costs of a business telephone line on your Schedule C tax form, while deductions for the business use of a home phone are severely limited. (Discuss this with your accountant.)

If you plan to connect to the Internet or install a fax machine, you will definitely need a second line to handle the load, but most crafters simply add an additional personal line instead of a business line. Once on the Internet, you may have even less need for a business phone than before since you can simply invite contact from buyers by advertising your e-mail address. (Always include your e-mail and Internet address on your business cards and stationery.)

If your primary selling methods are going to be consignment shops, craft fairs, or craft malls, a business phone number would be necessary only if you are inviting orders by phone. If you present a holiday boutique or open house once or twice a year, there should be no problem with putting your home phone number on promotional fliers because you are, in fact, inviting people to your home and not your business (similar to running a classified ad for a garage sale).

If and when you decide a separate line for your business is necessary, you may find it is not as costly as you think. Telephone companies today are very aware of the number of people who are working at home, and they have come up with a variety of affordable packages and second-line options, any one of which might be perfect for your craft business needs. Give your telephone company a call and see what's available.

Zoning Regulations

Before you start any kind of home-based business, check your home's zoning regulations. You can find a copy at your library or at city hall. Find out what zone you're in and then read the information under "home occupations." Be sure to read the fine print and note the penalty for violating a zoning ordinance. In most cases, someone who is caught violating zoning laws will be asked to cease and desist and a penalty is incurred only if this order is ignored. In other cases, however, willful violation could incur a hefty fine.

Zoning laws differ from one community to another, with some of them being terribly outdated (actually written back in horse-and-buggy days). In some communities, zoning officials simply "look the other way" where zoning violations are concerned because it's easier to do this than change the law. In other places, however, zoning regulations have recently been revised in light of the growing number of individuals working at home, and these changes have not always been to the benefit of home-based workers or self-employed individuals. Often there are restrictions as to (1) the amount of space in one's home a business may occupy (impossible to enforce, in my opinion), (2) the number of people (customers, students) who can come to your home each day, (3) the use of non-family employees, and so on. If you find you cannot advertise your home as a place of business, this problem can be easily solved by renting a P.O. box or using a commercial mailbox service as your business address.

Although I'm not suggesting that you violate your zoning law, I will tell you that many individuals who have found zoning to be a problem do ignore this law, particularly when they have a quiet business that is unlikely to create problems in their community.

Zoning officials don't go around checking for people who are violating the law; rather, they tend to act on complaints they have received about a certain activity that is creating problems for others. Thus, the best way to avoid zoning problems is to keep a low profile by not broadcasting your home-based business to neighbors. More important, never annoy them with activities that emit fumes or odors, create parking problems, or make noise of any kind.

While neighbors may grudgingly put up with a noisy hobby activity (such as sawing in the garage), they are not likely to tolerate the same noise or disturbance if they know it's related to a home-based business. Likewise, they won't mind if you have a garage sale every year, but if people are constantly coming to your home to buy from your home shop, open house, home parties, or holiday boutiques every year, you could be asking for trouble if the zoning laws don't favor this kind of activity.

5. General Business and Financial Information

This section offers introductory guidelines on essential business basics for beginners. Once your business is up and running, however, you need to read other craft-business books to get detailed information on the following topics and many others related to the successful growth and development of a home-based art or crafts business.

Making a Simple Business Plan

As baseball star Yogi Berra once said, "If you don't know where you are going, you might not get there." That's why you need a plan.

Like a road map, a business plan helps you get from here to there. It doesn't have to be fancy, but it does have to be in written form. A good business plan will save you time and money while helping you stay focused and on track to meet your goals. The kind of business plan a craftsperson makes will naturally be less complicated than the business plan of a major manufacturing company, but the elements are basically the same and should include:

- *History*—how and why you started your business
- *Business description*—what you do, what products you make, why they are special
- *Management information*—your business background or experience and the legal form your business will take
- *Manufacturing and production*—how and where products will be produced and who will make them; how and where supplies and materials will be obtained, and their estimated costs; labor costs (yours or other helpers); and overhead costs involved in the making of products
- *Financial plan*—estimated sales and expense figures for one year
- *Market research findings*—a description of your market (fairs, shops, mail order, Internet, etc.), your customers, and your competition
- *Marketing plan*—how you are going to sell your products and the anticipated cost of your marketing (commissions, advertising, craft fair displays, etc.)

If this all seems a bit much for a small crafts business, start managing your time by using a daily calendar/planner and start a notebook you can fill with your creative and marketing ideas, plans, and business goals. In it, write a simple mission statement that answers the following questions:

- What is my primary mission or goal in starting a business?
- What is my financial goal for this year?
- What am I going to do to get the sales I need this year to meet my financial goal?

The most important thing is that you start putting your dreams, goals, and business plans on paper so you can review them regularly.

It's always easier to see where you're going if you know where you've been.

When You Need an Attorney

Many business beginners think they have to hire a lawyer the minute they start a business, but that would be a terrible waste of money if you're just starting a simple art or crafts business at home, operating as a sole proprietor. Sure, a lawyer will be delighted to hold your hand and give you the same advice I'm giving you here (while charging you $150 an hour or more for his or her time). With this book in hand, you can easily take care of all the "legal details" of small business start-up. The day may come, however, when you do need legal counsel, such as when you:

Form a Partnership or Corporation

As stated earlier, an attorney's guidance is necessary in the formation of a partnership. Although many people have incorporated without a lawyer using a good how-to book on the topic, I wouldn't recommend doing this because there are so many details involved here, not to mention different types of corporate entities.

Defend an Infringement of a Copyright or Trademark

You don't need an attorney to get a simple copyright, but if someone infringes on one of your copyrights, you will probably need legal help to stop the infringer from profiting from your creativity. You can file your own trademark application (if you are exceedingly careful about following instructions), but it would be difficult to protect your trademark without legal help if someone tries to steal it. In both cases, you would need an attorney who specializes in copyright, patent, and trademark law. (If you ever need a good attorney who understands the plight of artists and crafters, contact me by e-mail at barbara@crafter.com and I'll refer you to

▼▼▼

Get a Safety Deposit Box

The longer you are in business, the more important it will be to safeguard your most valuable business records. When you work at home, there is always the possibility of fire or damage from some natural disaster, be it tornado, earthquake, hurricane, or flood. You will worry less if you keep your most valuable business papers, records, computer disks, and so forth off-premises, along with other items that would be difficult or impossible to replace. Some particulars I have always kept in my business safety deposit box include master software disks and computer back-up tapes; original copies of my designs and patterns, business contracts, copyrights, insurance policies, and a photographic record of all items insured on our homeowner's policy. Remember: Insurance is worthless if you cannot prove what you owned in the first place.

▲▲▲

the attorney who has been helpful to me in protecting my common-law trademark to *Homemade Money*, my home-business classic. The 6th edition of this book includes the details of my trademark infringement story.)

Negotiate a Contract

Many craft hobbyists of my acquaintance have gone on to write books and sell their original designs to manufacturers, suddenly finding themselves with a contract in hand that contains a lot of confusing legal jargon. When hiring an attorney to check any kind of contract, make sure he or she has experience in the particular field involved. For example, a lawyer specializing in real estate isn't going to know a thing about the inner workings of a book publishing company and how the omission or inclusion of a particular clause or phrase might impact the author's royalties or make it difficult to get publishing rights back when the book goes out of print. Although I have no experience in the licensing industry, I presume the same thing holds true here. What I do know for sure is that the problem with most contracts is not so much what's *in* them, as what *isn't.* Thus you need to be sure the attorney you hire for specialized contract work has done this kind of work for other clients.

Hire Independent Contractors

If you ever grow your business to the point where you need to hire workers and are wondering whether you have to hire employees or can use independent contractors instead, I suggest you to seek counsel from an attorney who specializes in labor law. This topic is very complex and beyond the scope of this beginner's guide, but I do want you to know that the IRS has been on a campaign for the past several years to abolish independent contractors altogether. Many small businesses have suffered great financial loss in back taxes and penalties because they followed the advice of an accountant or regular attorney who didn't fully understand the technicalities of this matter.

If and when you do need a lawyer for general business purposes, ask friends for a reference, and check with your bank, too, since it will probably know most of the attorneys with private practices in your area. Note that membership in some small business organizations will also give you access to affordable prepaid legal services. If you ever need serious legal help but have no funds to pay for it, contact the Volunteer Lawyers for the Arts (see resources in section 10).

Why You Need a Business Checking Account

Many business beginners use their personal checking account to conduct the transactions of their business, *but you must not do this* because the IRS does not allow co-mingling of business and personal income. If you are operating as a business, reporting income on a Schedule C form and taking deductions accordingly, the lack of a separate checking account for your business would surely result in an IRS ruling that your endeavor was a hobby and not a business. That, in turn, would cost you all the deductions previously taken on earlier tax returns and you'd end up with a very large tax bill. Don't you agree that the cost of a separate checking account is a small price to pay to protect all your tax deductions?

You do not necessarily need one of the more expensive business checking accounts; just a *separate account* through which you run all business income and expenditures. Your business name does not have to be on these checks so long as only your name (not your spouse's) is listed as account holder. You can save money on your checking account by first calling several banks and savings and loan institutions and comparing the charges they set for imprinted checks, deposits, checks written, bounced checks, and other services. Before you open your account, be sure to ask if the bank can set you up to take credit cards (merchant account) at some point in the future.

Accepting Credit Cards

Most of us today take credit cards for granted and expect to be able to use them for most everything we buy. It's nice to be able to offer credit card services to your craft fair customers, but it is costly and thus not recommended for beginning craft sellers. If you get into selling at craft fairs on a regular basis, however, at some point you may find you are losing sales because you don't have "merchant status" (the ability to accept credit cards as payment).

Some craftspeople have reported a considerable jump in sales once they started taking credit cards. That's because some people who buy with plastic may buy two or three items instead of one, or are willing to pay a higher price for something if they can charge it. Thus, the higher your prices, the more likely you are to lose sales if you can't accept credit cards. As one jewelry maker told me, "I always seem to get the customers who have run out of cash and left their checkbook at home. But even when they have a check, I feel uncomfortable taking a check for $100 or more."

A list follows of the various routes you can travel to get merchant status. You will have to do considerable research to find out which method is best for you. All will be costly, and you must have sufficient sales, or the expectation of increased sales, to consider taking credit cards in the first place. Understand, too, that taking credit cards in person (called face-to-face transactions where you have the card in front of you) is different from accepting credit cards by phone, by mail, or through a Web site (called non–face-to-face transactions). Each method of selling is treated differently by bankcard providers.

Merchant Status from Your Bank

When you're ready to accept credit cards, start with the bank where you have your business checking account. Where you bank, and where you live, has everything to do with whether you can get merchant status from your bank or not. Home-business owners in small towns often have less trouble than do those in large cities. One crafter told me Bank of America gave her merchant status with no problem, but some banks simply refuse to deal with anyone who doesn't operate out of a storefront. Most banks now insist that credit card sales be transmitted electronically, but a few still offer manual printers and allow merchants to send in their sales slips by mail. You will be given details about this at the time you apply for merchant status. All banks will require proof that you have a going business and will want to see your financial statements.

Merchant Status through a Crafts Organization

If you are refused by your bank because your business is home based or just too new, getting bankcard services through a crafts or home-business organization is the next best way to go. Because such organizations have a large membership, they have some negotiating power with the credit card companies and often get special deals for their members. As a member of such an organization, the chances are about 95 percent that you will automatically be accepted into an its bankcard program, even if you are a brand new business owner.

One organization I can recommend to beginning sellers is the National Craft Association. Managing Director Barbara Arena tells me that 60 percent of all new NCA members now take the MasterCard/VISA services offered by her organization. "Crafters who are unsure about whether they want to take credit cards over a long period of time have the option of renting equipment," says Barbara. "This enables them to get out of the program with a month's notice. NCA members can operate on a software basis through their personal computer (taking their laptop computer to shows and calling in sales on their cell phone), or use a swipe machine. Under NCA's program, crafters can also accept credit card sales on their Internet site."

For more information from NCA and other organizations offering merchant services, see "Crafts and Home-Business Organizations" on page 282.

Merchant Status from Credit Card Companies

If you've been in business for a while, you may find you can get merchant status directly from American Express or Novus Services, Inc., the umbrella company that handles the Discover, Bravo, and Private Issue credit cards. American Express says that in some cases it can grant merchant status immediately upon receipt of some key information given on the phone. As for Novus, many crafters have told me how easy it was to get merchant status from this company. Novus says it only needs your Social Security number and information to check your credit rating. If Novus accepts you, it can also get you set up to take VISA and MasterCard as well if you meet the special acceptance qualifications of these two credit card companies. (Usually, they require you to be in business for at least two years.)

Merchant Status from an Independent
Service Organization Provider (ISO)

ISOs act as agents for banks that authorize credit cards, promoting their services by direct mail, through magazine advertising, telemarketing, and on the Internet. Most of these bankcard providers are operating under a network marketing program (one agent representing one agent representing another, and so on). They are everywhere on the Internet, sending unsolicited e-mail messages to Web site owners. In addition to offering the merchant account service itself, many are also trying to get other Web site owners to promote the same service in exchange for some kind of referral fee. I do not recommend that you get merchant status through an ISO because I've heard too many horror stories about them. If you want to explore this option on the Internet, however, use your browser's search button and type "credit cards + merchant" to get a list of such sellers.

In general, ISOs may offer a low discount rate but will sock it to you with inflated equipment costs, a high application fee, and extra fees for installation, programming, and site inspection. You will also have to sign an unbreakable three- or four-year lease for the electronic equipment.

As you can see, you must really do your homework where bankcard services are concerned. In checking out the services offered by any of the providers noted here, ask plenty of questions. Make up a chart that lets you compare what each one charges for application and service fees, monthly charges, equipment costs, software, discount rates, and transaction fees.

Transaction fees can range from 20 to 80 cents per ticket, with discount rates running anywhere from 1.67 percent to 5 percent. Higher rates are usually attached to non–face-to-face credit card transactions, paper transaction systems, or a low volume of sales. Any rate higher than 5 percent should be a danger signal since you could be dealing with an unscrupulous seller or some kind of illegal third-party processing program.

I'm told that a good credit card processor today may cost around $800, yet some card service providers are charging two or three times that amount in their leasing arrangements. I once got a quote from a major ISO and found it would have cost me $40 a month to lease the terminal—$1,920 over a period of four years—or I could buy it for just $1,000. In checking with my bank, I learned I could get the same equipment and the software to run it for just $350!

In summary, if you're a nervous beginner, the safest way to break into taking credit cards is to work with a bank or organization that offers equipment on a month-by-month rental arrangement. Once you've had some experience in taking credit card payments, you can review your situation and decide whether you want to move into a leasing arrangement or buy equipment outright.

6. Minimizing the Financial Risks of Selling

This book contains a good chapter on how and where to sell your crafts, but I thought it would be helpful for you to have added perspective on the business management end of selling through various outlets, and some things you can do to protect yourself from financial loss and legal hassles.

First you must accept the fact that all businesses occasionally suffer financial losses of one kind or another. That's simply the nature of business. Selling automatically carries a certain degree of risk in that we can never be absolutely sure that we're going to be paid for anything until we actually have payment in hand. Checks may bounce, wholesale buyers may refuse to pay their invoices, and consignment shops can close unexpectedly without returning merchandise to crafters. In the past few years, a surprising number

State Consignment Laws

Technically, consigned goods remain the property of the seller until they are sold. When a shop goes out of business, however, consigned merchandise may be seized by creditors in spite of what your consignment agreement may state. You may have some legal protection here, however, if you live in a state that has a consignment law designed to protect artists and craftspeople in such instances. I believe such laws exist in the states of CA, CO, CT, IL, IA, KY, MA, NH, NM, NY, OR, TX, WA, and WI. Call your Secretary of State to confirm this or, if your state isn't listed here, ask whether this law is now on the books. Be sure to get full details about the kind of protection afforded by this law because some states have different definitions for what constitutes "art" or "crafts."

of craft mall owners have stolen out of town in the middle of the night, taking with them all the money due their vendors, and sometimes the vendors' merchandise as well. (This topic is beyond the scope of this book, but if you'd like more information on it, see my *Creative Cash* book and back issues of my *Craftsbiz Chat* newsletter on the Internet at www.crafter.com/brabec).

Now I don't want you to feel uneasy about selling or suspicious of every buyer who comes your way, because that would take all the fun out of selling. But I *do* want you to know that bad things sometimes happen to good craftspeople who have not done their homework (by reading this book, you are doing *your* homework). If you will follow the cautionary guidelines that follow, you can avoid some common selling pitfalls and minimize your financial risk to the point where it will be negligible.

Selling to Consignment Shops

Never consign more merchandise to one shop than you can afford to lose, and do not send new items to a shop until you see that payments are being made regularly according to your written consignment agreement. It should cover the topics of:

- insurance (see "Insurance Tips," section 7).
- pricing (make sure the shop cannot raise or lower your retail price without your permission).
- sales commission (40 percent is standard; don't work with shop owners who ask for more than this. It makes more sense to wholesale products at 50 percent and get payment in 30 days).
- payment dates.
- display of merchandise.
- return of unsold merchandise (some shops have a clause stating that if unsold merchandise is not claimed within 30 to 60 days after a notice has been sent, the shop can dispose of it any way it wishes).

Above all, make sure your agreement includes the name and phone number of the shop's owner (not just the manager). If a shop fails and you decide to take legal action, you want to be sure your lawyer can track down the owner. (See sidebar, "State Consignment Laws," page 244.)

Selling to Craft Malls

Shortly after the craft mall concept was introduced to the crafts community in 1988 by Rufus Coomer, entrepreneurs who understood the profit potential of such a business began to open malls all over the country. But there were no guidebooks and everyone was flying by the seat of his or her pants, making up operating rules along the way. Many mall owners, inexperienced in retailing, have since gone out of business, often leaving crafters holding the bag. The risks of selling through such well-known chain stores as Coomers or American Craft Malls are minimal, and many independently owned malls have also established excellent reputations in the industry. What you need to be especially concerned about here are new malls opened by individuals who have no track record in this industry.

I'm not telling you *not* to set up a booth in a new mall in your area—it might prove to be a terrific outlet for you—but I am cautioning you to keep a sharp eye on the mall and how it's being operated. Warning signs of a mall in trouble include:

- **less than 75 percent occupancy**
- **little or no ongoing advertising**
- **not many shoppers**
- **crafters pulling out (usually a sign of too few sales)**
- **poor accounting of sales**
- **late payments**

If a mall is in trouble, it stands to reason that the logical time for it to close is right after the biggest selling season of the year, namely Christmas. Interestingly, this is when most of the shady mall owners have stolen out of town with crafters' Christmas sales in their pockets. As stated in my *Creative Cash* book:

> If it's nearing Christmas time, and you're getting uncomfortable vibes about the financial condition of a mall you're in, it might be smart to remove the bulk of your merchandise— especially expensive items—just before it closes for the holidays. You can always restock after the first of the year if everything looks rosy.

Avoiding Bad Checks

At a crafts fair or other event where you're selling directly to the public, if the buyer doesn't have cash and you don't accept credit cards, your only option is to accept a check. Few crafters have bad check problems for sales held in the home (holiday boutique, open house, party plan, and such), but bad checks at craft fairs are always possible. Here are several things you can do to avoid accepting a bad check:

- Always ask to see a driver's license and look carefully at the picture on it. Write the license number on the check.

- If the sale is a for a large amount, you can ask to see a credit card for added identification, but writing down the number will do no good because you cannot legally cover a bad check with a customer's credit card. (The customer has a legal right to refuse to let you copy the number as well.)

- Look closely at the check itself. Is there a name and ad-dress printed on it? If not, ask the customer to write in this information by hand, along with his or her phone number.

- Look at the sides of the check. If at least one side is not perforated, it could be a phony check.

- Look at the check number in the upper right-hand corner. Most banks who issue personalized checks begin the num-bering system with 101 when a customer reorders new checks. The Small Business Administration says to be more cautious with low sequence numbers because there seems to be a higher number of these checks that are returned.

- Check the routing number in the lower left-hand corner and note the ink. If it looks shiny, wet your finger and see if the ink rubs off. That's a sure sign of a phony check because good checks are printed with magnetic ink that does not reflect light.

Collecting on a Bad Check

No matter how careful you are, sooner or later, you will get stuck with a bad check. It may bounce for three reasons:

> nonsufficient funds (NSF)
> account closed
> no account (evidence of fraud)

I've accepted tens of thousands of checks from mail-order buyers through the years and have rarely had a bad check I couldn't collect with a simple phone call asking the party to honor his or her obligation to me. People often move and close out accounts before all checks have cleared, or they add or subtract wrong, causing their account to be overdrawn. Typically, they are embarrassed to have caused a problem like this.

When the problem is more difficult than this, your bank can help. Check to learn its policy regarding bounced checks. Some automatically put checks through a second time. If a check bounces at this point, you may ask the bank to collect the check for you. The check needs to be substantial, however, since the bank fee may be $15 or more if they are successful in collecting the money.

If you have accepted a check for a substantial amount of money and believe there is evidence of fraud, you may wish to do one of the following:

- **notify your district attorney's office**
- **contact your sheriff or police department (since it is a crime to write a bad check)**
- **try to collect through small claims court**

For more detailed information on all of these topics, see *The Crafts Business Answer Book.*

7. Insurance Tips

As soon as you start even the smallest business at home, you need to give special attention to insurance. This section offers an introductory overview of insurance concerns of primary interest to crafts-business owners.

Homeowner's or Renter's Insurance

Anything in the home being used to generate income is considered to be business-related and thus exempt from coverage on a personal policy. Thus your homeowner's or renter's insurance policy will not cover business equipment, office furniture, supplies, or inventory of finished goods unless you obtain a special rider. Such riders, called a "Business Pursuits Endorsement" by some companies, are inexpensive and offer considerable protection. Your insurance agent will be happy to give you details.

As your business grows and you have an ever-larger inventory of supplies, materials, tools, and finished merchandise, you may find it necessary to buy a special in-home business policy that offers broader protection. Such policies may be purchased directly from insurance companies or through craft and home-business organizations that offer special insurance programs to their members.

Liability Insurance

There are two kinds of liability insurance. *Product* liability insurance protects you against lawsuits by consumers who have been injured while using one of your products. *Personal* liability insurance protects you against claims made by individuals who have suffered bodily injury while on your premises (either your home or the place where you are doing business, such as in your booth at a crafts fair).

Your homeowner's or renter's insurance policy will include some personal liability protection, but if someone were to suffer bodily injury while on your premises for *business* reasons, that coverage might not apply. Your need for personal liability insurance will be greater if you plan to regularly present home parties, holiday boutiques, or open house sales in your home where many people might be coming and going throughout the year. If you sell at craft fairs, you would also be liable for damages if someone were to fall and be injured in your booth or if something in your booth falls and injures another person. For this reason, some craft fair promoters now require all vendors to have personal liability insurance.

As for product liability insurance, whether you need it or not depends largely on the type of products you make for sale, how careful you are to make sure those products are safe, and how and where you sell them. Examples of some crafts that have caused injury to consumers and resulted in court claims in the past are stuffed toys with wire or pins that children have swallowed; items made of yarn or fiber that burned rapidly; handmade furniture that collapsed when someone put an ordinary amount of weight on them; jewelry with sharp points or other features that cut the wearer, and so on. Clearly, the best way to avoid injury to consumers is to make certain your products have no health hazards and are safe to use. (See discussion of consumer safety laws in section 8.)

Few artists and craftspeople who sell on a part-time basis feel they can afford product liability insurance, but many full-time craft professionals, particularly those who sell their work wholesale, find it a necessary expense. In fact, many wholesale buyers refuse to buy from suppliers that do not carry product liability insurance.

I believe the least expensive way to obtain both personal and product liability insurance is with one of the comprehensive in-home or craft business policies offered by a craft or home-business organization. Such policies generally offer a million dollars of both personal and product liability coverage. (See "Things to Do" Checklist on page 277 and Resources for some organizations you can contact for more information. Also check with your insurance agent about the benefits of an umbrella policy for extra liability insurance.)

Insurance on Crafts Merchandise

As a seller of art or crafts merchandise, you are responsible for insuring your own products against loss. If you plan to sell at craft fairs, in craft malls, rent-a-space shops, or consignment shops, you may want to buy an insurance policy that protects your merchandise both at home or away. Note that while craft shops and malls generally have fire insurance covering the building and its fixtures, this coverage cannot be extended to merchandise offered for sale because it is not the property of the shop owner. (Exception: Shops and malls in shopping centers are mandated by law to buy fire insurance on their contents whether they own the merchandise or not.)

This kind of insurance is usually part of the home-business/ crafts-business insurance policies mentioned earlier.

Auto Insurance

Be sure to talk to the agent who handles your car insurance and explain that you may occasionally use your car for business purposes. Normally, a policy issued for a car that's used only for pleasure or driving to and from work may not provide complete coverage for an accident that occurs during business use of the car, particularly if the insured is to blame for the accident. For example, if you were delivering a load of crafts to a shop or on your way to a crafts fair and had an accident, would your business destination and the "commercial merchandise" in your car negate your coverage in any

Insuring Your Art or Crafts Collection

The replacement cost insurance you may have on your personal household possessions does not extend to "fine art," which includes such things as paintings, antiques, pictures, tapestries, statuary, and other articles that cannot be replaced with new articles. If you have a large collection of art, crafts, memorabilia, or collector's items, and its value is more than $1,500, you may wish to have your collection appraised so it can be protected with a separate all-risk endorsement to your homeowner's policy called a "fine arts floater."

way? Where insurance is concerned, the more questions you ask, the better you'll feel about the policies you have.

8. Important Regulations Affecting Artists and Craftspeople

Government agencies have a number of regulations that artists and craftspeople must know about. Generally, they relate to consumer safety, the labeling of certain products and trade practices. Following are regulations of primary interest to readers of books in the For Fun & Profit series. If you find a law or regulation related to your particular art or craft interest, be sure to request additional information from the government agency named there.

Consumer Safety Laws

All product sellers must pay attention to the Consumer Product Safety Act, which protects the public against unreasonable risks of injury associated with consumer products. The Consumer Product Safety Commission (CPSC) is particularly active in the area of toys and consumer goods designed for children. All sellers of handmade products must be doubly careful about the materials they use for children's products since consumer lawsuits are common where products for children are concerned. To avoid this problem, simply comply with the consumer safety laws applicable to your specific art or craft.

Toy Safety Concerns

To meet CPSC's guidelines for safety, make sure any toys you make for sale are:

- too large to be swallowed
- not apt to break easily or leave jagged edges

- free of sharp edges or points
- not put together with easily exposed pins, wires, or nails
- nontoxic, nonflammable, and nonpoisonous

The Use of Paints, Varnishes, and Other Finishes

Since all paint sold for household use must meet the Consumer Product Safety Act's requirement for minimum amounts of lead, these paints are deemed to be safe for use on products made for children, such as toys and furniture. Always check, however, to make sure the label bears a nontoxic notation. Specialty paints must carry a warning on the label about lead count, but "artist's paints" are curiously exempt from CPS's lead-in-paint ban and are not required to bear a warning label of any kind. Thus you should *never* use such paints on products intended for use by children unless the label specifically states they are *nontoxic* (lead-free). Acrylics and other water-based paints, of course, are nontoxic and completely safe for use on toys and other products made for children. If you plan to use a finishing coat, make sure it is nontoxic as well.

Fabric Flammability Concerns

The Flammable Fabrics Act is applicable only to those who sell products made of fabric, particularly products for children. It prohibits the movement in interstate commerce of articles of wearing apparel and fabrics that are so highly flammable as to be dangerous when worn by individuals, and for other purposes. Most fabrics comply with the above act, but if you plan to sell children's clothes or toys, you may wish to take an extra step to be doubly sure the fabric you are using is safe. This is particularly important if you plan to wholesale your products. What you should do is ask your fabric supplier for a *guarantee of compliance with the Flammability Act*. This guarantee is generally passed along to the buyer by a statement on the invoice that reads "continuing guaranty under the Flammable Fabrics Act." If you do not find such a statement on your invoice, you should ask the fabric manufacturer, wholesaler, or distributor to furnish you with their "statement of compliance" with the flammability standards. The CPSC can also tell you if a particular manufacturer has filed a continuing guarantee under The Flammable Fabrics Act.

Labels Required by Law

The following information applies only to crafters who use textiles, fabrics, fibers, or yarn products to make wearing apparel, decorative accessories, household furnishings, soft toys, or any product made of wool.

Different governmental agencies require the attachment of certain tags or labels to products sold in the consumer marketplace, whether manufactured in quantity or handmade for limited sale. You don't have to be too concerned about these laws if you sell only at local fairs, church bazaars, and home boutiques. As soon as you get out into the general consumer marketplace, however—doing large craft fairs, selling through consignment shops, craft malls, or wholesaling to shops—it would be wise to comply with all the federal labeling laws. Actually, these laws are quite easy to comply with because the required labels are readily available at inexpensive prices, and you can even make your own if you wish. Here is what the federal government wants you to tell your buyers in a tag or label:

- **What's in a product, and who has made it. The Textile Fiber Products Identification Act (monitored both by the Bureau of Consumer Protection and the Federal Trade Commission) requires that a special label or hangtag be attached to all textile wearing apparel and household furnishings, with the exception of wall hangings. "Textiles" include products made of any fiber, yarn, or fabric, including garments and decorative accessories, quilts, pillows, place mats, stuffed toys, rugs, etc. The tag or label must include**

(1) the name of the manufacturer and (2) the generic names and percentages of all fibers in the product in amounts of 5 percent or more, listed in order of predominance by weight.

■ How to take care of products. Care Labeling Laws are part of the Textile Fiber Products Identification Act, details about which are available from the FTC. If you make wearing apparel or household furnishings of any kind using textiles, suede, or leather, you must attach a permanent label that explains how to take care of the item. This label must indicate whether the item is to be dry-cleaned or washed. If it is washable, you must indicate whether in hot or cold water, whether bleach may or may not be used, and the temperature at which it may be ironed. (See sample labels in sidebar)

■ Details about products made of wool. If a product contains wool, the FTC requires additional identification under a separate law known as the Wool Products Labeling Act of 1939. FTC rules require that the labels of all wool or textile products clearly indicate when imported ingredients are used. Thus, the label for a skirt knitted in the U.S. from wool yarn imported from England would read, "Made in the USA from imported products" or similar wordage. If the wool yarn was spun in the U.S., a product made from that yarn would simply need a tag or label stating it was "Made in the USA" or "Crafted in USA" or some similarly clear terminology.

The Bedding and Upholstered Furniture Law

This is a peculiar state labeling law that affects sellers of items that have a concealed filling. It requires the purchase of a license, and products must have a tag that bears the manufacturer's registry number.

Bedding laws have long been a thorn in the side of crafters because they make no distinction between the large manufacturing company that makes mattresses and pillows, and the individual crafts producer who sells only handmade items. "Concealed filling" items include not just bedding and upholstery, but handmade pillows and quilts. In some states, dolls, teddy bears, and stuffed soft sculpture items are also required to have a tag.

Fortunately, only twenty-nine states now have this law on the books, and even if your state is one of them, the law may be arbitrarily enforced. (One exception is the state of Pennsylvania, which is reportedly sending officials to craft shows to inspect merchandise to see if it is properly labeled.) The only penalty that appears to be connected with a violation of this law in any state is removal of merchandise from store shelves or craft fair exhibits. That being the case, many crafters choose to ignore this law until they are challenged. If you learn you must comply with this law, you will be required to obtain a state license that will cost between $25 and $100, and you will have to order special "bedding stamps" that can be attached to your products. For more information on this complex topic, see *The Crafts Business Answer Book*.

FTC Rule for Mail-Order Sellers

Even the smallest home-based business needs to be familiar with Federal Trade Commission (FTC) rules and regulations. A variety of free booklets are available to business owners on topics related to advertising, mail-order marketing, and product labeling (as discussed earlier). In particular, crafters who sell by mail need to pay attention to the FTC's Thirty-Day Mail-Order Rule, which states that one must ship customer orders within thirty days of receiving payment for the order. This rule is strictly enforced, with severe financial penalties for each violation.

Unless you specifically state in your advertising literature how long delivery will take, customers will expect to receive the product within thirty days after you get their order. If you cannot meet this shipping date, you must notify the customer accordingly, enclosing a postage-paid reply card or envelope, and giving them the option to cancel the order if they wish. Now you know why so many catalog sellers state, "Allow six weeks for delivery." This lets them off the hook in case there are unforeseen delays in getting the order delivered.

9. Protecting Your Intellectual Property

"Intellectual property," says Attorney Stephen Elias in his book, *Patent, Copyright & Trademark,* "is a product of the human intellect that has commercial value."

This section offers a brief overview of how to protect your intellectual property through patents and trademarks, with a longer discussion of copyright law, which is of the greatest concern to individuals who sell what they make. Since it is easy to get patents, trademarks, and copyrights mixed up, let me briefly define them for you:

- A *patent* is a grant issued by the government that gives an inventor the right to exclude all others from making, using, or selling an invention within the United States and its territories and possessions.

- A *trademark* is used by a manufacturer or merchant to identify his or her goods and distinguish them from those manufactured or sold by others.

- A *copyright* protects the rights of creators of intellectual property in five main categories (described in this section).

Perspective on Patents

A patent may be granted to anyone who invents or discovers a new and useful process, machine, manufacture or composition of matter, or any new and useful improvement thereof. Any new, original, and ornamental design for an article of manufacture can also be patented. The problem with patents is that they can cost as much as

$5,000 or more to obtain, and once you've got one, they still require periodic maintenance through the U.S. Patent and Trademark Office. To contact this office, you can use the following Web sites: www.uspto.com or www.lcweb.loc.gov.

Ironically, a patent doesn't even give one the right to sell a product. It merely excludes anyone else from making, using, or selling your invention. Many business novices who have gone to the trouble to patent a product end up wasting a lot of time and money because a patent is useless if it isn't backed with the right manufacturing, distribution, and advertising programs. As inventor Jeremy

A Proper Copyright Notice

Although a copyright notice is not required by law, you are encouraged to put a copyright notice on every original thing you create. Adding the copyright notice does not obligate you to formally register your copyright, but it does serve to warn others that your work is legally protected and makes it difficult for anyone to claim they have "accidentally stolen" your work. (Those who actually do violate a copyright because they don't understand the law are called "innocent infringers" by the Copyright Office.)

A proper copyright notice includes three things:

1. the word "copyright," its abbreviation "copr.," or the copyright symbol, ©

2. the year of first publication of the work (when it was first shown or sold to the public)

3. the name of the copyright owner. Example: © 2000 by Barbara Brabec. (When the words "All Rights Reserved" are added to the copyright notation, it means that copyright protection has been extended to include all of the Western Hemisphere.)

The copyright notice should be positioned in a place where it can easily be seen. It can be stamped, cast, engraved, painted, printed, wood-burned, or simply written by hand in permanent ink. In the case of fiber crafts, you can attach an inexpensive label with the copyright notice and your business name and logo (or any other information you wish to put on the label).

Gorman states in *Homemade Money,* "Ninety-seven percent of the U.S. patents issued never earn enough money to pay the patenting fee. They just go on a plaque on the wall or in a desk drawer to impress the grandchildren fifty years later."

What a Trademark Protects

Trademarks were established to prevent one company from trading on the good name and reputation of another. The primary function of a trademark is to indicate origin, but in some cases it also serves as a guarantee of quality.

You cannot adopt any trademark that is so similar to another that it is likely to confuse buyers, nor can you trademark generic or descriptive names in the public domain. If, however, you come up with a particular word, name, symbol, or device to identify and distinguish your products from others, you may protect that mark by trademark provided another company is not already using a similar mark. Brand names, trade names, slogans, and phrases may also qualify for trademark protection.

Many individual crafters have successfully registered their own trademarks using a how-to book on the topic, but some would say never to try this without the help of a trademark attorney. It depends on how much you love detail and how well you can follow directions. Any mistake on the application form could cause it to be rejected, and you would lose the application fee in the process. If this is something you're interested in, and you have designed a mark you want to protect, you should first do a trademark search to see if someone else is already using it. Trademark searches can be done using library directories, an online computer service (check with your library), through private trademark search firms, or directly on the Internet through the Patent & Trademark Office's online search service (see checklist and resources). All of these searches together could still be inconclusive, however, because many companies have a stash of trademarks in reserve waiting for just the right product. As I understand it, these "nonpublished" trademarks are in a special file that only an attorney or trademark search service could find for you.

Like copyrights, trademarks have their own symbol, which looks like this: ®. This symbol can only be used once the trademark has been formally registered through the U.S. Patent and Trademark Office. Business owners often use the superscript initials "™" with a mark to indicate they've claimed a logo or some other mark, but this offers no legal protection. While this does not guarantee trademark protection, it does give notice to the public that you are claiming this name as your trademark. However, after you've used a mark for some time, you do gain a certain amount of common-law protection for that mark. I have, in fact, gained common-law protection for the name of my *Homemade Money* book and successfully defended it against use by another individual in my field because this title has become so closely associated with my name in the home-business community.

Whether you ever formally register a trademark or not will have much to do with your long-range business plans, how you feel about protecting your creativity, and what it would do to your business if someone stole your mark and registered it in his or her own name. Once you've designed a trademark you feel is worth protecting, get additional information from the Patent & Trademark Office and read a book or two on the topic to decide whether this is something you wish to pursue. (See checklist and resources.)

What Copyrights Protect

As a serious student of the copyright law, I've pored through the hard-to-interpret copyright manual, read dozens of related articles and books, and discussed this subject at length with designers, writers, teachers, editors, and publishers. I must emphasize, however, that I am no expert on this topic, and the following information does not constitute legal advice. It is merely offered as a general guide to a very complex legal topic you may wish to research further on your own at some point. In a book of this nature, addressed to hobbyists and beginning crafts-business owners, a discussion of copyrights must be limited to three basic topics:

> **what copyrights do and do not protect**
> **how to register a copyright and protect your legal rights**
> **how to avoid infringing on the rights of other copyright holders**

One of the first things you should do now is send for the free booklets offered by the Copyright Office (see checklist and resources). Various free circulars explain copyright basics, the forms involved in registering a copyright, and how to submit a copyright application and register a copyright. They also discuss what you cannot copyright. Rather than duplicate all the free information you can get from the Copyright Office with a letter or phone call, I will only briefly touch on these topics and focus instead on addressing some of the particular copyright questions crafters have asked me in the past.

Things You Can Copyright

Some people mistakenly believe that copyright protection extends only to printed works, but that is not true. The purpose of the copyright law is to protect any creator from anyone who would use his creative work for his own profit. Under current copyright law, claims are now registered in seven classes, five of which pertain to crafts:

1. *Serials* (Form SE)—periodicals, newspapers, magazines, bulletins, newsletters, annuals, journals, and proceedings of societies.
2. *Text* (Form TX)—books, directories, and other written works, including the how-to instructions for a crafts project. (You

could copyright a letter to your mother if you wanted to—
or your best display ad copy, or any other written words that
represent income potential.)

3. *Visual Arts* (Form VA)—pictorial, graphic, or sculptural
   works, including fine, graphic, and applied art; photographs,
   charts; technical drawings; diagrams; and models. (Also included in this category are "works of artistic craftsmanship
   insofar as their form but not their mechanical or utilitarian
   aspects are concerned.")

4. *Performing Arts* (Form PA)—musical works and accompany-
   ing words, dramatic works, pantomimes, choreographic
   works, motion pictures, and other audiovisual works.

5. Sound Recordings (Form SR)—musical, spoken, or other
   sounds, including any audio- or videotapes you might
   create.

Selling How-To Projects to Magazines

If you want to sell an article, poem, or how-to project to a magazine, you need not
copyright the material first because copyright protection exists from the moment you
create that work. Your primary consideration here is whether you will sell "all rights"
or only "first rights" to the magazine.

The sale of first rights means you are giving a publication permission to print your article, poem, or how-to project once, for a specific sum of money. After publication, you
then have the right to resell that material or profit from it in other ways. Although it is
always desirable to sell only "first rights," some magazines do not offer this choice.

If you sell all rights, you will automatically lose ownership of the copyright to your
material and you can no longer profit from that work. Professional designers often
refuse to work this way because they know they can realize greater profits by publishing their own pattern packets or design leaflets and wholesaling them to shops.

Things You Cannot Copyright

You can't copyright ideas or procedures for doing, making, or building things, but the *expression* of an idea fixed in a tangible medium may be copyrightable—such as a book explaining a new system or technique. Brand names, trade names, slogans, and phrases cannot be copyrighted, either, although they might be entitled to protection under trademark laws.

The design on a craft object can be copyrighted, but only if it can be identified separately from the object itself. Objects themselves (a decorated coffee mug, a box, a tote bag) cannot be copyrighted.

Copyright Registration Tips

First, understand that you do not have to formally copyright anything because copyright protection exists from the moment a work is created, whether you add a copyright notice or not.

So why file at all? The answer is simple: If you don't file the form and pay the fee (currently $20), you'll never be able to take anyone to court for stealing your work. Therefore, in each instance where copyright protection is considered, you need to decide how important your work is to you in terms of dollars and cents, and ask yourself whether you value it enough to pay to protect it. Would you actually be willing to pay court costs to defend your copyright, should someone steal it from you? If you never intend to go to court, there's little use in officially registering a copyright; but since it costs you nothing to add a copyright notice to your work, you are foolish not to do this. (See sidebar, "A Proper Copyright Notice," page 258.)

If you do decide to file a copyright application, contact the Copyright Office and request the appropriate forms. When you file the copyright application form (which is easy to complete), you must include with it two copies of the work. Ordinarily, two actual copies of copyrighted items must be deposited, but certain items are exempt from deposit requirements, including all three-dimensional sculptural works and any works published only as reproduced in or on jewelry, dolls, toys, games, plaques, floor coverings, textile and other fabrics, packaging materials, or any useful article. In these cases, two photographs or drawings of the item are sufficient.

Note that the Copyright Office does not compare deposit copies to determine whether works submitted for registration are similar to any material already copyrighted. It is the sender's responsibility to determine the originality of what's being copyrighted. (See discussion of "original" in the next section, under "Respecting the Copyrights of Others.")

Protecting Your Copyrights

If someone ever copies one of your copyrighted works, and you have registered that work with the Copyright Office, you should defend it as far as you are financially able to do so. If you think you're dealing with an innocent infringer—another crafter, perhaps, who has probably not profited much (if at all) from your work—a strongly worded letter on your business stationery (with a copy to an attorney, if you have one) might do the trick. Simply inform the copyright infringer that you are the legal owner of the work and the only one who has the right to profit from it. Tell the infringer that he or she must immediately cease using your copyrighted work, and ask for a confirmation by return mail.

If you think you have lost some money or incurred other damages, consult with a copyright attorney before contacting the infringer to see how you can best protect your rights and recoup any financial losses you may have suffered. This is particularly important if the infringer appears to be a successful business or corporation. Although you may have no intention of ever going to court on this matter, the copyright infringer won't know that, and one letter from a competent attorney might immediately resolve the matter at very little cost to you.

Mandatory Deposit Requirements

Although you do not have to officially register a copyright claim, it *is* mandatory to deposit two copies of all "published works" for the collections of the Library of Congress within three months after publication. Failure to make the deposit may subject the copyright owner to fines and other monetary liabilities, but it does not affect copyright protection. No special form is required for this mandatory deposit.

Note that the term "published works" pertains not just to the publication of printed matter, but to the public display of any item. Thus you "publish" your originally designed craftwork when you first show it at a craft fair, in a shop, on your Web site, or any other public place.

Respecting the Copyrights of Others

Just as there are several things you must do to protect your "intellectual creations," there are several things you must not do if you wish to avoid legal problems with other copyright holders.

Copyright infringement occurs whenever anyone violates the exclusive rights covered by copyright. If and when a copyright case goes to court, the copyright holder who has been infringed upon must prove that his or her work is the original creation and that the two works are so similar that the alleged infringer must have copied it. This is not always an easy matter, for "original" is a difficult word to define. Even the Copyright Office has trouble here, which is why so many cases that go to court end up setting precedents.

In any copyright case, there will be discussions about "substantial similarity," instances where two people actually have created the same thing simultaneously, loss of profits, or damage to one's business or reputation. If you were found guilty of copyright infringement, at the very least you would probably be ordered to pay to the original creator all profits derived from the sale of the copyrighted work to date. You would also have to agree to refund any orders you might receive for the work in the future. In some copyright cases where the original creator has experienced considerable financial loss, penalties for copyright infringement have been as high as $100,000. As you can see, this is not a matter to take lightly.

This is a complex topic beyond the scope of this book, but any book on copyright law will provide additional information if you should ever need it. What's important here is that you fully understand the importance of being careful to respect the legal rights of others. As a crafts business owner, you could possibly infringe on someone else's designs when you (1) quote someone in an article, periodical, or book you've written; (2) photocopy copyrighted materials; or (3) share information on the Internet. Following is a brief discussion of the first three topics and a longer discussion of the fourth.

1. **Be careful when quoting from a published source.** If you're writing an article or book and wish to quote someone's words from any published source (book, magazine, Internet, and so on), you should always obtain written permission first. Granted, minor quotations from published sources are okay when they fall under the Copyright Office's Fair Use Doctrine, but unless you completely understand this doctrine, you should protect yourself by obtaining permission before you quote anyone in one of your own written works. It is not necessarily the quantity of the quote, but the value of the quoted material to the copyright owner.

   In particular, never *ever* use a published poem in one of your written works. To the poet, this is a "whole work," much the same as a book is a whole work to an author. While the use of one or two lines of a poem, or a paragraph from a book may be considered "fair use," many publishers now require written permission even for this short reproduction of a copyrighted work.

2. **Photocopying can be dangerous.** Teachers often photocopy large sections of a book (sometimes whole books) for distribution to their students, but this is a flagrant violation of the copyright law. Some publishers may grant photocopying of part of a work if it is to be used only once as a teaching aid, but written permission must always be obtained first.

   It is also a violation of the copyright law to photocopy patterns for sale or trade because such use denies the creator the profit from a copy that might have been sold.

3. **Don't share copyrighted information on the Internet.** People everywhere are lifting material from *Reader's Digest* and other copyrighted publications and "sharing" them on the Internet through e-mail messages, bulletin boards, and the like. *This is a very dangerous thing to do.* "But I didn't see a copyright notice," you might say, or "It indicated the author was anonymous." What you must remember is that *everything* gains copyright protection the moment it is created, whether a copyright notice is attached to it or not. Many "anonymous" items on the Internet are actually copyrighted poems and articles put there by someone who not only violated the copyright law but compounded the matter by failing to give credit to the original creator.

   If you were to pick up one of those "anonymous" pieces of information and put it into an article or book of your own, the original copyright owner, upon seeing his or her work in your publication, would have good grounds for a lawsuit. Remember, pleading ignorance of the law is never a good excuse.

   Clearly there is no financial gain to be realized by violating the rights of a copyright holder when it means that any day you might be contacted by a lawyer and threatened with a lawsuit. As stated in my *Crafts Business Answer Book & Resource Guide:*

Changing Things

Many crafters have mistakenly been led to believe that they can copy the work of others if they simply change this or that so their creation doesn't look exactly like the one they have copied. But many copyright court cases have hinged in someone taking "a substantial part" of someone else's design and claiming it as their own. As explained earlier, if your "original creation" bears even the slightest resemblance to the product you've copied—and you are caught selling it in the commercial marketplace—there could be legal problems.

Crafters often combine the parts of two or three patterns in an attempt to come up with their own original patterns, but often this only compounds the possible copyright problems. Let's imagine you're making a doll. You might take the head from one pattern, the arms and legs from another, and the unique facial features from another. You may think you have developed an original creation (and perhaps an original pattern

The best way to avoid copyright infringement problems is to follow the "Golden Rule" proposed by a United States Supreme Court justice: "Take not from others to such an extent and in such a manner that you would be resentful if they so took from you."

Using Commercial Patterns and Designs

Beginning crafters who lack design skills commonly make products for sale using commercial patterns, designs in books, or how-to instructions for projects found in magazines. The problem here is that all of these things are published for the general consumer market and offered for *personal use* only. Because they are all protected by copyright, that means only the copyright holder has the right to profit from their use.

That said, let me ease your mind by saying that the sale of products made from copyrighted patterns, designs, and magazine how-to projects is probably not going to cause any problems *as long*

you might sell), but you haven't. Since the original designer of any of the features you've copied might recognize her work in your "original creation" or published pattern, she could come after you for infringing on "a substantial part" of her design. In this case, all you've done is multiply your possibilities for a legal confrontation with three copyright holders.

"But I can't create my own original designs and patterns!" you moan. Many who have said this in the past were mistaken. With time and practice, most crafters are able to develop products that are original in design, and I believe you can do this, too. Meanwhile, check out Dover Publications' *Pictorial Archive* series of books (see the "Things to Do" checklist and Resources). Here you will find thousands of copyright-free designs and motifs you can use on your craft work or in needlework projects. And don't forget the wealth of design material in museums and old books that have fallen into the public domain. (See sidebar, "What's in the Public Domain?" on page 272.)

as sales are limited, and they yield a profit only to you, the crafter. That means no sales through shops of any kind where a sales commission or profit is received by a third party, and absolutely no wholesaling of such products.

It's not that designers and publishers are concerned about your sale of a few craft or needlework items to friends and local buyers; what they are fighting to protect with the legality of copyrights is their right to sell their own designs or finished products in the commercial marketplace. You may find that some patterns, designs, or projects state "no mass production." You are not mass producing if you make a dozen handcrafted items for sale at a craft fair or holiday boutique, but you would definitely be considered a mass-producer if you made dozens, or hundreds, for sale in shops.

Consignment sales fall into a kind of gray area that requires some commonsense judgment on your part. This is neither wholesaling nor selling direct to consumers. One publisher might consider such sales a violation of a copyright while another might not.

Whenever specific guidelines for the use of a pattern, design, or how-to project is not given, the only way to know for sure if you are operating on safe legal grounds is to write to the publisher and get written permission on where you can sell reproductions of the item in question.

Now let's take a closer look at the individual types of patterns, designs, and how-to projects you might consider using once you enter the crafts marketplace.

Craft, Toy, and Garment Patterns

Today, the consumer has access to thousands of sewing patterns plus toy, craft, needlework, and woodworking patterns of every kind and description found in books, magazines, and design or project leaflets. Whether you can use such patterns for commercial use depends largely on who has published the pattern and owns the copyright, and what the copyright holder's policy happens to be for how buyers may use those patterns.

To avoid copyright problems when using patterns of any kind, the first thing you need to do is look for some kind of notice on the pattern packet or publication containing the pattern. In checking some patterns, I found that those sold by *Woman's Day* state specifically that reproductions of the designs may not be sold, bartered, or traded. *Good Housekeeping*, on the other hand, gives permission to use their patterns for "income-producing activities." When in doubt, ask!

Whereas the general rule for selling reproductions made from commercial patterns is "no wholesaling and no sales to shops," items made from the average garment pattern (such as an apron, vest, shirt, or simple dress) purchased in the local fabric store *may* be an exception. My research suggests that selling such items in your local consignment shop or craft mall isn't likely to be much of a problem because the sewing pattern companies aren't on the lookout for copyright violators the way individual craft designers and major corporations are. (And most people who sew end up changing those patterns and using different decorations to such a degree that pattern companies might not recognize those patterns even if they were looking for them. See sidebar, "Changing Things," page 264.)

On the other hand, commercial garment patterns that have been designed by name designers should never be used without permission. In most cases, you would have to obtain a licensing agreement for the commercial use of such patterns.

Be especially careful about selling reproductions of toys and dolls made from commercial patterns or design books. Many are likely to be for popular copyrighted characters being sold in the commercial marketplace. In such cases, the pattern company will have a special licensing arrangement with the toy or doll manufacturer to sell the pattern, and reproductions for sale by individual crafters will be strictly prohibited.

Take a Raggedy Ann doll, for example. The fact that you've purchased a pattern to make such a doll does not give you the right to sell a finished likeness of that doll any more than your purchase of a piece of artwork gives you the right to re-create it for sale in some other form, such as notepaper or calendars. Only the original creator has such rights. You have simply purchased the *physical property* for private use.

How-To Projects in Magazines and Books

Each magazine and book publisher has its own policy about the use of its art, craft, or needlework projects. How those projects may be used depends on who owns the copyright to the published projects. In some instances, craft and needlework designers sell their original designs outright to publishers of books, leaflets, or magazines. Other designers authorize only a one-time use of their projects, which gives them the right to republish or sell their designs to another market or license them to a manufacturer. If guidelines about selling finished products do not appear somewhere in the magazine or on the copyright page of a book, you should always write and get permission to make such items for sale. In your letter, explain how many items you would like to make, and where you plan to sell them, as that could make a big difference in the reply you receive.

In case you missed the special note on the copyright page of this book, you *can* make and sell all of the projects featured in this and any other book in Prima's FOR FUN & PROFIT series.

As a columnist for *Crafts Magazine,* I can also tell you that its readers have the right to use its patterns and projects for money-making purposes, but only to the extent that sales are limited to places where the crafter is the only one who profits from their use. That means selling directly to individuals, with no sales in shops of any kind where a third party would also realize some profit from a sale. Actually, this is a good rule-of-thumb guideline to use if you plan to sell only a few items of any project or pattern published in any magazine, book, or leaflet.

What's in the Public Domain?

For all works created after January 1, 1978, the copyright lasts for the life of the author or creator plus 50 years after his or her death. For works created before 1978, there are different terms, which you can obtain from any book in your library on copyright law.

Once material falls into the public domain, it can never be copyrighted again. As a general rule, anything with a copyright date more than 75 years ago is probably in the public domain, but you can never be sure without doing a thorough search. Some characters in old books—such as Beatrix Potter's *Peter Rabbit*—are now protected under the trademark law as business logos. For more information on this, ask the Copyright Office to send you its circular on "How to Investigate the Copyright Status of a Work."

Early American craft and needlework patterns of all kind are in the public domain because they were created before the copyright law was a reality. Such old patterns may

In summary, products that aren't original in design will sell, but their market is limited, and they will never be able to command the kind of prices that original-design items enjoy. Generally speaking, the more original the product line, the greater one's chances for building a profitable crafts business.

As your business grows, questions about copyrights will arise, and you will have to do a little research to get the answers you need. Your library should have several books on this topic and there is a wealth of information on the Internet. (Just use your search button and type "copyright information.") If you have a technical copyright question, remember that you can always call the Copyright Office and speak to someone who can answer it and send you additional information. Note, however, that regulations prohibit the Copyright Office from giving legal advice or opinions concerning the rights of persons in connection with cases of alleged copyright infringement.

show up in books and magazines that are copyrighted, but the copyright in this case extends only to the book or magazine itself and the way in which a pattern has been presented to readers, along with the way in which the how-to-make instructions have been written. The actual patterns themselves cannot be copyrighted by anyone at this point.

Quilts offer an interesting example. If a contemporary quilt designer takes a traditional quilt pattern and does something unusual with it in terms of material or colors, this new creation would quality for a copyright, with the protection being given to the quilt as a work of art, not to the traditional pattern itself, which is still in the public domain. Thus you could take that same traditional quilt pattern and do something else with it for publication, but you could not publish the contemporary designer's copyrighted version of that same pattern.

10. To Keep Growing, Keep Learning

Everything we do, every action we take, affects our life in one way or another. Reading a book is a simple act, indeed, but trust me when I say that your reading of this particular book *could ultimately change your life.* I know this to be true because thousands of men and women have written to me over the years to tell me how their lives changed after they read one or another of my books and decided to start a crafts business. My life has changed, too, as a result of reading books by other authors.

Many years ago, the purchase of a book titled *You Can Whittle and Carve* unleashed a flood of creativity in me that has yet to cease. That simple book helped me to discover unknown craft talents, which in turn led me to start my first crafts business at home. That experience prepared me for the message I would find a decade later in the book, *On Writing Well* by William Zinsser. This author changed my life by giving me the courage to try my hand at writing professionally. Dozens of books later, I had learned a lot about the art and craft of writing well and making a living in the process.

Now you know why I believe reading should be given top priority in your life. Generally speaking, the more serious you become about anything you're interested in, the more reading you will need to do. This will take time, but the benefits will be enormous. If a crafts business is your current passion, this book contains all you need to know to get started. To keep growing, read some of the wonderful books recommended in the resource section of this book. (If you don't find them in your local library, ask your librarian to obtain them for you through the inter-library loan program.) Join one or more of the organizations recommended. Subscribe to a few periodicals or magazines, and "grow your business" through networking with others who share your interests.

Motivational Tips

As you start your new business or expand a money-making hobby already begun, consider the following suggestions:

- *Start an "Achievement Log."* Day by day, our small achievements may seem insignificant, but viewed in total after several weeks or months, they give us important perspective. Reread your achievement log periodically in the future, especially on days when you feel down in the dumps. Make entries at least once a week, noting such things as new customers or accounts acquired, publicity you've gotten, a new product you've designed, the brochure or catalog you've just completed, positive feedback received from others, new friendships, and financial gains.

- *Live your dream.* The mind is a curious thing—it can be trained to think success is possible or to think that success is only for other people. Most of our fears never come true, so allowing our minds to dwell on what may or may not happen cripples us, preventing us from moving ahead, from having confidence, and from living out our dreams. Instead of "facing fear," focus on the result you want. This may automatically eliminate the fear.

- *Think positively.* As Murphy has proven time and again, what can go wrong will, and usually at the worst possible moment. It matters little whether the thing that has gone wrong was caused by circumstances beyond our control or by a mistake in judgment. What does matter is how we deal with the problem at hand. A positive attitude and the ability to remain flexible at all times are two of the most important ingredients for success in any endeavor.

- *Don't be afraid to fail.* We often learn more from failure than from success. When you make a mistake, chalk it up to experience and consider it a good lesson well learned. The more you learn, the more self-confident you will become.

- *Temper your "dreams of riches" with thoughts of reality.* Remember that "success" can also mean being in control of your own life, making new friends, or discovering a new world of possibilities.

Online Help

Today, one of the best ways to network and learn about business is to get on the Internet. The many online resources included in the "Things to Do Checklist" in the next section will give you a jump-start and lead to many exciting discoveries.

For continuing help and advice from Barbara Brabec, be sure to visit her Web site at www.crafter.com/brabec. There you will find her monthly *Craftsbiz Chat* newsletter, reprints of some of her crafts marketing and business columns, recommended books, and links to hundreds of other art and craft sites on the Web. Reader questions may be e-mailed to barbara@crafter.com for discussion in her newsletter, but questions cannot be answered individually by e-mail.

You can also get Barbara's business advice in her monthly columns in *Crafts Magazine* and *The Crafts Report*.

Until now you may have lacked the courage to get your craft ideas off the ground, but now that you've seen how other people have accomplished their goals, I hope you feel more confident and adventurous and are ready to capitalize on your creativity. By following the good advice in this book, you can stop dreaming about all the things you want to do and start making plans to do them!

I'm not trying to make home-business owners out of everyone who reads this book, but my goal is definitely to give you a shove in that direction if you're teetering on the edge, wanting something more than just a profitable hobby. It's wonderful to have a satisfying hobby, and even better to have one that pays for itself; but the nicest thing of all is a real home business that lets you fully utilize your creative talents and abilities while also adding to the family income.

"The things I want to know are in books," Abraham Lincoln once said. "My best friend is the person who'll get me a book I ain't read." You now hold in your hands a book that has taught you many things you wanted to know. To make it a *life-changing book,* all you have to do is act on the information you've been given.

I wish you a joyful journey and a potful of profits!

"Things to Do" Checklist

INSTRUCTIONS: Read through this entire section, noting the different things you need to do to get your crafts business "up and running." Use the checklist as a plan, checking off each task as it is completed and obtaining any recommended resources. Where indicated, note the date action was taken so you have a reminder about any follow-up action that should be taken.

Business Start-Up Checklist

__Call City Hall or County Clerk

    __to register fictitious business name

    __to see if you need a business license or permit

    __to check on local zoning laws
    (info also available in your library)

    *Follow up:*_____

__Call state capitol

    __Secretary of State: to register your business name;
    ask about a license

    __Dept. of Revenue: to apply for sales tax number

    *Follow up:*_____

__Call your local telephone company about

    __cost of a separate phone line for business

    __cost of an additional personal line for Internet access

    __any special options for home-based businesses

    *Follow up:*_____

__Call your insurance agent(s) to discuss

    __business rider on house insurance
    (or need for separate in-home insurance policy)
    __benefits of an umbrella policy for extra liability insurance
    __using your car for business
    (how this may affect your insurance)

    *Follow up:*_____

__Call several banks or S&Ls in your area to

    __compare cost of a business checking account
    __ get price of a safe-deposit box for valuable business records

    *Follow up:*_____

__Visit office and computer supply stores to check on

    __manual bookkeeping systems, such as the
    Dome Simplified Monthly
    __accounting software
    __standard invoices and other helpful business forms

    *Follow up:*_____

__Call National Association of Enrolled Agents at (800) 424-4339

    __to get a referral to a tax professional in your area
    __to get answers to any tax questions you may have (no charge)

    *Follow up:*_____

__Contact government agencies for information
relative to your business.

    (See "Government Agencies" checklist.)

__Request free brochures from organizations

    (See "Craft and Home Business Organizations.")

__Obtain sample issues or subscribe to selected publications

    (See "Recommended Craft Business Periodicals.")

__Obtain other information of possible help to your business

  (See "Other Services and Suppliers.")

__Get acquainted with the business information available to you in your library

  (See list of "Recommended Business Books" and "Helpful Library Directories.")

Government Agencies

__Consumer Product Safety Commission (CPSC), Washington, DC 20207. Toll-free hotline: (800) 638-2772. Information Services: (301) 504-0000. Web site: www.cpsc.gov. (Includes a "Talk to Us" e-mail address where you can get answers to specific questions.) If you make toys or other products for children, garments (especially children's wear), or use any kind of paint, varnish, lacquer, or shellac on your products, obtain the following free booklets:

  __*The Consumer Product Safety Act of 1972*
  __*The Flammable Fabrics Act*

  Date Contacted:_____Information Received:_____

  *Follow up:*_____

__Copyright Office, Register of Copyrights, Library of Congress, Washington, DC 20559. To hear recorded messages on the Copyright Office's automated message system (general information, registration procedures, copyright search info, etc.), call (202) 707-3000. You can also get the same information online at www.loc.gov/copyright.

  To get free copyright forms, a complete list of all publications available, or to speak personally to someone who will answer your special questions, call (202) 797-9100. In particular, ask for:

  __Circular R1, *The Nuts and Bolts of Copyright*
  __Circular R2 (a list of publications available)

Date Contacted:_____Information Received:_____

*Follow up:*_____

__Department of Labor. If you should ever hire an employee
or independent contractor, contact your local Labor Department, Wage & Hour Division, for guidance on what you must
do to be completely legal. (Check your phone book under
"U.S. Government.")

Date Contacted:_____Information Received:_____

*Follow up:*_____

__Federal Trade Commission (FTC), 6th Street & Pennsylvania
Avenue., N.W., Washington, DC 20580. Web site: www.ftc.gov. Request
any of the following booklets relative to your craft or business:

__*Textile Fiber Products Identification Act*

__*Wool Products Labeling Act of 1939*

__*Care Labeling of Textile Wearing Apparel*

__*The Hand Knitting Yarn Industry* (booklet)

__*Truth-in-Advertising Rules*

__*Thirty-Day Mail Order Rule*

Date Contacted:_____Information Received:_____

Follow up _____

__Internal Revenue Service (IRS). Check the Internet at www
.irs.gov to read the following information online or call your
local IRS office to get the following booklets and other free tax
information:

__*Tax Guide for Small Business—#334*

__*Business Use of Your Home—#587*

__*Tax Information for Direct Sellers*

Date Contacted:_____Information Received:_____

*Follow up*_____

__Patent and Trademark Office (PTO), Washington, DC 20231. Web site: www.uspto.gov

For patent and trademark information 24 hours a day, call (800) 786-9199 (in northern Virgina, call (703) 308-9000) to hear various messages about patents and trademarks or to order the follow-ing booklets:

__*Basic Facts about Patents*
__*Basic Facts about Trademarks*

To search the PTO's online database of all registered trademarks, go to www.uspto.gov/tmdb/index.html.

Date Contacted:_____Information Received:_____

*Follow up:*_____

__Social Security Hotline. (800) 772-1213. By calling this number, you can hear automated messages, order information booklets, or speak directly to someone who can answer specific questions.

Date Contacted:_____Information Received:_____

*Follow up*_____

__U.S. Small Business Administration (SBA). (800) U-ASK-SBA. Call this number to hear a variety of prerecorded messages on starting and financing a business. Weekdays, you can speak personally to an SBA adviser to get answers to specific questions and request such free business publications as:

__*Starting Your Business* —#CO-0028

__*Resource Directory for Small Business Management*—#CO-0042
   (a list of low-cost publications available from the SBA)

The SBA's mission is to help people get into business and stay there. One-on-one counseling, training, and workshops are available through 950 small business development centers across the country. Help is also available from local district offices of the

SBA in the form of free business counseling and training from SCORE volunteers (see below). The SBA office in Washington has a special Women's Business Enterprise section that provides free information on loans, tax deductions, and other financial matters. District offices offer special training programs in management, marketing, and accounting.

A wealth of business information is also available online at www.sba.gov and www.business.gov (the U.S. Business Advisor site). To learn whether there is an SBA office near you, look under "U. S. Government" in your telephone directory, or call the SBA's toll-free number.

Date Contacted:_____Information Received:_____

*Follow up:*_____

__SCORE (Service Corps of Retired Executives). (800) 634-0245. There are more than 12,400 SCORE members who volunteer their time and expertise to small business owners. Many craft businesses have received valuable in-depth counseling and training simply by calling the organization and asking how to connect with a SCORE volunteer in their area.

In addition, the organization offers e-mail counseling via the Internet at www.score.org. You simply enter the specific expertise required and retrieve a list of e-mail counselors who represent the best match by industry and topic. Questions can then be sent by e-mail to the counselor of your choice for response.

Date Contacted:_____Information Received:_____

*Follow up:*_____

Crafts and Home-Business Organizations

In addition to the regular benefits of membership in an organization related to your art or craft (fellowship, networking, educational conferences or workshops, marketing opportunities, etc.), membership may also bring special business services, such as insurance programs, merchant card services, and discounts on supplies and materials. Each of the following organizations will send you membership information on request.

__The American Association of Home-Based Businesses, P.O. Box 10023, Rockville, MD 20849. (800) 447-9710. Web site: www.aahbb.org. This organization has chapters throughout the country. Members have access to merchant card services, discounted business products and services, prepaid legal services, and more.

Date Contacted:_____Information Received:_____

*Follow up:*_____

__American Crafts Council, 72 Spring Street, New York, NY 10012. (800)-724-0859. Web site: www.craftcouncil.org. Membership in this organization will give you access to a property and casualty insurance policy that will cost between $250 and $500 a year, depending on your city, state, and the value of items being insured in your art or crafts studio. The policy includes insurance for a craftsperson's work in the studio, in transit or at a show; a million dollars' coverage for bodily injury and property damage in studio or away; and a million dollars' worth of product liability insurance. This policy is from American Phoenix Corporation; staff members will answer your specific questions when you call (800) 274-6364, ext. 337.

Date Contacted:_____Information Received:_____

*Follow up:*_____

__Arts & Crafts Business Solutions, 2804 Bishop Gate Drive, Raleigh, NC 27613. (800) 873-1192. This company, known in the industry as the Arts Group, offers a bankcard service specifically for and tailored to the needs of the arts and crafts marketplace. Several differently priced packages are available, and complete information is available on request.

Date Contacted:_____Information Received:_____

*Follow up:*_____

__Home Business Institute, Inc., P.O. Box 301, White Plains, NY 10605-0301. (888) DIAL-HBI; Fax: (914) 946-6694. Web site: www.hbiweb.com. Membership benefits include insurance programs (medical insurance and in-home business policy that includes some liability insurance); savings on telephone services, office supplies, and merchant account enrollment; and free advertising services.

Date Contacted:_____Information Received:_____

*Follow up:*_____

__National Craft Association (NCA), 1945 E. Ridge Road, Suite 5178, Rochester, NY 14622-2647. (800) 715-9594. Web site: www.craft assoc.com. Members of NCA have access to a comprehensive package of services, including merchant account services; discounts on business services and products; a prepaid legal program; a check-guarantee merchant program; checks by fax, phone, or e-mail; and insurance programs. Of special interest to this book's readers is the "Crafters Business Insurance" policy (through RLI Insurance Co.) that includes coverage for business property; art/craft merchandise or inventory at home, in transit or at a show; theft away from premises; up to a million dollars in both personal and product liability insurance; loss of business income, and more. Members have the option to select the exact benefits they need. Premiums range from $150 to $300, depending on location, value of average inventory, and the risks associated with one's art or craft.

Date Contacted:_____Information Received:_____

*Followup:*_____

Recommended Craft Business Periodicals

Membership in an organizations generally includes a subscription to a newsletter or magazine that will be helpful to your business. Here are additional craft periodicals you should sample or subscribe to:

__*The Crafts Report—The Business Journal for the Crafts Industry,* Box 1992, Wilmington, DE 19899. (800) 777-7098. On the Internet at www.craftsreport.com. A monthly magazine covering all areas of craft business management and marketing (includes Barbara Brabec's "BusinessWise" column).

__*Craft Supply Magazine—The Industry Journal for the Professional Crafter,* Krause Publications, Inc., 700 East State Street, Iowa, WI 54990-0001. (800) 258-0929. Web site: www.krause.com. A monthly magazine that includes crafts business and marketing articles and wholesale supply sources.

__*Home Business Report,* 2949 Ash Street, Abbotsford, B.C., V2S 4G5 Canada. (604) 857-1788; Fax: (604) 854-3087. Canada's premier home-business magazine, relative to both general and craft-related businesses.

__*SAC Newsmonthly,* 414 Avenue B, P.O. Box 159, Bogalusa, LA 70429-0159. (800) TAKE-SAC; Fax: (504) 732-3744. A monthly national show guide that also includes business articles for professional crafters.

__*Sunshine Artist Magazine,* 2600 Temple Drive, Winter Park, FL 32789. (800) 597-2573; Fax: (407) 539-1499. Web site: www.sun shineartist.com. America's premier show and festival guide.

Each monthly issue contains business and marketing articles of interest to both artists and craftspeople.

Other Services and Suppliers

Contact any of the following companies that offer information or services of interest to you.

__American Express. For merchant account information, call the Merchant Establishment Services Department at (800) 445-AMEX.

Date Contacted:_____Information Received:_____

*Follow up:*_____

__Dover Publications, 31 E. 2nd Sreet, Mineola, NY 11501. Your source for thousands of copyright-free designs and motifs you can use in your craftwork or needlecraft projects. Request a free catalog of books in the *Pictorial Archive* series.

Date Contacted:_____Information Received:_____

*Follow up:*_____

__Novus Services, Inc. For merchant account information, call (800) 347-6673.

Date Contacted:_____Information Received:_____

*Follow up:*_____

__Volunteer Lawyers for the Arts(VLA), 1 E. 53rd Street, New York, NY 10022. Legal hotline: (212) 319-2910. If you ever need an attorney, and cannot afford one, contact this nonprofit organization, which has chapters all over the country. In addition to providing legal aid for performing and visual artists and craftspeople (individually or in groups), the VLA also provides a range of educational services, including issuing publications concerning taxes, accounting, and insurance.

Date Contacted:_____Information Received:_____

*Follow up:*_____

__Widby Enterprises USA, 4321 Crestfield Road, Knoxville, TN
37921-3104. (888) 522-2458. Web site: www.widbylabel.com.
Standard and custom-designed labels that meet federal labeling
requirements.

Date Contacted:_____Information Received:_____

*Follow up:*_____

Recommended Business Books

When you have specific business questions not answered in this
beginner's guide, check your library for the following books. Any
not on library shelves can be obtained through the library's inter-
library loan program.

__*Business and Legal Forms for Crafts* by Tad Crawford (Allworth
Press)

__*Business Forms and Contracts (in Plain English) for Crafts People*
by Leonard D. DuBoff (Interweave Press)

__*Crafting as a Business* by Wendy Rosen (Chilton)

__*The Crafts Business Answer Book & Resource Guide: Answers to
Hundreds of Troublesome Questions about Starting, Marketing &
Managing a Homebased Business Efficiently, Legally, & Profitably*
by Barbara Brabec (M. Evans & Co.)

__*Creative Cash: How to Profit from Your Special Artistry, Creativity,
Hand Skills, and Related Know-How* by Barbara Brabec (Prima
Publishing)

__*422 Tax Deductions for Businesses & Self Employed Individuals* by
Bernard Kamoroff (Bell Springs Publishing)

__*Homemade Money: How to Select, Start, Manage, Market and Multiply the Profits of a Business at Home* by Barbara Brabec (Betterway Books)

__*How to Register Your Own Trademark with Forms* by Mark Warda, 2nd ed. (Sourcebooks)

__*INC Yourself: How to Profit by Setting Up Your Own Corporation*, by Judith H. McQuown (HarperBusiness)

__*Patent, Copyright & Trademark: A Desk Reference to Intellectual Property Law* by Attorney Stephen Elias (Nolo Press)

__*The Perils of Partners* by Irwin Gray (Smith-Johnson Publisher)

__*Small Time Operator: How to Start Your Own Business, Keep Your Books, Pay Your Taxes & Stay Out of Trouble* by Bernard Kamoroff (Bell Springs Publishing)

__*Trademark: How to Name a Business & Product* by McGrath and Elias (Nolo Press)

Helpful Library Directories

__*Books in Print* and *Guide to Forthcoming Books* (how to find out which books are still in print, and which books will soon be published)

__*Encyclopedia of Associations* (useful in locating an organization dedicated to your art or craft)

__*National Trade and Professional Associations of the U.S.* (more than 7,000 associations listed alphabetically and geographically)

__*The Standard Periodical Directory* (annual guide to U.S. and Canadian periodicals)

__*Thomas Register of American Manufacturers* (helpful when you're looking for raw material suppliers or the owners of brand names and trademarks)

__*Trademark Register of the U.S.* (contains every trademark currently registered with the U.S. Patent & Trademark Office)

Appendix A

▼▼

More Odds and Ends About Soapmaking

Colorants for Soap on the FDA Approved List

Annatto (no restrictions)

Beta-carotene (no restrictions)

Caramel (no restrictions)

Chromium hydroxide greens (may be used externally, including in the eye area)

Chromium oxide greens (may be used externally, including in the eye area)

Iron oxides (no restrictions)

Manganese violet (no restrictions)

Mica (no restrictions)

Titanium dioxide (no restrictions)

Ultramarines: blue, green, pink, red, and violet (externally including eye area)

Zinc oxide (no restrictions)

Artists' Pigments

Chromium hydroxide green
—Viridian (Pigment Green 18)

Chromium oxide green
—Pigment Green 17

Iron oxides—Pigment Reds 101 & 102, Pigment Yellows 42 & 43, Pigment Brown 7

Manganese violet—Pigment Violet 16

Titanium dioxide—Pigment White 6

Ultramarine blue—Pigment Blue 29

Ultramarine pink, red, or violet
—Pigment Violet 15

Zinc oxide—Pigment White 4

Calibrating Your Scales for Smaller Measurements

I found this clever tip on an Internet soap mailing list. To find out if your scale is accurate, buy a pound of butter or margarine (the kind with four sticks). One stick weighs 4 ounces (or a quarter pound). Weigh one stick. The scale should read 4 ounces (1/4 pound). Then add another stick. The weight should read 8 ounces (1/2 pound). Then add the third stick. The scale should read 12 ounces (3/4 pound). Finally add the fourth stick. The scale should read 16 ounces (1 pound). A new scale should always be checked before using it.

Properties at a Glance

Common carrier oils: Sweet almond, apricot kernel oil, avocado oil, baby oil, California walnut oil, coconut oil, cottonseed oil, emu oil, grape seed oil, hazelnut, hemp seed oil, lard, lime oil, macadamia nut oil, olive oil, palm oil, pumpkinseed oil, safflower oil, soybean oil, sunflower oil, wheat germ oil.

Common saponification fats/oils: Almond oil, apricot kernel oil, avocado oil, beef fat/tallow, canola oil/canolive oil, castor oil, coconut oil, corn oil, emu oil, grape seed oil, hemp seed oil, lard, lime oil, macadamia nut oil, olive oil, palm oil, peanut oil, pumpkinseed oil, safflower oil, sesame oil, shortening/vegetable oil, soybean oil, sunflower oil.

Common superfatting oils: Almond oil, apricot kernel oil, avocado oil, baby oil, California walnut oil, canola oil/canolive oil, castor oil, cocoa butter, coconut oil, corn oil, cottonseed oil, emu oil, grape seed oil, hazelnut oil, hemp seed oil, lard, lime oil, macadamia nut oil, olive oil, palm oil, peanut oil, pumpkinseed oil, safflower oil, sesame oil, shortening/vegetable oil, soybean oil, sunflower oil, wheat germ oil.

Emollients: Castor oil, coconut oil, cottonseed oil, emu oil.

Fillers: Almonds, coffee, wheat germ, oatmeal, flower petals, herbs.

Fixatives: Clay, wax, dried herbs, groundnuts, base or carrier oils.

Hardeners: Beeswax, cocoa butter, coconut oil, lard, lime oil, macadamia nut oil, olive oil, palm oil.

Preservatives: Lemon (juice or peel), lime (juice or peel), vitamin E, grapefruit seed extract.

Appendix B

▼▼▼

Troubleshooting with Melt-and-Pour, Rebatching Cold-Process, or Hand-Milled Soap

1. **Soap is too soft to remove from mold?**

   Problem: Too much liquid was added to the batch.

   Solution: Allow to cure longer or add more water to make a liquid soap.

2. **Air bubbles in soap?**

   Problem: Stirred too much, stirred too fast, or re-melted at too high a temperature.

   Solution: Re-melt, rebatch, or hand-mill batch again. There is no problem with using the soap. This is just an appearance problem.

3. **White scumlike substance on soap?**

   Problem: Impurities in soap base or rebatched or hand-milled soap. Also can be caused by fragrance, essential oil, colorant, or any other additive.

   There is no problem with using the soap. This is just an appearance problem. Shaving small irregularities and bumps with a vegetable peeler can smooth out the soap. Also try lightly wetting soap with water and smoothing with your fingers.

Troubleshooting with Cold-Process Soapmaking

1. **Soap won't trace?**

   Problem: Not enough lye, too much water, wrong temperatures, or stirring too slowly.

   Solution: Double-check all your numbers with a lye calculator. Speed up stirring. After four hours of stirring, pour soap into molds and insulate. Inspect soap after 24 hours. If not setting or if soap separates, properly dispose of soap.

2. **Lye and fat separate while pouring into mold or while in mold?**

   Problem: Inaccurate measuring of ingredients.

   Solution: Reheat entire mixture to 110–120 degrees Fahrenheit. Stir until completely melted and trace begins. Pour soap into mold and wrap to insulate. If it separates again, properly dispose of soap.

3. **Soap seizes before pouring into mold?**

   Problem: The cooking temperature was too high or too low, soap reacted to fragrance or essential oil, or too much saturated fat was used.

   Solution: Pour or scoop quickly into mold. Smooth as best as possible with spatula.

4. **Soap curdles while making recipe or rebatching for hand-milled soaps?**

   Problem: Cooling recipe too fast, measuring ingredients inaccurately, adding dyes or additives with too much sodium, or stirring irregularly or not stirring briskly.

   Solution: If curdling comes from inaccurate measuring, see Question 1. If it is from too much sodium, try diluting it while re-melting. Weigh out another batch of soap and water and add it to the hand-milled soap. Reheat and combine. If curdling happens in this batch, properly dispose of soap.

5. **When cutting soap for rebatching or creating hand-milled soap there is clear liquid in the soap?**

   Problem: Too much lye in recipe.

   Solution: Remember to wear gloves at all times with cold-process soaps. This liquid is a lye pocket. If pockets are large, throw it out. When you find small pockets just cut up the soap for rebatching or hand-milling. Rinse off lye and allow soap to dry. Proceed with rebatching or hand-milled recipe.

6. **Soap in mold is grainy, streaky, or has air bubbles, cracks, or other irregularities?**

   Problem: Soap was stirred too long or too fast, or there was not enough lye or too much water.

   Solution: Test the pH of the soap with a pH strip. In most cases these problems only effect the soap's appearance and do not affect usage. Small irregularities and bumps can be shaved with a vegetable peeler. Also try lightly wetting soap and smoothing with your fingers.

7. **Soap is very soft or too soft to remove from mold without losing shape?**

   Problem: Either not enough lye or too much water was used.

Solution: Recheck all your measurements. Try curing for a couple more weeks. If still too soft, check the pH. If pH is within acceptable reading, you can add more water to make liquid soap. Otherwise properly dispose of soap.

8. **Soap is extremely hard or excessively brittle?**

   Problem: Too much lye was used.

   Solution: There is no way to correct this soap batch, properly dispose of soap.

9. **Soap is mottled or has shiny white spots or white powdery substance?**

   Problem: Too much lye was used, soap was stirred too slowly, or hard water was used and lye didn't dissolve properly.

   Solution: There is no way to correct this soap batch. Soap will be caustic, so properly dispose of soap.

Glossary

▼▼

Soapmaking

Abrasives: Gritty or rough substances added to soap to help scrub away dirt or dead outer skin cells. Also help remove excess oils from skin. Also considered an exfoliant. Avoid with delicate or dry skin types.

Absolute: Products, not strictly essential oils, obtained through chemical solvent extraction.

Allergy/Allergic: Hypersensitivity or reaction caused by a substance or an ingredient.

Antioxidant: Ingredient that retards the deterioration of the soap and prevents natural/fresh ingredients from combining with oxygen and becoming rancid.

Antiseptic: Ingredients that inhibit the growth of bacteria on living tissue or in soap.

Aroma/Aromatic: Having scent, flavor, or taste.

Aromatherapy: Using scents or essential oils to affect a person's mental or physical well being.

Aromatherapy benefit: The emotional or physical effect, including balance, energy, rejuvenation, cleansing, de-odorizing, and purifying, evoked by aromatic essential.

Astringents: Substances or additives to soap that tighten or close skin pores. The effect makes skin feel smoother.

Blenders: Additional scents combined with a main scent to enhance and fix the scents into a single blended fragrance.

Botanical name: Refers to the Latin name of the plant in the biological classification system. Is composed of the genus followed by the species.

Carrier oil: Oil base in which essential oils are diluted to create massage blends and body-care products. Has little or no scent.

Cold-press extraction: *See* Expression.

Dermal: Pertaining to the skin.

Disinfectant: Prevents or combats the spread of germs.

Emollients: Additives that soften skin.

Enfleurage: Age-old method of extracting essential oils using odorless fats and oils to absorb the oil from the plant material.

Essential oil: Highly concentrated, volatile, aromatic essences of plants.

Exfoliant: *See* Abrasives.

Expression: Method of obtaining essential oil from plant material, such as citrus fruit peel. The complete oil is physically forced from the plant material. Also known as cold-press extraction.

Extraction method: The method by which essential oils are separated from the plant. Common extraction methods include distillation, expression, and solvent extraction.

Fillers: Ingredients that add bulk or extend a soap's life.

Fixatives: Ingredients that stabilize volatile oils and prevent them from evaporating too quickly.

Food grade: Safe for use in food according to the Food and Drug Administration.

Fragrance oil: Fragrances and scents derived by synthetic means.

Herbal: Pertaining to natural botanicals and living plants.

Holistic: A natural approach to healing. Outside Western medicine conventions.

Homeopathy: Therapy that uses plant, animal, and mineral substances in dilutions to overcome illness by stimulating the body's natural immunity.

Hydrating: Restoring or maintaining normal proportion of fluid in the body or skin.

Insoluble: Unable to be dissolved in a liquid such as water.

Irritant: Substance or material that produces irritation or inflammation of the skin.

Main scent: Dominant scent to which other scents can be added to create a new single blended scent.

Nervine: Strengthening or toning the nerves or nervous system.

Olfactory: Relating to or connected with the sense of smell.

Potpourri: Fragrant mixture of dried herbs and flowers. Usually scented with synthetic fragrance oils.

Refrigerant: Ingredient that cools inflammation or eases muscle pain.

Relaxant: Ingredient that is soothing and that relieves strain or tension.

Rendering: The process of removing impurities in animal fats by heating. Creates tallow, or pure fat, used in soapmaking.

Sedative: Ingredient that reduces functional activity or calms.

Single note: Pure, 100% natural essential oil; no additives; no adulterations.

Soluble: Able to be dissolved in a liquid such as water.

Stimulant: Ingredient or substance that temporarily speeds the functional activity of a human tissue.

Synergistic: Characteristic in which the total effect is more effective than the individual parts.

Synergistic blend: Combination of multiple essential oils that produces a completely new aroma with a different therapeutic effect.

Synthetic: Artificially produced substance designed to imitate that which occurs naturally.

Viscosity: Pertaining to the thickness or thinness of a liquid.

Volatile: Essential oils that evaporate very easily or quickly. Fixatives stabilize oils, resulting in a longer lasting scent.

Volatilization: Rate of evaporation or oxidation of an essential oil.

Wild: Growing spontaneously, not cultivated.

Business Terms

Accounts payable: Money you owe for goods or services received.

Accounts receivable: Money owed to your business for goods or services delivered.

Back order: Items not shipped in an order may be sent at a later date to buyer.

Break-even: Point at which business is not making or losing money. Total revenue equals total expenses.

Budget: Financial plan to control spending.

CCD: Certified Craft Designer

COD account: Cash or check on delivery. Payment is due upon receipt from a common carrier.

Common carrier: Transportation service or company that delivers supplies. For example, UPS.

Consumer: End user

Cost of good sold: Direct cost to business owner of items that will in turn be sold to consumer.

CPD: Certified Professional Demonstrator

Dealer minimum: Also called minimum order. Lowest quantity of an item(s) that must be purchased or the lowest dollar amount that must be spent to place an order with a supplier.

Distributor: Middleman who markets and sells to retailers.

Gross price: Price of product before discounts, deductions, or allowances.

Invoice: Itemized statement from supplier/vendor stating charges for merchandise.

Manufacturer: Business that makes product(s) from raw materials.

Net price: Actual price paid for products/supplies after deductions, discounts, and allowances are subtracted.

Open account: Credit extended to a business for a specific billing period.

Purchase order: Record of agreement made with supplier from buyer.

Retailer: Business that sells directly to the consumer.

Sales representative: Person who sells a product(s) usually in a specific geographic area for a commission. Company representatives work for a specific manufacturer/distributor and independent representatives work for more than one line.

SKU: Stock Keeping Unit. Unit assigned to a product or an item, usually designated with a bar code, for inventory control.

Terms of sale: The conditions concerning who can purchase goods and payment of purchase.

Trade association: An organization of businesses in the same line of work promoting common interests.

Trade publication: Printed material intended for trade-only consumption.

Trade show: Gathering of individuals and businesses in a common industry to display, educate, and sell products/services to other members within the common industry.

Wholesaler: Business that sells to others for resale.

Resources

▼▼▼

Recommended Books

Brabec, Barbara. *Creative Cash*, 6th Edition. Rocklin, CA: Prima, 1998.

Cameron, Julia. *The Artist's Way.* New York, NY: Putnam, 1992.

Edwards, Betty. *Drawing on the Artist Within.* New York, NY: Simon & Schuster, 1989.

Edwards, Betty. *Drawing on the Right Side of the Brain.* New York, NY: Simon & Schuster, 1989.

Edwards, Paul, and Sarah Edwards. *Working from Home.* New York, NY: Putnam, 1994.

Field, Edwin M., and Selma G. Field. *Promoting & Marketing Your Crafts.* New York, NY: Macmillan, 1994.

Ganim, Barbara. *The Designer's Common Sense Business Book.* Cincinnati, OH: North Light Books, 1994.

Gerhards, Paul. *How to Sell What You Make: The Business of Marketing Crafts.* Mechanicsbury, PA: Stackpole Books, 1996.

Jefferson, Brian T. *Profitable Crafts Marketing: A Complete Guide to Successful Selling.* Portland, OR: Timber Press, 1985.

Landman, Sylvia. *Crafting for Dollars.* Rocklin, CA: Prima, 1996.

Lehmkuhl, Dorothy, and Dolores Cotter Lamping. *Organizing for the Creative Person.* New York, NY: Crown Trade Paperbacks, 1993.

Manolis, Argie. *Crafts Market Place: Where and How to Sell Your Crafts.* Cincinnati, OH: Betterway Books, 1985.

Nadeau, Alyce. *Making & Selling Herbal Crafts.* New York, NY: Sterling, 1996.

Oberrecht, Ken. *How to Open and Operate a Home-Based Craft Business.* Saybrook, CT: The Globe Pequot Press, 1994.

Platt, Ellen. *How to Profit from Flower and Herb Crafts.* Mechanicsburg, PA: Stackpole Books, 1996.

Seitz, James E. *Selling What You Make: Profit from your Handcrafts.* Blue Ridge Summit, PA: TAB Books, 1993.

Aromatherapy, Soapmaking, and Essential Oils

Allardice, Pamela. *The Art of Aromatherapy.* Avenel, NJ: Crescent Books, 1995.

Browning, Marie. *Beautiful Handmade Natural Soaps.* New York, NY: Sterling, 1998.

Cavitch, Susan Miller. *The Natural Soap Book.* Pownal, VT: Storey, 1995.

Cavitch, Susan Miller. *The Soapmaker's Companion*. Pownal, VT: Storey, 1997.

Duff, Gail. *A Book of Herbs & Spices*. Topsfield, MA: Beaufort Books, 1987.

Duff, Gail. *A Book of Pot-Pourri*. Topsfield, MA: Beaufort Books, 1985.

Lawless, Julia. *The Encyclopaedia of Essential Oils*. Rockport, MA: Element, 1996.

Purchon, Nerys. *Health and Beauty the Natural Way*. New York, NY: Metro Books, 1997.

Reno, Kelly. *Soaps, Shampoos & Other Suds*. Rocklin, CA: Prima, 1996.

Reno, Kelly. *Oils, Lotions & Other Luxuries*. Rocklin, CA: Prima, 1996.

Recommended Magazines

Craftrends (Trade Only)
Editor: Bill Gardner
Publisher: PRIMEDIA Special Interest Group
741 Corporate Circle, Suite A
Golden, CO 80401
Phone: 309-682-6626
Fax: 309-682-7394
Web site: www.craftrends.com

Fairs and Festivals
Division of Continuing Education, University of Massachusetts, Amherst, MA 01003
Phone: 413-545-2360

Fax: 413-545-3351
E-mail: aes@admin.umass.edu
Web site: www.umass.edu

Potpourri Simple & Easy Update
Publisher: Prosperity & Profits Unlimited Distribution Services
Box 416, Denver, CO 80201-0416
Phone: 303-575-5576

Sunshine Artist Magazine
2600 Temple Drive, Winter Park, FL 32789
Phone: 407-539-1399
Toll-free phone: 800-804-4607
Fax: 407-539-1499

Art and Craft Suppliers and Product Resources

Specialty Suppliers

Environmental Lighting Concepts
(True Spectrum Lighting)

3923 Coconut Palm Drive
Tampa, FL 33619

Toll-free phone: 800-842-8848

Fiskars
(Ergonomically Correct Tools)

7811 West Stewart Avenue
Wausau, WI 54402-8027

Phone: 715-842-2091

Fax: 715-848-3657

Soap Base, Soap, Herbs, Scents, Spices, and Essential Oils Suppliers

Action Bag Co.
(packaging)

Phone: 900-824-BAGS

Alameen Fragrances
P.O. Box 2904, Kingston, NY 12401

Phone: 914-338-4398

Toll-free phone: 800-914-4398

Anderson Country Products
Kim Anderson

P.O. Box 451

Coeur d'Alene, ID 83816

Phone: 208-687-5012

E-mail: Kawolf430@aol.com

Web site: www.angelfire.com/yt/
AndersonCountryProd/index.html

Aroma Vera
5901 Rodeo Road,
Los Angeles, CA
90016-4312

Toll-free phone: 800-669-9514

Associated Bag Company
(packaging)

Toll-free phone: 800-926-6100

Aura Cacia
P.O. Box 399, Weaverville, CA 96093

Toll-free phone: 800-437-3301

Avena Botanicals
20 Mill Street, Rockland, ME 04841

Phone: 207-594-0694

B & B Products, Inc.
(Etching Supplies)

18700 North 107th Avenue #13,
Sun City, Arizona 85373-9759

U.S. toll-free phone: 888-382-4255

U.S. toll-free fax: 877-329-3824

International fax: 602-815-9095

Botanical Beauty Products
2870-E NE Hogan Road, Dept. 247,
Gresham, OR 97030

Buty Wave Products Co.
7323 Beverly Boulevard,
Los Angeles, CA 90036

Phone: 213-936-2191

Camden-Grey Essential Oils
8567 Coral Way, #178, Miami, FL 33155
Toll-free phone: 877-232-7662

Caswell-Massey Co., Ltd.
100 Enterprise Place, Dover, DE 19901
Toll-free phone: 800-326-0500

Chem Lab (pH test strips)
Costello Imports
561 Broadway, Sonoma, CA 95476
Toll-free phone: 800-388-7273

Creative Fragrances Manufacturing
10890 Alder Circle, Dallas, TX 75238
Phone: 214-341-3666

Delta Technical Coatings (paint, stencils, brushes)
2550 Pellissier Place, Whittier, CA 90601

Devonshire Apothecary
P.O. Box 160215, Austin, TX 78716-0215
Phone: 512-442-0019

Dragon Marsh
3737 6th Street, Riverside, CA 92501
Phone: 909-276-1116

Earthen Scents
RR 3 Box 450, Glouster, OH 45732
Phone: 740-767-2885
E-mail: DrFrog@frognet.net

Edmund Scientific
101 East Gloucester Pike
Barrington, NJ 08007

The Essential Oil Company
P.O. Box 206, Lake Oswego, OR 97034
Toll-free phone: 800-729-5912

ETI/Environmental Technology, Inc
PO Box 365, Fields Landing, CA 95537
Phone: 707-443-9323
Fax: 707-443-7962
Web site: www.eti-usa.com

Eye of the Cat
3314 East Broadway,
Long Beach, CA 90803
Phone: 310-438-3569

The Fanning Corp.
2450 West Hubbard Street,
Chicago, IL 60612
Phone: 312-248-5700
Toll-free phone: 800-FANNING

Fragrant Fields
128 Front Street, Dongola, IL 62926
Toll-free phone: 800-635-0282

Gaia Products
62 Kent Street, Brooklyn, NY 11222
Phone: 212-532-4188

Herbs & Such
15922 76th Street, Live Oak, FL 32060
Phone: 904-362-6903
E-mail: jenkins@glenbrookfarm.com

Greenfield Herb Garden
1135 Woodbine, Oak Park, IL 60302
Phone: 219-768-7110

The Herbfarm
32804 Issaquah-Fall City Road,
Fall City, WA 98024
Phone: 206-784-2222

Indiana Botanic Gardens, Inc.
3401 West Thirty-Seventh Avenue,
Hobart, IN 46342
Phone: 219-947-4040

International Imports
236 West Manchester Avenue
Los Angeles, CA 90003
Phone: 213-778-2233
OR
2637-45 Webster Avenue, Bronx, NY 10458
Phone: 718-933-7700

Jancas Jojoba Oil and Seed Co
Phone: 602-497-9494

Kamala Perfumes
712 West Park Avenue
Champagne, IL 61820
Phone: 217-355-8555

Lavender Lane
6715 Donerail Drive
Sacramento, CA 95842
Phone: 916-334-4400

Lebermuth
P.O. Box 4103, South Bend, IN 46634
Toll-free phone: 800-648-1123

Logee's Greenhouse
North Street, Danielson, CT 06239

Lorann Oils
4518 Aurelius Road, P.O. Box 22009,
Lansing, MI 48909-2009
Toll-free phone (outside Michigan):
800-248-1302
Toll-free phone (within Michigan):
800-862-8620

Mann Lake Supply
County Road 40 & First Street
Hackensack, MN 56452
Toll-free phone: 800-233-6663

Meadows Direct
13805 Highway 136, Onslow, IA 52321
Phone: 319-485-2723

Mountain Rose
Box 2000, Redway, CA 95560
Toll-free phone: 800 879-3337

Nature's Herb Co.
1010 Forty-Sixth Street
Emeryville, CA 94608
Phone: 415-601-0700

The Original Swiss Aromatics
PO Box 6842, 28 Paul Drive, Suite F
San Rafael, CA 94903
Phone: 415-459-3998

PT BAG (packaging)
Toll-free phone: 800-448-5891

Penn Herb Co., Ltd.
603 North Second Street
Philadelphia, PA 19123-3098
Toll-free phone: 800-523-9971

Pourette
PO Box 15220, Seattle, WA 98115
Phone: 206-525-4488

The Preferred Source
3637 West Alabama, Suite 160
Houston, TX 77027
Phone: 713-622-2190

Renaissance Acres
4450 Valentine, Whitmore Lake, MI 48189

San Francisco Herb Company
250 14th Street, San Francisco, CA 94103
Toll-free phone: 800-227-4530

Sappo Hills Soapworks
654 Tolman Creek Road
Ashland, OR 97520
Phone: 503-482-4485

Scent from the Heart
8001 NE Mesa #106, El Paso, TX 79932
Phone: 915-584-7871

Soap Crafters Company
2944 South West Temple
Salt Lake City, UT 84115
Phone: 801-484-5121
Fax: 801-487-1958

The Soap Opera
319 State Street, Madison, WI 53703
Phone: 608-251-4051
Toll-free phone: 800-251-7627
Fax: 608-251-1703
Web site: www.thesoapopera.com

SoapMeister Marsh
P.O. Box 231, Ardenvoir, WA 98811
Phone: 509-784-2033
Fax: 509-784-1706

Soap Saloon
7309 Sage Oak Court,
Citrus Heights, CA 95621
Phone: 916-723-6859

St. John's Herb Garden, Inc.
7711 Hillmeade Road, Bowie, MD 20720
Phone: 301-262-5302
Fax: 301-262-2489

Sugarplum's Sundries
5152 Fair Forest Drive,
Stone Mountain, GA 30088
Phone: 404-297-0158

Sunburst Bottle Company
7001 Sunburst Way
Citrus Heights, CA 95621
Phone: 916-722-4632

Sunfeather Herbal Soap Co.
HCR 84, Box 60A-Q, Potsdam, NY 13676
Phone: 315-365-3648

Sunflower Soap and Herb Co.
2411 Robley Street, Pasadena, TX 77502
E-mail: Soaponia@aol.com

Sunrise Herb Co.
4808 Dreams End Drive
Louisville. KY 40291
Phone: 502-493-7132

Sunshine Soapworks
Cari Bourassa
5703 Red Bug Lake Road, PMB 266
Winter Springs, FL 32708
Phone: 407-695-6969
E-mail: soapworks@email.com
Web site: www.sunshinesoapworks.com

Super Soap Company
2655 Ingalls Street
San Francisco, CA 94124
Phone: 415-822-7363

Valley Hills Press
1864 Ridgeland Drive
Starkville, MS 39759
Toll-free phone: 800-323-7102

Violet Star Aromatics
6700 South Dairy Ashford, Suite 503,
Houston, TX 77072
Phone: 713-575-6080
E-mail: violetstar@earthlink.net

Walnut Acres Farm
Toll-free phone: 800-433-3998

Warsaw Chemical Co., Inc.
P.O. Box 858, 390 Argonne Road
Warsaw, IN 46580
Toll-free phone: 800-548-3396
Fax: 219-267-3884
E-mail: WCC@WARSAW-CHEM.COM

Weleda, Inc.
P.O. Box 249, Congers, NY 10920

Phone: 914-268-8572
Toll-free phone: 800-241-1030

The Whole Herb Company
19800 8th Street East, P.O. Box 1203,
Sonoma, CA 95476
Phone: 707-935-1077

Wood Violet Books
3814 Sunhill Drive, Madison, WI 53704
Phone: 608-837-7207

Wyndham Soapworks
Christin Ocasio
PMB #259, 177 W. Alexander Street
Plant City, FL 33566-7155
Phone: 813-754-7523
E-mail: tabbi@ns.icubed.net
Web site: www.angelfire.com/biz2/
Wyndham Soapworks

General Supplies (Carry Most Supplies Needed in Packaging or Decorating Soaps)

Alpine Import Crafts Supplies
7106 North Alpine Road
Rockford, IL 61111
Phone: 815-654-2746
Toll-free phone: 800-654-6114
E-mail:
customer_service@alpineimport.com

Craft King
PO Box 90637, Lakeland, FL 33804
Toll-free phone: 888-272-3891

National Artcraft
7996 Darrow Road, Twinsburg, OH 44087
Toll-free phone: 888-937-2723
E-mail: nationalartcraft@worldnet.att.net

Sax
P.O. Box 510710, New Berlin, WI 53151-0710
U.S. fax (toll-free): 800-328-4729
Canada fax: 905-356-3700

Sunshine Discount Crafts
12335 62nd Street North, Largo, FL 33773
Toll-free phone: 800-729-2878

Zim's
Box 57620, Salt Lake City, UT 84157
Phone: 801-268-2505
E-mail: ranae@interserv.com

Waxes

Candle Cents
673 Street, Highway 165,
Branson, MO 65616
Phone: 417-336-3915
Toll-free: 888-336-3915
Fax: 417-336-4955

Candlechem Co., Inc.
56 Intervale Street, Brockton, MA 02302
Phone: 508-586-1880
Fax: 508-586-1784
E-mail: candlechem@mediaone.net

Glorybee Foods, Inc.
120 North Seneca Road, Eugene, OR 97402

Honey Wax
CR 40 & 1st Street,
Hackensack, MN 56452
Toll-free phone: 800-880-7694
Fax: 218-675-6156
E-mail: honeywax@mannlakeltd.com
Web site: www.mannlakeltd.com

Mid-Con
8883 Lenexa Drive,
Overland, KS 66215-3913
Toll-free phone: 800-547-1392

Yaley
7672 Avianca Drive, Redding, CA 96002
Phone: 916-365-5252
Fax: 916-365-6483
E-mail: info@yaley.com
Web site: www.yaley.com

Recommended Web Sites

Amnesi: www.amnesi.com
If you can't remember the exact URL of a Web site, tell Amnesi what you remember. It will provide of list of sites that it thinks match. The Java interface is a bit clunky and slow, but the results are impressive.

Ask Jeeves: www.askjeeves.com
A human-powered search service that aims to direct you to the exact page to answer your question. If it fails to find a match within its own database, then it will provide matching Web pages from various search engines.

Art and Craft Show Net:
www.artandcraftshows.net

Search database of more than 2000 shows

DejaNews: www.dejanews.com

Devoted to searching newsgroup discussions, with archives stretching back to March 1995.

FindMail: www.egroups.com

Similar to DejaNews, but only for mailing lists. FindMail allows you to search for mailing lists of interest or to read actual messages and post via an online interface.

Information Please: www.infoplease.com

Information Please almanacs are favorites among researchers who need trustworthy facts. This site allows searching across Information Please's various almanacs, its encyclopedia, and its dictionary.

List of Lists: catalog.com/vivian /interest-group-search.html

Search or browse for lists of interest.

Liszt: www.liszt.com

Long a favorite for those looking for mailing lists.

Publicly Accessible Mailing Lists (PAML): www.neosoft.com/internet/paml

Another well-known place to find mailing lists.

U.S. Trademark Search Page: trademarks.uspto.gov/access /search-mark.html

Enter a few words, and you can quickly discover if a trademark has been registered in the United States containing those words. It is free and easy and comes courtesy of the U.S. Patent and Trademark Office. The link provided is to the "Combined Marks" search page, which is very easy to use.

When.com: www.when.com

An events directory and personal calendar Web site. Users can browse event listings, ranging from Internet chat sessions to upcoming trade shows. Events can then be linked to a Web-based personal calendar.

World Wide Art Resources: wwar.com/index.html

Artists, museums, galleries, art history, arts education, antiques, performing arts ranging from dance to opera, classified ads, résumé postings and more.

General Soapmaking

hometown.aol.com/ALather1/news.htm

www.snowdriftfarm.com

www.esosoft.com/thelibrary/index.htm

www.angelfire.com/mi/soapnutshome /index.html

www.gentleridge.com

www.teleport.com/~liberty/soapmakr .html

www.angelfire.com/biz/Countryman /index.html

soapcrafters.com

www.utec.net/bhcs/candle.htm

gaylor-web.com/index.html

www.execpc.com/~bcsupply/soaptemp
.html

waltonfeed.com/old/soaphome.html

www.soapguild.org

www.soapmakersreview.com

www.thepetalpusher.com/sap.html

www.silverlink.net/~timer/soapinfo
.html

www.angelfire.com/fl2/flsoapers/index
.html

www.angelfire.com/mi/countrypetaler
/indexsoap.html

www.dejanews.com/~soapaddicts

www.maxpages.com/killmastersoap

www.soapmakingtoday.com

www.ziggurat.org/soap

www.delphi.com/iasoap

members.aol.com/jillspc/soap/soap.htm

www.lis.ab.ca/walton/old/soaphome.html

www.ajtsc.com

www.ajtsc.com/update/index.html

candleandsoap.miningco.com

www.fragrant.demon.co.uk/makesoap
.html

www.seasoaps.com/soapbook.html

www.craftcave.com/candle/soapsupply
.shtml

www.compusmart.ab.ca/sbra/lynden
/soap.htm

www.sweetcakes.com/

www.chem.wsu.edu/Chem102
/102-LipFatSoap.html

ironman.linkport.com/~wshay1

Lye

www.teleport.com/~liberty/soapmakr
.html

www.chemlab.com/soap.ASP

members.tripod.com/adm/popup
/roadmap.shtml

www.the-sage.com/services/NaOH.html

www.pathcom.com/~newmoon/soap
.htm

www.zetatalk.com/shelter/tshlt05d.htm

danpatch.ecn.purdue.edu/~epados/waste
/house/lye.htm

www.the-sage.com/services/NaOH.html

Essential Oils, Fragrance Oils, Herbs, and Scents

www.thesoapopera.com/dir.htm

www.essentialoil.net

www.angelfire.com/mi/soapnutshome
/inci.html

www.rainbowcrystal.com/oils/oils1.html

www.webbusinesspages.com
/aromaspring/pureoil.html

www.cloudninehi.com/shop/oils

www.medicineflower.com/html
/essential_oil.htm

www.rainbowmeadow.com
/Aromatherapy.html

www.amaranthine.com/product/essentl2
.html

www.kamala.com/essent.html

www.fast.net.au/wwalker/aroma.html

www.sunshine-bodyworks.com/oils.htm

www.fragrant.demon.co.uk/main.html

www.frontiercoop.com/aromatherapy
/potpourri/formulas/citrus.html

www.frontiercoop.com/aromatherapy
/aro.gate.html

www.botanical.com

www.botanical.com/botanical/links.html

www.herbnet.com

www.fragrant.demon.co.uk/main.html

www.essenceofthings.com
/AromatherapyIntroPage.htm

www.essentialoil.net

www.rainbowcrystal.com/oils/oils1.html

www.webbusinesspages.com
/aromaspring/pureoil.html

www.cloudninehi.com/shop/oils

www.kamala.com/essent.html

www.ccdaroma.com/aroe.htm

www.fast.net.au/wwalker/aroma.html

www.jcrows.com/

www.sunshine-bodyworks.com/oils.htm

spiralup.com/graphics.htm

www.fragrant.demon.co.uk/main.html

www.nursehealer.com/Spice.htm

www.artitude.com/fssoapworks
/fragrance_a-f.html

www.artitude.com/fssoapworks
/fragrance_g-z.html

www.xmission.com/ ~ mmtnsage
/services/fragcalc.html

www.halcyon.com/kway/uses.htm

Colorants

www.prime-online.com/ ~ colors

members.aol.com/pigmntlady/index.htm

Lye Calculators

waltonfeed.com/old/soap/soaptabl.html

www.therepertoire.com/ccc/conv.htm

www.foodwine.com/cgi-bin
/hts?convcalc.hts + usequiv + new

www.lis.ab.ca/walton/old/soap
/soaptabl.html

www.xmission.com/ ~ mmtnsage
/services/fragcalc.html

Soap Recipes

www.sugarplum.net

www.pathcom.com/~ newmoon
/soap.htm

libertynatural.com/info/soaprecipes.htm

gaylor-web.com/index.html

washington.xtn.net/%7Eauthor
/soapgoat.htm

members.aol.com/oelaineo/directions
.html

www.silverlink.net/~timer/botched.html

www.silverlink.net/~timer/soapallveg
.html

www.maxpages.com/soapshoppe
/Favorite_Recipes

Soapmakers or Handmade Soaps for Sale

www.angelfire.com/ut/earthsoaps/index
.html

www.raincountry.com

www.sweetcakes.com

angelfire.com/sys/toolbar.html

www.webring.org/cgi-bin
/webring?ring = soap&list

Mail Lists, Bulletin Board Services, and Newsgroups

gaylor-web.com/index.html

www.onelist.com

www.xmission.com/~mmtnsage
/services/fragcalc.html

Business

www.fda.gov

www.sunshineartist.com

www.geocities.com/ad_container
/pop.html?cuid = 23803&keywords = none;

www.cebsys.com/kbrews.htm

www.ebay.com

vm.cfsan.fda.gov/~dms/cos-toc.html

www.monmouth.com/~ocularium

www.maxpages.com/ancientarts

www.britsoap.co.uk

Trade and Consumer Associations, Societies, and Guilds

You will not have a need for every one of these groups, but the following list is a great reference. An asterisk (*) precedes the trade-only groups, which means you must qualify for membership within the trade of the craft industry. Trade associations are for promoting the business of a trade.

American Society of Artists
Box 1326, Palatine, IL 60078

Artists and Craftsmen Associated
9420 Shoreview, Dallas, TX 75238
Phone: 214-348-0829

*Canadian Craft & Hobby
Box 44, 4044 12th Street NE,
Calgary, Alberta, Canada T2E-6K9
Phone: 403-291-0559
Fax: 403-291-0675

*HIA/Hobby Industry Association
319 East 54th Street
Elmwood Park, NJ 07407
Phone: 201-794-1133
Fax: 201 797-0657

National Academy of Design
1083 Fifth Avenue, New York, NY 10028

National Artists Equity Association
P.O. Box 28068, Central Station
Washington, DC 20038-8068

The National Arts Club
15 Gramercy Park South
New York, NY 10003

*ACCI/Association of Craft and Creative Industries
Contact: Offinger Management
P.O. Box 2188, Zanesville, OH 43702
Phone: 614-452-4541

Acknowledgments

Many thanks to the special people and companies who provided quality products, witty advice, great tips, wonderful hints, brilliant ideas, insightful wisdom, sage advice, endless patience, pep talks, a listening ear, quick responses, and much appreciated support to me in writing this book:

Ken Nerius, Bo, Sam, and Max; Ron Given, Jim Given, and Bill Given; Elizabeth Conklin and Nancee Bee MacAteer; Denise Sternad, Anya Lawler, Michelle McCormack, and Prima Publishing; David Folsen, Environmental Technology, Inc.; Chuck Bauer, Chuck Beckwith and The Soap Opera; Bill Gardner; Richard Kenepaske, Debbie Garner, George Smith, Tracia Ledford, and Delta Technical Coatings; Sandra Cashman, Desi Hart, and Fiskars; MPR Associates; David Ladd, Chris Wallace, Betty Auth and Walnut Hollow; Deirdra A. Silver and Silver Brush; Bruce Burnstein and Environmental Lighting Concepts; Carolyn Ricker and Adhesive Technologies, Inc.

Special thoughts to Karen Ancona, Wanda Cusack, Susie Berg, Heather MacAteer, and Crystal Maldonado.

Index

8/11/16
0

To Order Books

Please send me the following items:

Quantity	Title	U.S. Price	Total
_____	Decorative Painting For Fun & Profit	$ 19.99	$ _____
_____	Holiday Decorations For Fun & Profit	$ 19.99	$ _____
_____	Woodworking For Fun & Profit	$ 19.99	$ _____
_____	Knitting For Fun & Profit	$ 19.99	$ _____
_____	Quilting For Fun & Profit	$ 19.99	$ _____
_____	Soapmaking For Fun & Profit	$ 19.99	$ _____
_____	_____	$ _____	$ _____
_____	_____	$ _____	$ _____

Subtotal $ _____

Deduct 10% when ordering 3–5 books $ _____

7.25% Sales Tax (CA only) $ _____

8.25% Sales Tax (TN only) $ _____

5% Sales Tax (MD and IN only) $ _____

7% G.S.T. Tax (Canada only) $ _____

Shipping and Handling* $ _____

Total Order $ _____

*Shipping and Handling depend on Subtotal.

Subtotal	Shipping/Handling
$0.00–$29.99	$4.00
$30.00–$49.99	$6.00
$50.00–$99.99	$10.00
$100.00–$199.99	$13.50
$200.00+	Call for Quote

Foreign and all Priority Request orders:
Call Customer Service
for price quote at 916-632-4400
This chart represents the total retail price of books only
(before applicable discounts are taken).

By Telephone: With American Express, MC, or Visa,
call 800-632-8676 or 916-632-4400. Mon–Fri, 8:30–4:30.
www.primapublishing.com
By E-mail: sales@primapub.com
By Mail: Just fill out the information below and send with your remittance to:
Prima Publishing · P.O. Box 1260BK · Rocklin, CA 95677

Name _____

Address _____

City _____ State _____ ZIP _____

MC/Visa/American Express# _____ Exp. _____

Check/money order enclosed for $ _____ Payable to Prima Publishing

Daytime telephone _____

Signature _____

About the Author

BILL ADAMS, THINGS TO REMEMBER

MARIA GIVEN NERIUS graduated with a degree in Advertising and worked in that field briefly before discovering her love of crafting. She sells her original folk wood dolls at craft shows in Florida and has published over 1,000 of her designs. Maria has helped establish education and information resources for the crafter in consumer magazines, on television, and on the Internet. In Maria's own words, "Crafting is the expression of care, love, and joy straight from the heart." Feel free to contact Maria Nerius at: PO Box 100205, Palm Bay, FL 32907 or by e-mail at: Mnerius@aol.com.

About the Series Editor

BARBARA BRABEC is one of the world's leading experts on how to turn an art or crafts hobby into a profitable home-based business. She regularly communicates with thousands of creative people through her Web site and monthly columns in *Crafts Magazine* and *The Crafts Report*.